The Whole Dog Catalog

Also by the Author
The Whole Kitty CATalog

The
Whole Dog
Catalog

More Than 700 Terrific Toys, Treats, and True Dog Tales— For You and Your Dog!

John Avalon Reed

Three Rivers Press   New York

Published by Three Rivers Press, a division of Crown Publishers, Inc., 201 East 50th Street, New York, New York 10022. Member of the Crown Publishing Group.

Random House, Inc. New York, Toronto, London, Sydney, Auckland
http://www.randomhouse.com/

Three Rivers Press and Colophon are trademarks of Crown Publishers, Inc.

Printed in the United States of America

Library of Congress Cataloging-in-Publication Data
    The whole dog catalog : more than 700 terrific toys, treats, and true dog tales—for you and your dog! / John Avalon Reed.—1st ed.
        p.   cm.
    1. Dogs. 2. Dogs—Equipment and supplies.
    3. Dogs—Anecdotes.
    I. Title.
    SF426.R44   1997
    636.7—dc21   97-8077
                                                        CIP

ISBN 0-609-88037-X

10   9   8   7   6   5   4   3   2   1

First Edition

For Susan Ruth Huegel and Sunny

Contents

Acknowledgments

My sincere thanks to all the individuals, artists, and companies who helped make this book a reality. Many went well out of their way to take photographs or to send me literature, samples, and enthusiastic letters. Mary Jo has been a champ with my odd-hour writing life and rambling brainstorms; Addison's a sophomore in high school and a beautiful young man; Abbie's going to college and figuring it all out; Mike's about to exit high school, heading out the door; and Lisa, living in San Francisco, wants—more than any-thing—a dog.

Last, a big thank-you to California. If it didn't exist, they'd have to invent it.

Introduction:
A Handful of Dogs

Welcome to an amazing collection of quality products, books, and services for dog owners. In this catalog, you'll find incredible one-of-a-kind products from North America, celebrating dogs and their owners. Though I call them products, most are truly works of art—lovingly produced crafts and inspirations that mean as much to their creators as they do to you. Many are made by small to tiny companies that have put their hearts in their work. They love dogs. They care deeply about what they make, often starting their business as a hobby, believing fully in the precept "Do what you like, and the money will follow."

On the beach in Cabo San Lucas, at the very tip of Baja, Mexico, where the Pacific Ocean pounds on one side and the Sea of Cortez swells on the other, you'll find The Office restaurant.

You can sit here for dinner, in ninety-degree desert heat and an ocean breeze, plunked down on white plastic chairs in the sand, on the beach, and eat lobster and salad that won't make you sick and watch the sun go down. Sometimes a big wave sloshes in under your feet. Tourists eat with their shoes on.

Not so long ago I was here with my wife and three teenage kids. The teenage girl was having her hair braided for twenty dollars. The boys dug into the food. My wife and I, calm and relaxed, taking it in, worked our way through fresh papaya margaritas.

Useless signs in Spanish were stuck in the sand around the tables, warning off the beach vendors who came staggering up with twenty-five hats on their heads, or twenty carpets on their shoulders, cases of jewelry, African carvings, whatever. They hovered just outside the ring of tables, on the beach, waiting. With the slightest eye contact, they advanced, and you either waved them off or braced yourself for bargaining.

As the evening got darker, torches were lit, and I noticed out of the corner of my eye a very small young boy—five or six years old, all of three feet tall—working the noisy, happy crowd, holding up something small and white, way above his head, mumbling. Small kids in Mexico sometimes peddle Chiclets—little clear-plastic packets of pink or green or white gum—for a peso, so I didn't think much of it. Wandering about, he moved closer to our table.

Held in his hand above his head, mumbling "perro," he was selling dogs. Little white dogs, one at a time, carved out of translucent stone. He looked our way. I waved him over. We pointed, stumbled around the language. I asked, "How much for the dog?" He was just a little boy, very soft spoken, and it wasn't easy—with the uproar of the place—to figure out much of what he said, so we used sign language. He pointed to a peso coin, about fourteen cents, on the table. That was the price. "Got any more?" I asked. Reaching into his pocket, he produced tonight's inventory—seven little stone dogs. One measly dollar for a whole pack of dogs arduously carved out of rock.

I thought to myself, "Of all the things this kid could sell, why dogs?" So I asked him. His halting response, barely audible, one word at a time: "My best friends."

Struck by his statement—in the midst of all that noise, music, food, margaritas, and "end of the land" anarchy—I folded a five-dollar bill, handed it to him, pointed to the menu, and offered a free dinner—anything he wanted. He declined, and then he went into the night, up the beach, into the fading light, outside the light of the torches, just a little richer.

Even at his tender age, living a tough life, he got it right. The children of the world—and fortunate adults—know it: Your dog will stand with you. Through thick or thin. Prince or pauper. Always glad to see you.

Loyalty and kindness seem rather scarce these days. In an age when every-thing's for sale—an age of exaggerated, fleeting emotions, new highs and lows, instant gratification—these things can't be bought, or found on the seven o'clock news, in the newspapers, or on the Internet.

These are the beautiful feelings we can always count upon—since humanity's first meeting with the dog more than twelve thousand years ago. The dog's gift to mankind lives in our hearts and gives us perspective and hope.

That little boy is walking the beach tonight, dogs in his pocket.

If you've picked up this book, chances are you understand and share their passion. It's natural for dog lovers to want only the best for their companions. I put this book together because I wanted the best for my own dog. So in these pages you'll find more than 700 fabulous toys, furnishings, and canine clothing (for you and the dog!); wonderful expressive dog art; the best natural-health products to be found anywhere; gourmet doggy treats and some exciting gifts and surprises; 125 terrific fiction and nonfiction dog books for adults and children; and 100 True Dog Facts—intriguing and useful dog trivia and all-natural tips for the care and well-being of your dog.

You'll notice that for all of these products, I've provided specific addresses and phone numbers for contacting the makers and/or distributors. Here are some very simple ordering guidelines.

1. In general, check your local pet or specialty store for those items I've marked with an . This means you're reasonably likely to find the item sold at retail. If you're unable to find a product at retail, call or write the manufacturer to learn where you can find it or if you can order directly from them. Most of the books I've reviewed here are available through bookstores when you see the , but you can contact the publisher to order if you'd prefer.

2. If there's no by a product, contact the manufacturer directly to discuss your purchase. You may find the item at retail, but the manufacturer will help you direct-order, if you'd like.

3. If I've provided detailed shipping-and-handling information for a product, it means you're not likely to find the item at retail, and the manufacturer is set up to take your order through the mail or over the telephone. Call or write to place your order.

Finally, since I've selected only a few of the best products from each manufacturer, you should be sure to ask about a catalog of their other products if you're interested. Most will be happy to send you a free catalog if you ask.

Enjoy this wonderful celebration of our best friend!

The Whole Dog Catalog

Chapter One

The Best Toys

Soft Bite! ®

This fuzzy, fleecy flexi-flyer is a super fetch toy for your playmate. It's flexible and flies like a Frisbee; it's tough (the fleece is bonded to a rubber ring) and—ta da—it floats! Lots of play fun, easy on the teeth!

Fleecy Flyer, $7.99 + UPS (IL res. add sales tax)

Flexi-Mat
2244 S. Western Ave.
Chicago, IL 60608
(773) 376-5500

Big Mouth Toys ®

Open wide! These giant rubber toys require a big mouth. Fire Hydrant (upper left) is 10″ tall, as is the Giant Hedgehog, in bright red with blue quills. Nubby Football stretches 9″, Dumbbell, in blue and red is 10″, far-out Space Capsule lifts 10″ off the ground. A serious mouthful for every dog!

Super Colossal Fire Hydrant, $8.99
Super Colossal Giant Hedgehog, $8.99
Super Colossal Nubby Football, $8.99
Super Colossal Dumbbell, $8.99
Super Colossal Space Capsule, $8.99
+ UPS (NJ res. add sales tax)

Vo-Toys
400 S. Fifth St.
Harrison, NJ 07029
(800) 272-0088

The Dogs Who Came to Stay ®

A stray dog arrives in the night. The author—a quiet, gentle professor of philosophy at Princeton University—shines his light under the shed, seeing a dog who's just given birth to puppies. Thus begins a true love story between a man and his dogs: a humorous, touching exploration of unconditional love and the renewal of feelings he thought were lost to him forever.

By George Pitcher, 1995, 163 pp., $18.95 + UPS (NY res. add sales tax)

Dutton
Penguin USA
375 Hudson St.
New York, NY 10014
(212) 366-2000

Dem Bones, De Dem Cotton Bo

These great cotton—yes, cotton—bones are wound with 4,000 lbs. of pressure . . . so tight they're hard as a bone. Perfect toy for chewing and tugging matches. Two choices—regular or Christmas (with colored threads)—in all-natural cotton. Good chewy toy, chokeproof, helps clean teeth, machine washable, lasts up to four months with heavy use. Made in the USA.

Bowser Bone, $3.90 (sm.), $5.25 (med.), $7.65 (lg.) + UPS (MO res. add sales tax)

Benepet Pet Care Products
P.O. Box 8111
St. Joseph, MO 64508
(800) 825-0341

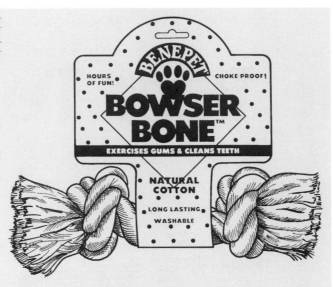

"If you pick up a starving dog and make him prosperous, he will not bite you. This is the principal difference between a dog and a man."

—Mark Twain

The Five-Dog Night ®

Old Betty lives just down the hill from crusty retired bachelor Ezra and his five dogs. In this amusing book for children, winter's coming and the nights are getting colder and colder. Betty's worried about Ezra, except that the clever old guy has his own ways of keeping warm. How's he do it? Just add an extra dog to the bed!

By Eileen Christelow, 1993, 36 pp., $14.95 + UPS (MA res. add sales tax)

Clarion Books
Houghton Mifflin
222 Berkeley St.
Boston, MA 02116
(800) 225-3362

Biting Me Softly ®

My mother's Shih Tzu won't touch latex toys. She prefers to sink her pearly whites into soft, chewy material she can chew to shreds. Simple happiness. This collection of toys is perfect for the "sensitive" dog who won't be fooled by latex. Soft and Cuddle Plush Turtle, Parrot, Lion, and Fish include a built-in squeaker for satisfaction in every bite. Canvas and rope toys Pull n' Tug Canvas Ball (4" dia.) and Canvas Disk (9" dia.) are perfect for play. Very cool canvas toys include a Bunny, Cat, Frog, Worm, Apple, and Dog. Each is soft, tough, and eminently chewable and includes a squeaker. Chewy fun.

Soft and Cuddle Plush Turtle, Parrot, Lion, or Fish, $7.99
Pull n' Tug Canvas Ball, $13.99
Pull n' Tug Canvas Disk, $15.69

Canvas Bunny, Cat, Frog, Worm, Apple, or Dog, $6.49–$12.99 + UPS (NJ res. add sales tax)

Vo-Toys
400 S. Fifth St.
Harrison, NJ 07029
(800) 272-0088

Stuffed Mouth ®

This cool, soft flying disk is made from simulated sheep-skin, but it's tough enough to throw for months and months. Toss it in the washing machine when you can't stand it any-more. Easy on the teeth, great texture, a fun toy!

Large Flying Disk,
$6.99 + UPS
(IL res. add sales tax)

Flexi-Mat
2244 S. Western Ave.
Chicago, IL 60608
(773) 376-5500

Doggie Adventure

Will your dog watch TV? Here's the videotape you can use to find out. The entire 25-minute film was shot from a height of about 2′ above ground. The camera races around the house, out the door, and through the park, hopping onto a pickup truck, nosing around some pigs—and all of it at dog's eye level. You see it just as the dog sees it. Here's a perfectly intelli-gent German Shepherd staring at the TV! Sound track of pigs grunting, music, the dog panting, crazy fun—especially for kids!

Doggie Adventure
(VHS videotape), $19.95 + UPS
(MN res. add sales tax)

Made-for-Dog Videos
P.O. Box 300122
Minneapolis, MN 55403
(612) 377-8981

Big Fun Dog Toys!

Great crazy shapes—from cows to bunnies, a dinosaur, toes!!!—make these durable, wash-able plush toys with squeakers a monster hit with the pup. Wow! Eighteen to choose from, including a rein-deer, Christmas tree, and goose for the holiday season! Ask for their cool brochure.

Tough Plush Toys,
$3.50–$7 + UPS
(NJ res. add sales tax)

Fawn Run Corp.
1122 Ramapo Valley Rd.
Mahwah, NJ 07430
(800) 998-3331

Tennis, Anyone?

This is tricky. Toss the tennis ball—attached to the rope—to your dog. Let him catch the ball. Toss it again, only this time pull on the rope that slides through the handle. Suddenly the ball's going all over the place. Loops around in the air, bounces off the ground. Intense workout. Ease into it until the dog catches on.

Nifty Pet Exerciser and Toy, $8 + $2 S&H
(MN res. add 6.5% sales tax)

T&L Nifty Products
P.O. Box 606
Cambridge, MN 55008
(612) 396-4400

Disco Fetch ®

Dog love to fetch? Bright yellow supertough Frisbee includes a cone-shaped nubby knob that makes the disk land right-side up. It's easy for the dog to pick it up, even on pavement. And it floats!

Disc-O-Dog, $9.99 + UPS
(TX res. add sales tax)

Ani Mate
1300 S. Frazier
Suite 303
Conroe, TX 77301
(800) 725-4333

TRUE DOG TALE

The Saint Bernard Keg

We're all familiar with stories of Saint Bernards carrying wooden kegs of brandy to stranded travelers. The part about the wooden kegs is debatable, but there's no question this breed has saved many, many lives in the Alps. Since the middle of the 15th century, monks of the Hospice of Saint Bernardine have been raising these huge dogs (up to 200 lbs.) to rescue travelers making difficult crossings through the mountain passes of Switzerland. Perhaps the most famous Saint Bernard is Barry, an extraordinary rescue dog credited with saving more than 35 lives. He actually carried a child clinging to his back through miles of snow to safety at the monastery. His exploits are a permanent part of Swiss history.

TRUE DOG TALE

The Fastest Dog

Except for the dog running away from your garbage can, Greyhounds are generally accepted to be the fastest dogs on earth. They reach top speeds of just under 40 mph. Whippets come in a close second at nearly 35 mph.

My Dog's the World's Best Dog ®

Tapping into the rampant excesses of dog ownership, whimsical illustrations reflect the wit and wisdom of dog owners who are utterly convinced there is no dog like their dog. Great fun for all dog owners who will see themselves—and their pets—in these pages!

By Suzy Becker, 1995, 96 pp., $6.95 + UPS
(NY res. add sales tax)

Workman Publishing
708 Broadway
New York, NY 10003
(212) 254-5900

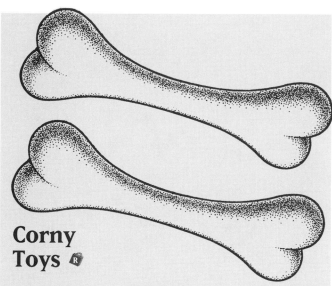

Corny Toys ®

Booda Velvets are superchewy dog bones that are actually made of corn. Three flavors (premium mix, chicken, and beef and vegetables) contain absolutely no animal by-products or additives. Gobbling down the unique, patented cornstarch material won't upset your dog's stomach. Very different, all-natural treat worth asking for!

Booda Velvets, $3.15 (sm), $5 (med), $6.30 (lg) + UPS (CO res. add sales tax)

Aspen Pet Products
11701 E. 53rd Ave.
Denver, CO 80239
(800) BUY-4-PET

Baseball Tug ®

Put a beef-flavored base-ball on the end of a tough, twisted rope, and you have a great tug toy. Super for pull-and-fetch contests, even at the lake or beach (the baseball floats!), and dogs love gnawing that beefy flavor. Just rinse it off when it gets dirty. Made of safe, nontoxic materials in two sizes: Major League (for big dogs) and Pee Wee League (small dogs). What's next? Hamburger on a stick?

Tug-a-Beefy Baseball, $6.50 (Pee Wee), $7.50 (Major League) + UPS (no sales tax in NH)

Omega Products
292 Old Dover Rd.
Rochester, NH 03867
(800) 258-7148

Indoor/Outdoor Plush Toys ®

Humorous hot dog, pizza, rocket, and paintbrush toys in wild colors are made from rugged plush fabric, meant for extended romps and repeated machine washings. Soft enough to play with indoors. Chomp-after-chomp, fetch-after-fetch fun, "op art" play toys. Brilliant colors.

Plush Toss n' Fetch Toys, $3.99–5.99 + UPS (IL res. add sales tax)
Flexi-Mat
2244 S. Western Ave.
Chicago, IL 60608
(773) 376-5500

Your Favorite Breeds ®

Breeds on Parade is a new line of soft, chewy dog toys. Each is lifelike in appearance and made of plush fur, filled with Poly-Fil batting. There's a soft, durable plastic squeaker inside, and you can toss it into the washing machine. They look nice on a bed full of pillows.

Breeds on Parade, $9 each (Dachshund, Golden Retriever, Lab Retriever, Poodle, Schnauzer, Scottish Terrier, and Miniature Pinscher); $11 (Afghan, German Shepherd, Samoyed, Great Dane, Saint Bernard, and Great Pyrenees) + UPS (Calif. sales tax included)

R.V.B. Creations
2461 Vineyard Rd.
Novato, CA 94947
(800) 892-3192

Pull, Tug, Toss, and Pacify ®

Uh-oh. Puppy having a rough day? Maybe a good walk followed by a pacifier would help. Check out these big Pacifiers (upper left) for a relaxing, stress-releasing chew. The perfect gift for an adult nondog whiner as well. Somebody at work won't shut up? Just leave one on his desk! Relieve anxiety with the Super Ball, toss a triangle-shaped Satellite, start some action with the Pull Strap, which has a spot for your hand as the dog yanks away. Figure 8 Tugs (lower left), Toss and Chew Rings, Balls, and Dumbbells round out this rubber, tough-toys exercise collection.

Pacifier, $5.95 (6″)
Super Ball, $10.99 (3″)
Satellite, $8.95
Pull Strap, $11.95 (12″), $15.99 (14″)
Figure 8 Tug, Toss and Chew Ring, Ball, or Dumbbell, $4.99–$12.99 + UPS (NJ res. add sales tax)

Vo-Toys
400 S. Fifth St.
Harrison, NJ 07029
(800) 272-0088

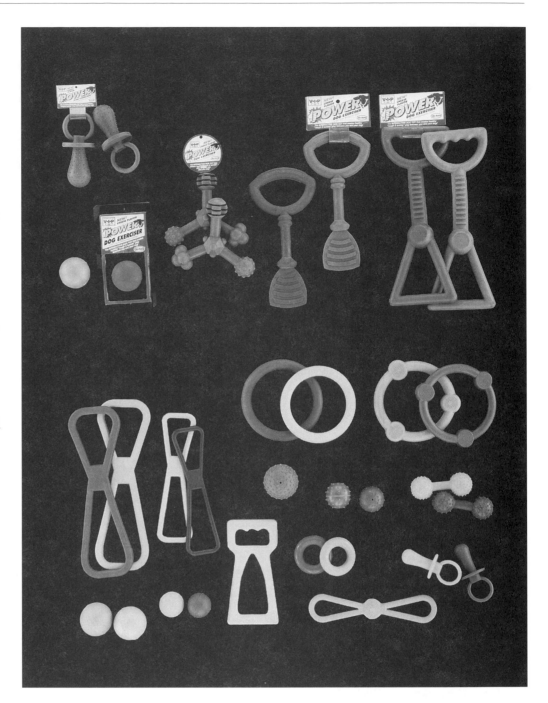

Fresh Mint Tennis Balls!

Grab your bat or tennis racket, head to a big park, and whack these great minty tennis balls for exercise and fresh breath too! Superb idea. Dogs love crunching down on tennis balls, and these come in Mint or VanillaMint flavors. Keep them and other dog toys (or your dry dog food) in this fun Toy Box with words like "fetch" and "top dog" painted on the removable roof. Available in forest green or Snoopy red.

Spearmint Tennis Balls (pkg. of 2), $7 + $3.50 S&H

Dog House Toy Box, $90 + $10 S&H (GA res. add 6% sales tax)

Melia Enterprises
2103 N. Decatur Rd.
Suite 222
Decatur, GA 30033
(404) 315-6377

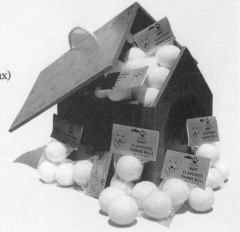

Fleecy Toys ®

Soft toys are hot these days, because they help prevent injuries to a dog's teeth. Each of these toys is a nuzzly sherpa that's nice and soft in your dog's mouth. Just under the heart is a squeaker. The Doghouse Mouse proves that mice aren't just for cats. Teddy Buddy is a bear the size of a bunny. Heart 'o Mine is an especially endearing gift for your best friend. My Best Friend is a cuddly kitty with a fluffy tail. ChowHound is a cool, soft, three-sided bone toy. There's no such thing as too many toys!

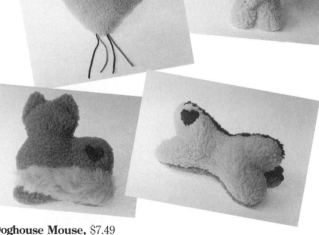

Doghouse Mouse, $7.49
Teddy Buddy, $9.95
Heart 'o Mine, $6.29
My Best Friend, $9.99
ChowHound, $7.99
+ $2 S&H
(CA res. add sales tax)

Hound Alley
4811 Venner Rd.
Martinez, CA 94553
(888) 255-4322

The Dog of the Aborigines

Untamed and illegal to keep as pets in most of Australia, Dingoes arrived with the Aborigines over 4,000 years ago. A hybrid of the Asiatic Wolf or the Indian Plains Wolf, this breed comes into mating season only once a year. (Domestic dogs enter season twice a year.) Though they spend time in proximity to people, they have a wildness that puts them on the edge of consideration as a "domesticated" dog. Of medium build, brown color, weighing 20–40 lbs. and standing up to 20″ tall, Dingoes are highly intelligent, resourceful dogs, with keen reasoning powers. Packs of them live wild in the immense Australian Outback, and they also live with natives, serving as sentries, camp scavengers, and in times past, a source of food when the going got tough. They are so deeply disliked by ranchers that an enormous fence was erected across Australia to keep them from herds of cattle and sheep. Considered vermin to be shot on sight, they are thriving despite efforts at eradication.

Tug for Exercise and Fun! ®

The patented design behind this simple toy includes two hidden balls tucked inside durable, stretchable fabric, so they never damage teeth. You grab one end, the dog grabs the other. When necessary, just toss into the washer and dryer. Simulated lambswool. Four neon colors. Beats that old sock you've been using. . . .

Tammi-Tug, $6.99 + UPS
(IL res. add sales tax)

Flexi-Mat
2244 S. Western Ave.
Chicago, IL 60608
(312) 376-5500

Soft Squeaks ®

Your dog will adore chomping on the soft simulated-fleece exterior of this toy. Looks like lambswool, but it's a tough, nonallergenic synthetic. Each shape is stuffed with a squeaker. Happiness you can hear, as your dog plays.

Poochsmooch for Dogs,
$7.99 and up + UPS
(AZ res. add sales tax)

Pet Affairs
691 E. 20th St.
Building 111
Tucson, AZ
85719
(800) 777-9192

Crazy Barking Bone

Nutty 7″ white nylon bone sits there, ready to be chewed. The dog comes up, grabs it with his mouth, and "*BARK, BARK*." It's a barking bone! The dog drops the bone and steps back to think it over. The barking sound is activated by movement of the bone. Requires 2 AA batteries. The human race has invented a bone that barks back!

Barking Bone, $11.95 + $5 S&H
(PA res. add 6% sales tax)

Fun-damental Too Ltd.
2381 Philmont Ave.
Suite 119
Huntingdon Valley, PA 19006
(800) 922-3110
http://www.shopperusa.com/Fundamental

The Official Dog I.Q. Test

Is your dog smarter than you? Through a series of amusing, often hilarious multiple-choice questions, this book helps you assign points to your dog through a handy rating scale in order to determine his IQ—from genius to severely retarded. Harmless, nutty fun. Includes semiofficial-looking framable certificate for you to complete.

By Peter Mandel, 1995, 60 pp., $6.95 + $4 S&H
(IL res. add sales tax)

Bonus Books
160 E. Illinois St.
Chicago, IL 60611
(312) 467-0580

Jumpy, Bumpy Toy ®

Ever try to predict where a football will bounce? The weird shape of this wild exercise toy makes it bounce and hop all over the place. Throw it and start the action. Made of non-toxic materials, long-lasting, available in fire engine red or marine blue. Scrambles dogs in every direction!

The Wobbler, $5.13 + UPS
(CA res. add sales tax)

Classic Products
1451 Vanguard Dr.
Oxnard, CA 93033
(800) 228-0105

Take Me out to the Park ®

These soft fleece balls are made of sturdy acrylic lambswool for rough-and-tumble play. Detailed with a heart sewn over the squeaker. Leather tassels fly through the air. Add a faux lambswool baseball cap and glove (not shown), and you have three amusing sporting dog toys. Chew 'em up.

PuppyLeague (1 ball, glove, and cap), $25.95 + $4.95 S&H
(CA res. add sales tax)

Hound Alley
4811 Venner Rd.
Martinez, CA 94553
(888) 255-4322

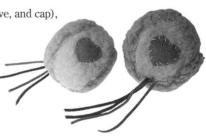

Pet Names of the Rich and Famous ®

David Letterman is famous for his late-night television show's stupid pet tricks; however, his dog Stan has never appeared in one. Ivana Trump's dog Tiapka II (means "paw" in Czech) never gets left behind, instead jumping into a certain gray suitcase whenever Ivana's about to leave. Kirk, named by William Shatner after his character in *Star Trek,* was taken to famous pet healer Beatrice Lydecker. You get the drift: Hundreds of dog names and brief stories about pets owned by famous folks. Interesting trivia.

By Robert Davenport, 1995, 192 pp., $5.95 + UPS (CA res. add sales tax)

General Publishing Group
2701 Ocean Park Blvd.
Suite 140
Santa Monica, CA 90405
(800) 745-9000

Inflite Entertainment ®

Zoom this baby through the air for hours of fun. Toss it just like a Frisbee. Constructed of durable nylon canvas, it's decked out in popular summer-bright colors. The handle makes for easy pickup and retrieval. Two sizes: 7″ dia. for small dogs, 9″ dia. for large dogs. Holiday? Birthday? Time for a new toy!

Flitemaster, $4.88 (7″),
$5.55 (9″) + UPS
(CA res. add sales tax)

Classic Products
1451 Vanguard Dr.
Oxnard, CA 93033
(800) 228-0105

TRUE DOG TALE

Japanese Prairie Dogs

In an endless quest for the new, unusual, and expensive, an American company in Texas uses a giant vacuum cleaner to suck prairie dogs out of the ground, then ships them to Japan. Seems the Japanese consider prairie dogs to be prime pets. It works like this: A giant vacuum truck pulls up to a prairie dog hole, sticks the nozzle in, and sucks up all the young prairie dogs (adults are too heavy) into an enclosure. From there they go to Japan, where the asking price is $700 each.

Where's My Slipper?

Missing a slipper? That's a common refrain if you own a puppy (or puppyish dog) who loves to take stuff and hide it. Solution? Get him his own. This plush slipper is a dog's dream toy. Multipatterned fabrics, fleece lined, packaged in a decorative shoebox. Leave the box open on the floor—he'll find it!

Super Toy: Plush Puppy's Plaything Slipper, $15 + UPS
(IL res. add 8% sales tax)

Baxter and Charming, Ltd.
11 W. Main
Carpentersville, IL 60110
(800) 569-2761
E-mail: Baxterpets @aol.com

No Chipped Teeth ®

Ever bitten into the hard crust of French bread? Your dog gets the same feeling when she bites down on a hard toy. The SofTug is a braided sherpa tugging toy with soft, sturdy knots for maximum fun *and* happy teeth. Colorful and durable.

SofTug, $7.99 (sm), $9.99 (lg) + $4.95 S&H
(CA res. add sales tax)

Hound Alley
4811 Venner Rd.
Martinez, CA 94553
(888) 255-4322

Vacationing with Your Pet: ®

Eileen's Directory of Pet-Friendly Lodging (U.S. and Canada)

Fifty-eight million U.S. households have family pets. Something like 10 million pet owners always take their pets on trips. The question is, where to stay? If you've ever traveled with a dog and tried to rent a room, you know it can get dicey. Many years ago I carried my large 65-lb. Gordon Setter in my arms, under a coat, through a major hotel lobby and onto a crowded elevator, pushed the button with my elbow, and waited it out until we got to the 16th floor. She didn't make a sound. Same thing, back and forth, for three days. Hopefully this mammoth book with over 20,000 pet-friendly hotel, B&B, inn, motel, and resort listings in the U.S. and Canada—from rustic to ritzy—will save you some paranoia when you check in with your best friend.

By Eileen Barish, 1995, 688 pp.,
$19.95 + $3.95 S&H
(AZ res. add sales tax)

Pet-Friendly Publications
P.O. Box 8459
Scottsdale, AZ 85252
(800) 638-3637

Slingshot, Tennis Ball Launcher!

Wow! This lightweight (under 2 lbs.) wooden slingshot can hurl a tennis ball more than 120 feet before it bounces! No more tennis elbow or injuries from repetitive throwing. Just place a tennis ball (2 come free with your order) in the rubberized canvas pouch (good for up to 2,000 launches, replaceable), pull it back, and launch away. Balls go incredibly far, with the dog in hot pursuit. Bright red stain finish. Great for ages 10 and up; also those with modest physical limitations who want to give their dog a good workout—and anyone who wants to be able to shake hands the next day.

Fetch Boy's Ball Launcher, $30 (includes S&H + sales tax)

Fetch Boy
P.O. Box 30126
Seattle, WA 98103
(206) 783-BALL

Tuff It Out ®

Got a real chewer on your hands who destroys toys in minutes? Try these Tuff Bite molded-vinyl toys in cool colors and fun shapes. Flexible vinyl bends with the bites. Your choice of "grunt" and "roar" noisemakers inside. Good quality, humorous designs.

Tuff Bite Dog Toys, $16 and up + UPS
(CO res. add sales tax)

Aspen Pet Products
11701 E. 53rd Ave.
Denver, CO 80239
(800) BUY-4-PET

Torn Dreams

No mail today? Ask the dog what he's been up to. The U.S. Postal Service estimates that dogs bite 28 mail carriers every day. The Service might lose your letters, but it doesn't forgive abuse: In aggravated and persistent cases, the U.S.P.S. sues dog owners (they also stop delivering the mail).

"Love me, love my dog."
—Saint Bernard

The Wonders of Wood

Patrick Keen, bless him, has not forgotten how to make a good, old-fashioned, high-quality, *imaginative* wooden toy. Try to find something comparable nowadays—it's almost impossible. Notice the quality of these wooden dog toys for young children. They're made of hand-sanded ponderosa pine, with real leather ears and lifelike eyes. The wheels are of hard birch for durability. All are nontoxic and child-safe. Bone Dog comes with his own bone and a magnet under his chin to "retrieve" the bone. Sophie is a wide-eyed, lovable Basset Hound with big, big leather ears and a cute flopped-over leather tail. Both follow along when you pull on their durable pull cord. Dependable friends for a young child.

Bone Dog or **Sophie the Basset Hound,** $20 each + $4.50 S&H
(CA res. add sales tax)

Keen Toys
520 North St.
Lompoc, CA 93436
(805) 735-1754

A Toy for Every Dog ®

The toy should fit the dog. This incredible collection includes some of the best soft toys found anywhere and offers sizes to suit any dog. I've tried out many, on both big and small dogs. My favorites are the Teddies. Ted, Big Ted, and Tiny Ted (top row) are available in heavy-duty genuine faux sheepskin or acrylic. The Standard Bone is made of fleece. The round white fleece Basketball is nice and big to roll around and play with! Squirrels are remarkably lifelike and superior toys. Super, flop-around fun.

Tiny Ted (6″), $6.99
Big Ted (11″), $11.10
Ted (15″), $25
Big Bone (12″), $7.80
Standard Bone (8″), $5.80
Tiny Ball (6″), $6
Basketball (11″), $15
Squirrel (13″), $8
Medium Squirrel (17″), $9.95
Large Squirrel (21″), $14.99
+ UPS (Calif. res. add sales tax)

Air Creations
Concord Dog Toys
601A Stone Rd.
Benicia, CA 94510
(707) 745-4500

Grunt Toys! ®

At last—a toy that sounds like a truck driver's grunt! Dog owners fall in love with these. I got a box of samples, handed them out, gave some to my dog, and hoarded a few on the desk, next to the phone. Each has a squeaker that gives out a nice, deep, earthy grunt, and they all sound a little different. No wimpy squeaks! Washable, synthetic, bright colors. Grunt and play.

Soft Bite Toys—Grunt Series, $5.40–$13 and up + UPS
(CO res. add sales tax)

Aspen Pet Products
11701 E. 53rd Ave.
Denver, CO 80239
(800) BUY-4-PET

Barking at Prozac ®

Wrapped in bologna, Buck the Beagle downs what he thinks is Prozac for his not-so-up mood, then proceeds to give us a neurotic, Woody Allen self-examination of his life as a dog. Funny—his owner's Prozac pills are white, like his, only much smaller! When all is said and done, there are several major conclusions: All white pills aren't the same, they weren't necessary,

and life is all right just the way it is. Who needs this stuff? We all have ups, we all have downs. Prozac contemplation in and out of the doghouse.

By Tom McNichol, 1996,
120 pp., $9 + UPS
(NY res. add sales tax)

Crown Trade Paperbacks
201 E. 50th St.
New York, NY 10022
(212) 572-6117

In the Dark ®

Why let nightfall stop you from playing with your dog? Find a big open lawn and toss this glowing ball until the dog's had enough. Durable, made of nontoxic materials that recharge when left under any light source. Ridges help the dog grip the ball . . . and bring it back to you for another nighttime throw!

Glo-Fetch, $7.95 + $1.50 S&H
(NY res. add sales tax)

Rockywoods
P.O. Box 1406
Fairport, NY 14450
(716) 425-3763
http://www.spidermen.com
/rockywoods

Outrageous Exerciser ®

This thing is wild. Flip it up in the air, spin it around, zig and zag while the dog tries to grab it! Tough 36″ flexible wand with soft toy (synthetic lambswool) and replaceable squeaker on the end. Very strong 36″ nylon rope. The whole thing is guaranteed not to fall apart during normal play with any size dog, Chihuahua to Great Dane.

Chase 'n Pull Interactive Toy,
$12 + $3 S&H
(CA res. add sales tax)

Vee Enterprises
1066 S. Ogden Dr.
Los Angeles, CA 90019
(800) 733-1903

Playtime ®

Ten million dogs in America are a little pudgy around the waistline from a few too many late-night snacks. If yours is among them, maybe you need some exercise equipment. The Booda Tug is a dual-action toy you can use for interactive play or as a solo chew toy for the dog. The Solo Tug is designed for tough interactive play—meaning your dog grabs the toy and pulls while you hold on for dear life. Machine washable, made of supertightly wound rope, with a custom rubber grip that saves your hand from laceration. A necessity for any playful dog. Play Bounce and Tug with the Ball 'n Bone is a combo toy with a genuine rubber ball for chewing and tough, woven fibers for tugging and gnawing. Or, with his bright red lips and denim clothes, the Booda Buddy is not only charming but practical, made of the same tough woven stuff that dogs love to chew and fetch. Boy or girl. Makes a great gift.

Booda Tug, $8.50
Solo Tug, $10.50
Ball 'n Bone, $5.35–$15
(sm–xlg)
Booda Buddy, $12–$13
+ UPS (CO res. add sales tax)

Aspen Pet Products
11701 E. 53rd Ave.
   Denver, CO 80239
    (800) BUY-4-PET

Frisbee Dogs: How to Raise, Train, and Compete

What a sport! Dogs catching Frisbees is a big business, with 115 annual community competitions plus regional, open, and a world final competition held in Washington, D.C. Here's a how-to book that tells you all about getting into the fun. Plus the scoop on the history of the sport, basic and advanced training, throwing skills you'll need, competition rules, tips, and lots more. (FYI: The record for the longest Frisbee throw and catch is 130 yards by Cheyenne Ashley Whippet, who ran the distance at 35 mph and caught the Frisbee in midair.) Unbelievable photos of dogs flying through the air with reckless abandon, vaulting off the backs of trainers, some soaring as high as nine feet. Author is the world champion and owner/trainer of World Canine Champion Whirlin' Wizard. Wow!

By Peter Bloeme, 1994, 184 pp., $14.95 + $5 S&H
(GA res. add 5% sales tax)

PRB and Associates
4060-D Peachtree Rd.
Suite 326F
Atlanta, GA 30319
(800) 786-9240

TRUE DOG TALE

Virtual Dogs

Grab some coffee, type in the word DOG, and you're off on the Internet for everything from dog pictures to FAQ (frequently asked questions), dog breeder directories, cartoons, self-publications, homemade dog stories, pictures of kids' dogs, health advice, and almost everything conceivable about dogs you would expect from millions of dog owners with computers and home pages. Japanese, Australian, Swedish, Eskimo—meet the dogs of the world with just a local phone call.

Big Barkersville Benefits! ®

Tired of that same old red-rubber-steak squeaker toy? Meet the fun toys of Barkersville, complete with a "Key to the City" rawhide treat. Purchase the On-the-Go Dog Phone (left), Private Jet, Computer, or Happy Sax, and you'll get more than just a great dog toy: A mini 8-page story-book comes attached to each. On the last page is an application for Barkersville citizenship. Fill it out, and you get coupons, newsletters, treats, surprises, and lots of other goodies by mail. The storybook's free!

Barkersville Dog Toy,
$5.99 + UPS
(NJ res. add sales tax)

Multipet International
626 16th St.
Carlstadt, NJ 07072
(800) 900-6738

Avoiding-the-Dentist Toys ®

Dogs dislike dentists as much as we do. But dental care is a big, expensive issue, especially with older dogs. You can help reduce those office visits with the durable cotton-fiber shank of Booda's Dental Bone. It massages and flosses gums, helping to fight plaque and disperse odor-causing bacteria. Scented knuckles (4 flavors: original, bubblegum, mint, and cinnamon) are made from a tough, premium thermo-plastic material that helps control tartar buildup while satisfying the most demanding chewers. Krackling Bone also helps clean teeth, giving the dog a crunchy, crackling sound with every bite. For quiet nib-blers consider the Booda Bone Denim Chew. It's made of very tightly wound denim in bright multicolored patterns that can withstand many hours of contemplative chewing.

Booda Two-Way Dental Bones, $6.30 (sm), $13 (lg) + UPS
(CO res. add sales tax)

Aspen Pet Products
11701 E. 53rd Ave.
Denver, CO 80239
(800) BUY-4-PET

My Puppy's Record Book ®

Oh boy, a puppy! All that fun and energy and sweetness! Here's the place for your first puppy picture, the family history, and just like a baby book, all the important moments as your puppy grows into a dog. The author is renowned for her award-winning "Carl" dog books for young children. Beautiful hardcover includes a special keepsake medal medallion for your puppy's collar. Ages 5 and up.

By Alexandra Day, 1994,
24 pp., $9.95 + UPS
(NY res. add sales tax)

Farrar Straus Giroux
19 Union Sq. West
New York, NY 10003
(212) 741-6900

Montana Dogs ®

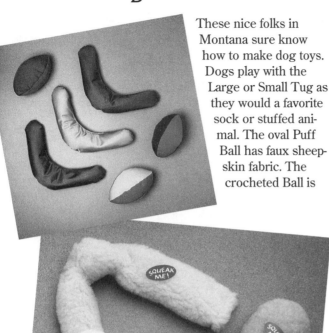

These nice folks in Montana sure know how to make dog toys. Dogs play with the Large or Small Tug as they would a favorite sock or stuffed animal. The oval Puff Ball has faux sheepskin fabric. The crocheted Ball is hand-crocheted, using double strands of rug yarn in a variety of patterns. All come with squeakers. Get out the old pigskin with the soft Football, in assorted bright colors. Give him something to chomp into.

Large Tug, $6
Small Tug, $5
Oval Puff Ball
(5″ l. × 4″ dia.), $5
Crocheted Ball (4″ dia.), $5
Football (9″ l. × 4½″ dia.), $7
+ UPS (no sales tax in MT)

Pet Pals
107 Sun Ave.
Livingston, MT 59047
(800) 999-5366

TRUE DOG TALE

Your Used Car Is Their Ride Home!

Many nonprofit humane societies will welcome your used car as a donation. They sell it, and you receive a nice tax deduction. Your donation helps reunite lost animals with worried owners, gives sick and injured animals a second chance at life, and places unwanted animals into new loving homes. Everybody wins! Call your local humane society (see your Yellow Pages), give 'em those old wheels, take the tax deduction.

Give a Dog a Bone ®

Let's have some fun! Here's a great hardcover collection of happy stories, rhymes, jokes, and riddles about dogs. Lively artwork illustrates amusing bedtime stories for young children under 8.

Compiled by Joanna Cole and Stephanie Calmenson, 1996, 90 pp., $16.95 + UPS
(NY res. add sales tax)

Scholastic
555 Broadway
New York, NY 10012
(800) 289-3694

Flying Fun ®

The Soft Bite Floppy Disc makes hard plastic throwing disks obsolete. Soft, safe and gentle for dog's teeth and gums. Two sizes, in various bright colors. The dog loves chasing it, and you'll become a Frisbee master.

Soft Bite Floppy Disc, $11.50 (7″ dia.), $16.50 (10″ dia.) + UPS (CO res. add sales tax)

Information:
Aspen Pet Products
11701 E. 53rd Ave.
Denver, CO 80239
(800) BUY-4-PET

FLEXIBLE

DURABLE

IT FLIES

IT FLOATS

Doggerel: Great Poets on Remarkable Dogs ®

Dylan Thomas, Ogden Nash, Erica Jong, James Dickey, Lawrence Ferlinghetti—these and other literary greats write odes to great dogs they have known, accompanied by Martha Paulos's black and white linocuts. Putting in a good word for the dogs.

By Fly Productions, 1990, 64 pp., $14.95 + UPS (CA res. add sales tax)

Chronicle Books
275 Fifth Ave.
San Francisco, CA 94013
(800) 722-6657

Underwater Retrieve Toy!

Splunky is an underwater retrieve toy named for the sound it makes when you drop it in the water. If your dog loves to swim, he'll enjoy a game of Splunk in the shallows. Toss it in, let him find it (3 handles make it easy to grab), and slowly work your way up to chest-deep water. Splunky also has an unpredictable bounce on land that will have the dog scurrying in all directions. Bring this toy to the lake.

Splunky, $7.25 + UPS (PA res. add 6% sales tax)

Dog Works
14297 Curvin Dr.
Stewartstown, PA 17363
(800) 787-2788

TRUE DOG TALE

Where Are the Spots?

You've decided on a Dalmatian puppy. Surprise of surprises, you show up a day after the puppies are born and—oops, no spots! Dalmatian pups are born pure white, but they quickly develop the spots that kids and firemen love.

Chapter Two

The Finest Furniture and Furnishings

Chilly Night Cuddle-Up ®

Cold coming? Brrrr. Choose the Highland Plaid or Teddy Bear print for a warm, snug nap in this Cuddler dog bed. Cozy fleece provides total comfort from cold, damp floors, and the cover is fully washable and dryable. Available in sizes from 21″ to 43″. A good night's rest.

Cuddler (Highland Plaid or Teddy Bear print), $29.95–$59.95 + UPS
(IL res. add sales tax)

Flexi-Mat
2244 S. Western Ave.
Chicago, IL 60608
(773) 376-5500

TRUE DOG TALE

The Wolf Ancestor

It's believed that dogs were the first domesticated animals, sharing their lives with humans more than 12,000 years ago. Amazingly, all domestic dogs—from big to small—are related to wolves, part of the canine family, which also includes coyotes and foxes. In the canine family, only the wolf became domesticated enough to live with people. Since wolves are pack animals, they have transferred their loyalties and need for hierarchy to the top dog, the "alpha" leader—you, the owner. This relationship enables you to train your dog.

The Dog Who Rescues Cats ®

Personality quirks aren't unique to people. This very unusual, true-life dog story centers on the personality and sixth sense of Ginny, a one-year-old previously abused dog, adopted from a shelter, who immediately begins dragging her new owners into vacant lots and abandoned buildings to rescue injured and starving cats. Incredibly, Ginny's owners now feed and care for more than 40 stray cats. They've taken as many as 15 cats at once into their home, and they've arranged for more than 60 adoptions. Wonderful story of a canine Mother Teresa. Wow!

By Philip Gonzalez and Leonore Fleischer, 1995, 160 pp., $16 + UPS (NY res. add sales tax)

HarperCollins Publishers
10 E. 53rd St.
New York, NY 10022
(800) 242-7737

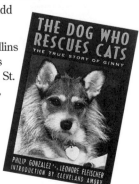

Highland Plaid for Me, Puleeeze! ®

What a bed! The Highland Plaid Collection includes a poly/cedar fill that helps repel fleas, along with a zippered cover and inner liner that's machine washable and dryable. Beautiful bed in a distinctive Scottish plaid, your choice of barnside red or Delft blue. Sizes from 27″ × 36″ to 36″ × 48″. This is a happy dog.

Petnapper, $29.95–$59.95 + UPS
(IL res. add sales tax)

Flexi-Mat
2244 S. Western Ave.
Chicago, IL 60608
(773) 376-5500

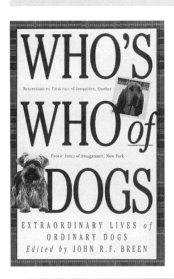

Who's Who of Dogs ®

Ministories, bite-size bits of hundreds of dog's lives and what makes them special. A few choice words for each, just about half a page, from AAgelyn's Lady Kate Losquadro (New York City) to the biography of Zuma Jay Risenhoover of Nashville, Tennessee. Dogs' lives as told by their owners, from Alaska to New York City.

Edited by John Breen, 1995, 504 pp., $7.95 + UPS
(NY res. add sales tax)

Workman Publishing,
708 Broadway
New York, NY 10003
(212) 254-5900

> *"To his dog, every man is Napoleon; hence the constant popularity of dogs."*
>
> —Aldous Huxley

TRUE DOG TALE

Where the Dogs Live

Nearly 38% of all U.S. households have a dog, and many have more than one. So the best guesstimate of total pet dogs in the U.S.: 58 million. Dogs gobble up more than $3.5 billion in food each year, and their veterinary bills exceed $4.8 billion annually. Are dogs the most popular pet? Nope. That distinction goes to fish.

Sign It

Okay, it's not glamorous, but maybe you need a dog sign. And where do you get a sign made, anyway? These nonrusting, 3″ × 12″ aluminum plaques have embossed black letters on a white background and include one hole in each corner. Very inexpensive, and they should last forever. Just nail or screw them on your wall, fence, etc. Thirty messages—from humorous "Pets Are Welcome" to serious "Guard Dog on Duty." Entire list is in Sirgo's free catalog.

Aluminum Pet Signs,
$2 + $1.50 S&H
(IN res. add 5% sales tax)

The Sirgo Company
Box 58
Schererville, IN 46375
(219) 865-6092

Stella's Pretty Beds

Stella Mitson from Santee, California, makes very nice four-poster canopy beds. They measure 22″l. × 21″w. × 15″h. and are constructed of 8-gauge galvanized wire with four dark wood posts. A 100% cotton cover (Symmetry and Dalmania models shown) comes with the beds, is fully removable and washable, and is available in a variety of prints and colors. The plush pillow is color-coordinated with cover, and custom beds can be ordered to match your decor. Made in the USA. Your small dog will love to snuggle on the plush pillow and peek out from beneath the canopy. She'll also look cute. Get out the camera.

Complete Princess Pet Bed, $104.95
Additional Covers Ordered with Bed, $44.95 + UPS (CA res. add 7.75% sales tax)

Stella's Princess Pet Beds
P.O. Box 92072
Santee, CA 92072

Luxury Pet Carrier ®

How do you go about choosing a great dog carrier? The Sherpa Roll-Up has reinforced handles, all-brass hardware, a roomy zippered pocket for snacks, an adjustable shoulder strap (which doubles as a leash, handy while waiting at the airport), mesh panels on three sides for good ventilation, and roll-up flaps for privacy when the pup needs a nap while traveling. An accessory pouch holds toys, food, and grooming supplies and slides onto the handles on the side of the bag. Optional Biscuit Bag holds any little extras you'll need. Three sizes, two colors (black and forest green diamond piqué with caramel trim). Just the best for your best friend.

Sherpa Roll-Up, $90 (sm., 15″l. × 9″h. × 8″w.) + UPS (NY res. add sales tax)

Sherpa's Pet Trading Co.
357 E. 57th St.
New York, NY 10022
(800) 743-7723
http://www.
acmepet.com/sherpa

THE SHERPA ROLL-UP

Ins and Outs

Magnets help this clever dog door to open and close. Flap is made of a Lexan material that cannot be chewed, won't warp or crack, and has a brush strip all the way around to close securely. Quiet operation, lockable, self-lining for doors up to 2″ thick; other liners available for installing in walls of any thickness. It's available in white, brown, or gray for dogs up to 18″ shoulder height.

Medium Dog Door,
$52.99 + UPS
(TX res. add sales tax)

Ani Mate
1300 S. Frazier
Suite 303
Conroe, TX 77301
(800) 725-4333

Transporter or Dog Bed? ®

Actually, both. You can buckle it into a car's seat-belts while traveling, or remove the doors and use as a nifty pet bed. Clean space-age design comes in three colors: smokey gray, blue, and rose. There's a molded handle on top for easy carrying; a sturdy slide-latch snaps into the closed position. Good air ventilation, measures 26½″ tall × 19″. See-through design, raised platform, 5-year limited warranty.

Alyssa Transporter,
$44.95 + UPS
(IN res. add sales tax)

Alyssa Industries
P.O. Box 4533
Elkhart, IN 46514
(219) 522-0795

Off Limits

Keep your wildly friendly dog off your dinner guests with the sliding hardwood panels of this indoor gate, which expands to fit openings from 53″ to 96″. Because it unlatches at either end, the gate can swing open in both directions. Quick-release hardware permits instant removal for use in other locations or for storage. The gate is 24″ high; the slat spacing is 2¾″. Must be bolted to an inner doorway.

Superwide All-Hardwood Gate, $39.99 + $6.99 S&H
(WI res. add 5% sales tax)

Drs. Foster and Smith
2253 Air Park Rd.
P.O. Box 100
Rhinelander, WI 54501
(800) 826-7206 (24 hours)

German Shepherd ®

Though in comparison the Labrador Retriever is considered slightly more trainable and less likely to chew up other dogs, most behavior profiles show the German Shepherd to be the best all-around large dog. They are smart and intensely loyal, natural protectors, and great companions, and they fit in well with most families. This attractive, full-color hardcover book of illustrations and photographs provides the basics of care: feeding and grooming, health and breeding, showing your Shepherd, working your Shepherd. Shepherd coloration varies dramatically, from the typical black-and-tan to all-black and even all-white. A useful book fact: Feeding your dog too much red meat or other rich food may make him too

aggressive. Too rich a diet provides too much food energy. Add carbohydrates, vegetables, or even a meat substitute like tofu instead.

By Bruce Fogle, D.V.M., 1996, 80 pp., $14.95 + UPS (NY res. add sales tax)

Dorling Kindersley Publishing
95 Madison Ave.
New York, NY 10016
(212) 213-4800

Easy Ups and Downs

Sometimes it's difficult for older dogs to get around, much less make the leap onto the sofa. Here's a carpeted, ramp/stool combo that gives your dog easy access to her favorite resting place. Plus, lift the lid and the stool holds her favorite toys! This company also makes a practical, foldable pet ramp for helping the dog in and out of your car.

Pet Ramp with Stool, $99.50 (11″), $129.50 (13″), $149.50 (15″) + $15 S&H
Vehicle Pet Ramp, $99.50 + $20 S&H (GA res. add 5% sales tax)

Petramp
4727 Lawrenceville Hwy.
Tucker, GA 30084
(770) 934-1053

Rosie— A Visiting Dog's Story ®

People thrive on companionship. It's been proven over and over again that having a pet helps add length and joy to people's lives. Rosie is a working dog who belongs to the Delta Society's Pet Partners Program and an organization called Therapy Dogs International. Her job is simple: She cheers up people in homes, hospitals, schools, and nursing homes. Great hardcover

book on the fabulous contribution dogs make to all of our lives.

By Stephanie Calmenson, 1994, 48 pp., $15.95 + UPS (MA res. add sales tax)

Clarion Books
Houghton Mifflin
222 Berkeley St.
Boston, MA 02116
(800) 225-3362

22

Bunk Buddies

This cool bunk bed is large enough for most dogs, measuring 28″ l. × 19″ w. The detachable bunks can be used as single beds. The ladder is also detachable, plus the bed will be personalized with your dog's name (up to 10 letters). Complete with mattress pads, but be nice and add a queen-size pillow for extra comfort! Nice for sleepovers—perhaps give the dogs a soothing chapter from Lassie as they drift off to sleep.

Dog Bunk Bed, $199 (includes S&H + sales tax)

Smart Dog Products
P.O. Box 1036
Picayune, MS 39466
(800) 264-DOGS

Hot Dog Weenie Bed!

This is a scream! Wildly happy Dachshund reclines in a simulated Hot Dog Bed, made of hot-dog-bun-colored cotton with a bright red weenie pillow sticking out both ends! Measures 26″ l. × 15″ w. Check out the Taco Bed too, made of cotton tortillalike fabric on the outside and plush fake fur on the inside, trimmed with cotton "lettuce" and "cheese." Machine washable, hang to dry, 20″ dia. The Burrito Bed is 30″ dia., made of cotton tortilla-like fabric, with Velcro closure so your pup can burrow into the Burrito tunnel. Machine washable, hang to dry. Food beds, California-style.

Hot Dog Bed,
$30 + $5 S&H
Taco Dog Bed,
$30 + $4 S&H
Burrito Dog Bed,
$30 + $4 S&H
(CA res. add $2.25 sales tax)

Small Town Ideas
P.O. Box 1905
Lower Lake, CA 95457
(800) 994-0552

Airport Mobility ®

Your dog is getting heavier and heavier with each step as you trudge miles to the gate at the airport. Sound familiar? The big advantage of this carrier is its wheels. You simply hook your leash onto a pin for easy towing. Many sizes, from small (21″ l. × 16¾″ w. × 18″ h.) to extra-large (40″ l. × 27″ w. × 27½″ h.). Plus it comes with

a built-in washable food and water bowl. Excellent ventilation, with a solid, lockable metal gate. The small unit has wheels and a carrying handle. If you remove the bottom and add a cushion, you have a cozy travel bed. Hunter green.

Kennel Express,
$29.95–$72.95 + UPS
(PA res. add 6% sales tax)

Stylette
P.O. Box 190
Oakdale, PA 15071
(412) 693-9484

Animals, Our Return to Wholeness

The entire field of animal communications has exploded during the past several years, heading east across America from California. Animal communication specialist Penelope Smith relates to animals as teachers, healers, and guides. In this book she records stories and principles communicated telepathically to her by animals, revealing their spiritual understanding, life purpose, and symbiotic relationship with humans. This book can be a real eye-opener, since she actually communicates with animals, claiming to know their thoughts and feelings. It's not as fringe as you might think. Besides, anything that develops compassion and understanding of animals can only be good.

By Penelope Smith, 1993, 355 pp., $ 19.95 + $2.50 S&H (CA res. add sales tax)

Pegasus Publications
P.O. Box 1060
Pt. Reyes Station, CA 94956
(800) 356-9315

Roll-It-Up Dog Pen

Traveling? Visiting the relatives? Need a quick enclosure for the pup? You can get your hands on this pen two ways. Buy the plans for $5 and buy the materials (pipe, end caps, #10 clothesline wire), and get a PVC cutter or handsaw, pliers, and drill to make it yourself. Or buy the pen preassembled. Made of long-lasting white PVC pipes with caps, the average size is 4′ in diameter and 2½′ high. Simply roll it up and put it under your arm when you want to move it. You can also have a custom model made in almost any size.

Portable Dog Pen (preassembled, 4′ dia.), $250 + UPS (NC res. add 6% sales tax)

Unique Ideas
153 E. Southwind Dr., Newport, NC 28570
(919) 726-8256

Happy Dog Pillow ®

Happy, wagging-tail pillow measures 16″ square and is made from 100% unbleached cotton, accented with black cording and silk-screened in black with water-based inks. Removable cover is machine washable.

Dog Pillow, $45
(includes S&H)
(CA res. add 8.5% sales tax)

Objects
1920 Union St.
Oakland, CA 94607
(510) 835-2728

The Meal with Legs

Recycled margarine tubs fit perfectly into this clever feeding-dish holder. The small holder (for toy breeds) uses ½-lb. margarine cups as food or water dishes. The large holder (for medium-size and larger dogs) accommodates 1-lb. margarine tubs. Fantasy Farm Products supplies the holder in a choice of 24 breeds. You supply the margarine dishes!

Feed Dish Holder,
$27.95 (sm.) + $5.85 S&H; $37.95 (lg.) + $6.85 S&H (WA res. add 7.8% sales tax)

Fantasy Farm Products Co.
P.O. Box 1262
Bellingham, WA 98227
(360) 734-9770

"Even a dog knows the difference between being tripped over and being kicked."

—Oliver Wendell Holmes

Those Creaking Joints

Special padding in this cushion distributes a dog's weight, reducing pressure on the joints of an ailing or convalescing dog. For a healthy pet, the pad is just a comfortable sleeping or resting place. Soft polyester and convoluted foam allows air to flow through the cushion to keep your dog drier. Cover (also sold separately) with a full-length zipper is easily removable for machine laundering.

Comfort Cushion, $20.25 (20″ × 20″), $25.50 (20″ × 30″), $42 (30″ × 40″), $58.50 (30″ × 60″) + $2 S&H (MN res. add 6.5% sales tax)

Four Flags over Aspen
34402 15th St.
Janesville, MN 56048
(800) 222-9263
E-mail: ffoa@ic.mankato.mn.us

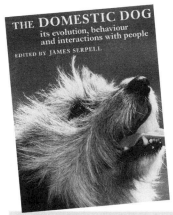

The Domestic Dog

This is perhaps the most scientific, best-researched book on dog history and behavior you'll ever find. It's a curious, scholarly approach to dogs, with hundreds of references, charts, and graphs, such as the one on the comparative sizes of their skull area and another detailing the "excitability" of common breeds. Fascinating, exquisite details. Technical pup talk.

Edited by James Serpell, 1995, 268 pp., $19.95 + UPS (NY res. add sales tax)

Cambridge University Press
110 Midland Ave.
Port Chester, NY 10573
(800) 872-7423

Senior Comfort ®

Any dog—especially an older dog—will appreciate the support provided by this remarkable bed. It combines a supersoft, polyester lambswool with convoluted, medical-grade polyfoam. Together they help provide pressure reduction for your dog's entire body. Sizes from 20″ square to 36″ × 48″. One of the most comfortable dog beds made.

Supersoft Orthopedic Dog Bed, $24.95–$55.95 + UPS (IL res. add sales tax)

Flexi-Mat
2244 S. Western Ave.
Chicago, IL 60608
(773) 376-5500

Easy Ins and Outs

You know the picture. The dog sits with his nose pressed to the screen door. Okay, time to let him out. But, with just a hammer and a knife, you can install this handy screen door into a door or window screen and stay seated. Made of durable lightweight plastic, it measures 8″ × 10″ and includes a security lock as well as preinstalled magnets to keep it from swinging in the wind. Fresh air without a hassle.

Pet Screen Door,
$25.95 + $4 S&H
(CA res. add 7.75% sales tax)

Borwick Innovations
P.O. Box 30345
Santa Barbara, CA 93130
(800) 365-5657

Happy, Warm Bed ®

Do you live in an army barracks? No? Then why have a boring dog bed? Four large fleecy bones in hot pink and purple decorate the corners of this terrific new Polarfleece dog bed. The happy design takes the boredom out of beds forever. Add in the hot pink and purple Polarfleece rattle ball, and you have both comfort and play. The best will do just fine.

Pawsitively Polar Bed,
$85 + $7.50 S&H
Pawsitively Rattle Ball,
$13 + $3.50 S&H
(MN res. add sales tax)

L. Coffey Ltd.
4244 Linden Hills Blvd.
Minneapolis, MN 55410
(800) 448-4PET

Plush Sleeping Comfort

Critter Rugs are resting mats made of dense, plush synthetic lambswool, filled with a single layer of Poly-Fil batting. Completely machine washable and dryable. Six attractive colors: mauve, blue, tan, white, gray, or mint. Sizes from 13″ × 18″ to 30″ × 40″. Each includes a small plush toy bone! Handcrafted quality.

Critter Rugs, $14–$60 + UPS
(includes CA sales tax)

R.V.B. Creations
2461 Vineyard Rd.
Novato, CA 94947
(800) 892-3192

Dog People ®

Some books have so much personality that reading one of them is like settling down with an old friend for a long talk. They can change your day and even your outlook on life. This is such a book. Twenty-two writers and artists talk about their lives with dogs, including their visual artistry. Jamie Wyeth's dog paintings and hilarious photos by William Wegman are side by side, followed by Edward Albee's deeply moving story of Irish Wolfhounds in "Harry Sighing." All profits from sales of this book benefit humane agencies across the country. Adoring portraits and prose.

By Michael J. Rosen, 1995,
160 pp., $25 + UPS
(NY res. add sales tax)

Artisan Books
Workman Publishing
708 Broadway
New York, NY 10003
(800) 722-7202

How's the View?

Mental stimulation is the best cure for a bored dog. This window box installs from the inside much like a portable air conditioner. Stress-tested to 120 lbs., it won't deface your window with brackets, screws, or holes. You can use it in any window. I suggest installing one facing the street for maximum viewing activity. It's available in 6 sizes and has 2 screens on the ends, to allow in fresh air and sounds. The floor and watertight ceiling are completely clear, for viewing pleasure. Regular size is 22″ w. × 18″ h. × 24″ dia. Acrylic, UV resistant, strong plastic, replacement parts if you ever need them, 3-year frame guarantee. Any weather, all-year viewing fun. A dog's view of the world.

Regular Pet Patio,
$189 + $27 S&H
(NJ res. add 6% sales tax)

Angora Industries
P.O. Box 17
Metuchen, NJ 08840
(800) 804-3451
E-mail: PetPatio@aol. com

Pillow for Two

Cozy comfort for two little cuties or one big dog. Handmade from designer dog-pattern fabrics in two styles: Original pillow has piping along the side, with bottom zippers; deluxe pillow has fabric side border with piping on both the top and bottom. Dry clean. Removable cover, replacement covers available. Luxurious comfort.

Lov Bedzz
Small (21″ × 21″) $52 (original), $80 (deluxe)
Medium (28″ × 28″) $64 (original), $110 (deluxe)
Large (38″ × 38″) $90 (original), $150 (deluxe)
+ UPS (Tex. res. add sales tax)

PetLink
13164 Memorial Dr., #134
Houston, TX 77079
(888) PET-LINK

The Big Moment ®

For most dogs, meals are the highlight of the day. If you have an enthusiastic, eager eater, you'll need a mat to put under his food dish. You know what I'm talking about. Minimalist art mats keep cleanup simple.

Happy Dog or Crazy Cat Mats, $2.95 + UPS
(WA res. add 8.2% sales tax)

Keller Design
P.O. Box 3854
Seattle, WA 98154
(800) 683-1227
E-mail: Petbuds@ix.netcom.com

TRUE DOG TALE

Monk's Companion

The gorgeous Lhasa Apso originated in Tibet. For hundreds, perhaps thousands of years, it was the companion pet of Buddhist monks. It was also a resident of the Potala, the thousand-room palace of the Dalai Lama. A gift of this dog—treasured for its watchful temperament—conferred good luck on the recipient. Tibetans did not part with the Lhasa Apso easily—it's been in the West for only 80 years.

Flying Saucer Bed? ®

Star Trek bed? Well, not really, but this "ultimate in dog bedding" has lots of space-age benefits. The special poly/cedar fill helps repel fleas, while the superior resilience and softness of the fill maximizes comfort. Heavy-duty nylon zipper on the completely removable, machine-washable and -dryable cover. Bolster back protects your walls while providing a convenient headrest. A superior big bed for one (or more) lucky dogs.

Teddy Bed (23″–57″ dia.), $24.95–$59.95 + UPS (IL res. add sales tax)

Flexi-Mat
2244 S. Western Ave.
Chicago, IL 60608
(773) 376-5500

R&R Dribbler Pad

Good old rest and relaxation. You might as well make it as pleasant as possible for your dog with this waterproof (great for dribblers), cushioned, flannel-covered rest pad. Perfect for a nap or to protect your sofa or car seat. Machine washable and dryable, measures 26″ × 33″.

Pup Pad, $19.95 + $5.25 S&H (no sales tax in OR)

Pampered Pups Extraordinaire
647 S. 44th St.
Springfield, OR 97478
(541) 746-3801
E-mail: cavlady@pond.net

Bichon Frise ®

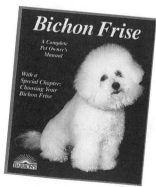

Is this the cutest dog in the world? Every owner of a Bichon Frise says so. That sweet face and diminutive size originated back in the time of the Romans, when a medium-size dog called the Barbet was crossed with a small white lapdog. From this cross came the Poodle, Maltese, and four varieties of the Bichon. This lovely book, with color illustrations, contains information about the purchase, care, nutrition, breeding, behavior, and training of your beautiful Bichon.

By Richard G. Beauchamp, 1996, 96 pp., $6.95 + UPS (NY res. add sales tax)

Barron's Educational Series
250 Wireless Blvd.
Hauppauge, NY 11788
(800) 645-3476

Overnight Rest Stop

Overnight canine guests? Thoughtful hosts pull out this handy Dog Futon for a comfortable party! The cushion measures 24″ × 30″, and the pine frame (it requires some modest, idiotproof assembly) measures 22″ × 30″. The soft cotton futon has a washable cover. Spare comfort when you need it, or your dog just might claim it as her permanent bed!

Dog Futon and Cushion,
$92 + UPS
(CA res. add sales tax)

Hound Alley
4811 Venner Rd.
Martinez, CA 94553
(888) 255-4322

Welcome Home!

Here's the best pet-door solution for sliding-glass doors. The panel fits into the door's frame, leaving the door partially open (adjusts to a frame height of 77½″ to 82½″). The door can be locked with the panel in place. Easily installed aluminum-frame door includes weather stripping for an airtight seal. Shatterproof tempered glass above the pet door lets the light through. Alterations are not necessary for installation on most door frames. Keep it simple.

Johnson Patio Panel
Toy breeds (Pug, Fox Terrier, Maltese, etc.), $163
Medium breeds (Basset, Cocker, etc.), $169.99
Large breeds (German Shepherd, Boxer, etc.), $187.99
+ $9.99 S&H
(WI res. add 5% sales tax)

Drs. Foster and Smith
P.O. Box 100
Rhinelander, WI 54501
(800) 826-7206 (24 hours)

The Rich Look of Tapestry ®

Upscale stylish carriers feature a chic tapestry design, a mesh opening for ventilation and air circulation, and a clever, removable soft-padded floor for easy cleaning. Available in two sizes: small (15″ l. × 8″ h. × 10″ w.) and large (18″ l. × 10½″ h. × 11⅕″ w.). Great for a trip to the vet or flying across the country. Both sizes meet the pet carry-on requirements of most major airlines.

Tapestry Design Pet Carrier, $33.66 (sm.), $41.16 (lg.) + UPS
(CA res. add sales tax)

Classic Products
1451 Vanguard Dr.
Oxnard, CA 93033
(800) 228-0105

Let's Hit the Road, Pup

Thinking of taking a trip with the dog? Here are some helpful hints to make it work for both of you. Before your trip:

1. Check with the vet to make sure your dog is healthy. If the vet suggests tranquilizers, try them on the dog before you leave.

2. Bring along your dog's health certificates. Airlines, international customs, and kennels will expect to see them. Depending upon where you're going, ask your vet about special vaccines and areas with epidemics and quarantines.

3. Call the airline before traveling with your dog. Advance reservations for dogs are required, and there are rules about crate size and documents. Most airlines will allow a small dog in a pet carrier into the passenger compartment. Insist upon this to prevent trauma to your dog in the luggage compartment from flight delays, pressurization problems, and heat and cold dangers.

4. Hold back on food before traveling, to prevent upset. A 2-hour fast is best if you are traveling by car, 6 hours when flying. Never try new dog foods when traveling.

5. Heat is dangerous to dogs. Bring along adequate water and ice cubes for drinking. Never leave a dog alone in a hot car, even with the windows cracked in the shade. If necessary, leave the air conditioner on. In an emergency wet the dog down with water.

Just Loungin' Around ®

Do these dogs look comfortable or what? The Pet Couch has a nice form-fit design so a dog can lean right into it. A durable foam border with removable, reversible, and washable cushion, with your choice of polycotton or faux sheepskin lining. Sizes: small (16″ × 22″), medium (21″ × 27″), and large (26″ × 34″). The Flopper bed is great for maximum comfort and durability, plus the nylon shell is water resistant. Filled with tiny polystyrene pellets (like a beanbag chair), it molds to your dog's shape! Zippered end, inner-printed polycotton shell. Colors: hunter green, navy blue, burgundy, and black. Sizes: small (19″ × 22″), medium (26″ × 34″), large (shown, 28″ × 41″), x-large (32″ × 46″), and jumbo (36″ × 53″). Don't be surprised if the kids wind up sitting on the dog's bed! The Cloud features superlofty polyester fill with aromatic cedar as a natural insect repellent and for freshness. One side is sheepskin, the other polycotton. The zippered cover, which removes for cleaning, comes in a wide choice of patterns. It will look like the dog's floating on a soft cloud. One big, wonderful size: 45″ dia.

Pet Couch (large), $44.99
Flopper (jumbo), $49.99
The Cloud, $39.99
+ UPS (shipped in U.S.)
(Includes sales tax)

Cloud "K" Nine Pet Products
Kwilt Kraft
4765 Blvd. de Grandes Prairies
St. Leonard, Quebec
Canada H1A 1A5
(514) 327-2460, ext. 203

Travelin' Bedroll

Perfect for traveling, this extra-large, 4' × 6', 100% cotton quilt is designed for rugged everyday use. Looks sharp with braided latigo leather handling strap and nickel bolt snap. Deep blue with black edging. First class all the way.

Cotton Bedroll Quilt,
$58 + $5.50 S&H
(IL res. add 8% sales tax)

Baxter and Charming, Ltd.
11 W. Main
Carpentersville, IL 60110
(800) 569-2761
E-mail: Baxterpets@aol.com

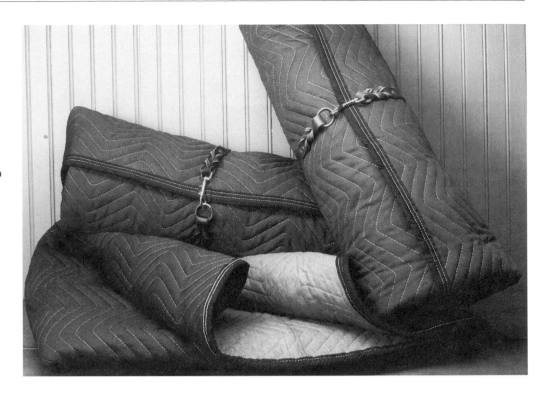

Easy Access ®

Mount this Pet Door almost anywhere. The telescoping frame adapts itself to all hollow-core and solid doors of 1¼" to 1¾" thickness. Installation time

averages 30 minutes. No extra hardware or framing necessary. Lockable clear flap. You can paint the frame to match your house or trim color. Five sizes: small (5" × 8"), medium (7" × 11¼"), large (9" × 15"), extra-large (10½" × 15") and extra,-extra-large (15" × 20"). Ask about patio doors and the Pet Passage for screen doors and windows. Color brochure in English and Spanish.

Ideal Pet Door,
$24.99 and up + UPS
(CA res. add sales tax)

Ideal Pet Products
24735 Ave. Rockefeller
Valencia, CA 91355
(800) 378-4385

Hammock for the Road

Are you traveling? Going to a show? Keeping your friend in a wire crate while you do? This hammock hooks into wire crates with a width of 18" or 21", suspending the dog off the floor in sumptuous jungle comfort. Made of Sunbrella 100% acrylic woven fabric, it includes four hooks for hanging. You can make it fit a plastic kennel if you lengthen the suspension with ropes or chains. Colors: red/white stripe, light/dark brown stripe, light/dark green stripe. Vastly more comfy than a hard floor. Cool leisure look.

The Original Creature Cradle, $27 + $3 S&H
(VA res. add sales tax)

Meco Enterprises
1145 Hanover Ave.
Norfolk, VA 23508
(804) 489-8024

Let's Get Comfortable! ®

Who doesn't like comfort? For starters, try out the Pet Pillow for your dog, available in 4 styles and a variety of colors. Convenient zippered cover removes for washing; options include the exclusive UltraSuede (extra-soft) or a delightful cotton pattern. Your choice of feather or polyfiber filling. Festive holiday prints, too!

UltraSuede Pet Pillow
(with down and feathers),
$200 + S&H
UltraSuede Pet Pillow
(with fiberfill), $140 + S&H
Cotton Pet Pillow
(with down and feathers),
$150 + S&H
Cotton Pet Pillow
(with fiberfill), $50 + S&H
(MI res. add 5% sales tax)

UltraMouse, Ltd.
1442 E. Park Place
Ann Arbor, MI 48104
(800) 573-8869

Wild and Crazy Furs ®

Now you can choose from 5 sensational decorative animal patterns on a *totally washable* dog bed. No removing covers. You toss the entire bed into your washer and dryer. The cover is 100% acrylic, and the filling material is "memory fiber"

bonded polyester. Sizes from 18″ × 28″ to 38″ × 48″. Cuddly soft, exotically styled, big bed fun.

Flexi-Furs, $29.95–$44.95
+ UPS
(IL res. add sales tax)

Flexi-Mat
2244 S. Western Ave.
Chicago, IL 60608
(773) 376-5500

"Why that dog is practically a Phi Beta Kappa. She can sit up and beg, and she can give her paw—I don't say she will, but she can."

—Dorothy Parker

Stuffed Dalmatians

Whimsical caricatures of tail-wagging Dalmatians make this plush, poly-fiber-fill pillow with piping

pleasing to the eye. Pattern on the reverse side is a solid or print, color coordinated with the design on the front.

Dalmatians Pillow,
$20 + $3 S&H ($5 S&H for 2)
(PA res. add sales tax)

Up the Creek
1209 Rose Glen Rd.
Gladwyne, PA 19035
E-mail:
jsmith4287@aol.com
http://home.navisoft.
com/utc/utc.htm

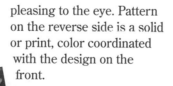
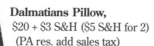

Wild Puppies ®

Goodness. A nicely photographed book of cute pups in the wild. With Mom. Growing up. Learning to hunt. Includes Gray Wolf, Gray Fox, Red Fox, Swift Fox, Arctic Fox, Coyote, African Wild Dog, Bat-eared Fox, Black-backed Jackal, Dhole, Dingo, Ethiopian Wolf, Fennec Fox, Iberian Wolf, Maned Wolf, Raccoon Dog, and Red Wolf pups in their natural environments around the world.

By Peggy Bauer, 1995,
78 pp., $10.95 + UPS
(CA res. add sales tax)

Chronicle Books
275 Fifth Ave.
San Francisco, CA
94013
(800) 722-6657

Feel the Field

At last! A magnetic dog bed! Sewn inside a quality foam pad are ceramic magnets, covered with removable, dark blue fabric. The pad is available in 3 sizes: small, 16″ square, with 25 magnets; medium, 24″ × 32″, with 42 magnets; large, 32″ × 36″, with 56 magnets. As your dog rests and sleeps, these magnets (according to the company) help promote blood circulation, which increases oxygen and helps reduce inflamed joints, arthritis, rheumatism, and hip dysplasia. It's called magnetic therapy. Ask your holistic vet.

Magnetic Dog Pad,
$39 (sm.), $49 (med.),
$69 (lg.) + $5 S&H
($5 add. for Canadian shipments)
(IL res. add 6.5% sales tax)

American Health Service Magnetics
531 Bank Ln.
Highwood, IL 60040
(800) 544-7521

Austrian Dog Blanket

Don't be surprised if your dog refuses to part with his blankie. This superb, very soft blanket is made in Austria of 95% cotton, with 5% viscose added for soft fluffy texture. Resilient and long-lasting; available in multiple colors and designs; manufactured from raw cotton without dyes, bleaches, or chemicals. Throw it over your dog's favorite chair. An attractive, superior blanket for chilly nights—and it keeps the hair off your furniture.

Royal Pet Blanket,
$14.90–$21.25 (med.),
$19.75–$27.50 (lg.) + UPS
(CA res. add sales tax)

Carry Me
130 E. Grand Ave.
Escondido, CA 92025
(619) 480-8444

The Height of Luxury

This fabulous Victorian-inspired chaise in muted French pinks and blues provides a lucky dog with a superb resting and observation place. Featuring a tufted polyester pillow top, it's perfect for the pet connoisseur. The base is a resilient 100% polyurethane foam core. The one-piece cover is removable and machine washable. Measures 14″ w. × 12″ h. × 31″ l. For the queen (or king) of the house. Prepare yourself for compliments.

Pet Chaise, $44.95 + UPS
(CA res. add sales tax)

Lazy Pet Products
540 W. Lambert Rd.
Brea, CA 92621
(800) 622-1288

Igloo and Pyramid Dreams

Here's the perfect escape to dog-dreamland. The Igloo is perfect for the dog who likes to cuddle up out of sight. The medium Igloo is 21″ dia., with a 8½″ × 9½″ door opening and a 14″ floor-to-ceiling height. The large Igloo is 24″ dia., with an 11″ × 12″ door opening and an inside height of 17″. The stunning Pyramid is just about the coolest dog shack in town, measuring 24″ square, with a door opening of 11″ × 10½″ and an inside height of 17″. Both houses have a base of 2″ foam, with a removable, machine-washable fleece cover. Available in a variety of solid colors and prints. You can lift off the top in warm weather and let Pooch sleep on the fleece base. In cold weather the top traps the dog's body heat, keeping him warm. Suitable for use indoors, or perhaps on a covered patio. It's not waterproof, and it'll disappear down the road in a stiff wind, so keep it inside. Every dog needs some space.

Dog Igloos, $48 (med.), $54 (lg.)
Dog Pyramid, $52 (includes S&H; no sales tax in NV)

Cozy Critters
P.O. Box 5173
Gardnerville, NV 89410
(702) 265-2260
E-mail: CozyCritrs@aol.com

The Complete Book of Dogs ®

Lavish color photography makes this a beautiful general reference for most of the popular dog breeds. There's plenty of useful canine information: history, sizes and shapes of breeds, puppy care, and dog health and safety. But it's the pictures that make the book a real winner. Packed with adorable puppy photos and big, bright shots of our favorite dogs, in a large format. A must-have hardcover gift book for any dog lover.

By Yvonne Rees, 1993, 124 pp., $19.95 + UPS
(NJ res. add sales tax)

Crescent Books
Outlet Book Co.
Random House
40 Engelhard
Ave.
Avenel, NJ 07001
(800) 793-2665

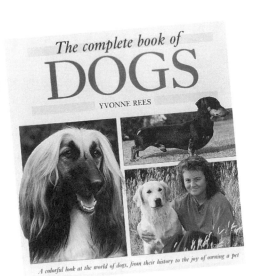

The complete book of **DOGS** YVONNE REES

A colorful look at the world of dogs, from their history to the joy of owning a pet

Canopy Comfort

There it is at the gift show: a tiny exquisite canopy bed for dogs in ultramodern, high-tech steel, next to its much larger twin version for adults. Its luxurious fabrics include washable cream silk, gold silk Tissue Crunch with pearls. Measuring 20″ w. × 27″ d. × 27″ h., it includes a comfy mattress as well as lavish fabrics. Now there's adorable luxury for your little one—right next to your own bed.

Doggie Bed, $750 + $20 S&H
(CA res. add sales tax)

Anne Gish
3529 Old Conejo Rd.
Suite 117
Newbury Park, CA 91320
(805) 498-4447

Flip for Comfort!

Wow! Imagine your dog in this Flip Chair or Flip Couch with a beautiful floral-print cover, which is completely washable and zippered for easy removal. The Flip Chair opens to 33½″ l. × 18½″ h. × 29″ d., while the couch (for larger dogs or two small dogs) measures a big 50″ l. × 18½″ h. × 29″ d. The amusing flip feature is perfect for overnight guests!

Flip Chair, $44.95 + UPS
Flip Couch, $59.95 + UPS

Flexi-Mat
2244 S. Western Ave.
Chicago, IL 60608
(773) 376-5500

What's a House Without a Dog?

Catinka knows. She makes a great Little Pillow and a Big Dog Bed, each bearing the inscription: "Home Is Where the Dog Is." That's her own "dog-pound-wonder-dog" Stymie with the faux leopard pillow, which includes gold and silver tasseling with lettering on a white background. The Big Dog Bed is of blue material with a red heart and dark blue lettering. Around the heart, yellow bones fly with blue wings. Fun, upbeat dog products. Catinka's color catalog is a wild mélange of exuberant life and cool, from-the-heart stuff for pets.

Little Pillow, $60 + $6 S&H
Big Dog Bed,
$80 + $6 S&H
(CA res. add sales tax)

Catinka
245 Longfellow
Hermosa Beach, CA 90254
(310) 318-5222

Let in Some Cool Air

You need one of these if your dog travels in the car. A temperature of 80° outside can mean a temperature of 120° inside your car within 30 minutes—well within the danger zone of brain damage and heatstroke. This vent lets in air but prevents theft. It installs and removes in seconds; self-locks in the window channel; adjusts to fit any four-door car and most pickups; made of unbreakable plastic. Fold it up and leave it in the trunk when you don't need it.

Pet Vent, $11.18 + UPS
(FL res. add sales tax)

Hamilton Products
P.O. Box 770069
Ocala, FL 34477
(352) 237-6188

The Quotable Canine

In golden brown duotones a dog looks out at us from each spread, accompanied by a few memorable words. In this hardcover are the thoughts of Winston Churchill on pugs, Madame de Sévigné on the obvious deficiencies of men compared with any dog, Groucho Marx's dog humor, Edith Wharton on her little dog, and so on. The man from Missouri, Harry S. Truman, said it best: "Children and dogs are as necessary to the welfare of the country as Wall Street and the railroads." Amen.

Edited by Jim Dratfield and Paul Coughlin, 1995, 90 pp., $20 + UPS
(NY res. add sales tax)

Doubleday
1540 Broadway
New York, NY 10036
(800) 223-6834

TRUE DOG TALE

A Growing Hazard

Decorating? Many common (and not so common) house plants are poisonous to dogs. Ask your vet about poisonous house plants in your area. Here's a partial list of indoor plants that don't belong in a house with a dog:

Amaryllis	Holly
Asparagus fern	Ivies (most)
Azalea	Japanese yew
Bird of paradise	Lily of the valley (often
Castor bean (potentially	fatal)
fatal)	Mistletoe (often fatal)
Cherry (Jerusalem and	Mother-in-law's tongue
ordinary)	Ornamental yew
Creeping Charlie	Philodendron (often fatal)
Crown of thorns	Poinsettia (leaves often
Dieffenbachia	fatal)
Dragon tree	Pot or spider chrysanthe-
Easter lily (often fatal)	mum
Elderberry	Rhubarb
Elephant ears	Sprangeri fern
Foxglove	Umbrella plant

Dog Tales: Lessons in Love from Guideposts ®

Dogs can teach us valuable life lessons. These heartwarming stories contain religious insights into how dog friendship, loyalty, forgiveness, acceptance, nurturing, trust, help, loving, and grieving can help us, as people, cope with life when trouble arrives at our door. Scriptural quotations from the King James Bible. Dogs, thankfully, can be steady anchors in a heavy wind.

Foreword by Marjorie Holmes; reprinted from *Guideposts* magazine and *Daily Guideposts*, 1995, 96 pp., $7 + UPS (Tenn. res. add sales tax)

Dimensions for Living
Abingdon Press
Division of the United
Methodist Publishing House
201 Eighth Ave. South
Nashville, TN 37203
(800) 251-3320

Buckwheat Bed ®

The Sobagara Buckster dog bed changes shape because it's filled with buckwheat hulls. Cool in summer, warm in winter, it won't attract odors or retain moisture. The buckwheat hulls are durable and won't break down. The zippered case is removable, so the hulls can be aired naturally. Made of 100% durable cotton fabric, with your choice of designer prints. Very light, with an interesting feel. The shape changes as you squeeze the hulls. Interesting, very comfortable natural product.

Sobagara Buckster,
$45.95 + UPS
(CA res. add 7.5% sales tax)

Sobagara Enterprises
70A W. North St.
Healdsburg, CA 95448
(800) 369-2000

Who Put a Bone in the Chair?

You did! This snazzy Bone Pillow, in a classic shape, is a wonderful adornment to a dog lover's chair or sofa. Perfect on your dog's bed, too. Print shows a variety of dogs; elegant brocade trim. Pile 'em on.

Bone Pillow,
$32 + $4.50 S&H
(IL res. add sales tax)

Creature Comforts
Tyler & Russell, Ltd.
357 W. Erie St.
2nd Floor
Chicago, IL 60610
(312) 266-0907

Rustic Log Cabin Living

You might want to rename your dog Abe when he takes up residence in this Lincoln-esque log cabin. The log walls contain steel rods for strength. Each house is stained in red oak, cherry, or mahogany—then coated with polyurethane for durability. Or you can opt for the no-stain, natural look and let it age with the elements. It has easy-to-clean, wall-to-wall carpeting—just lift one of the log walls and vacuum. The manufacturers are very nice folks who will gladly build you a custom Log Cabin Dog House. They resist the phone, so write or fax.

Log Cabin Dog House,
$117–$228 + UPS
(NY res. add 7% sales tax)

Mini-Log Structures
P.O. Box 0230
Hammond, NY 13646
(315) 324-5518 (fax)

Way Beyond the Ordinary

These exquisite dog beds are just a sampling of the upscale, attractive dog furniture offered by Beastly Beds. The elegant Regency is a solid mahogany four-poster with "ebonized" uprights and gold finials. The mahogany has a rich finish and will look smart in the most stylish of room decors. The tailored, machine-washable green velvet cushion slips easily off its foam base. The Country Cottage is an old-fashioned, comfy, handpainted, white wooden bed. Rounded feet and ball finials, combined with a red-and-cream-checked cushion, give the bed a country feeling. The entire cushion is machine washable. Both beds are for owners with attractive homes and apartments who expect attractive dog furniture to match their decor. Ask about the wrought-iron French Provincial bed and the Shaker Box beds (not shown). Quality speaks for itself.

Regency Dog Bed, $395
Country Cottage Dog Bed,
$325 + UPS (appx. 45 lbs.)
(NY res. add sales tax)

Beastly Beds
P.O. Box 498
Pine Plains, NY 12567
(518) 398-6617

A Ride with a View ®

Is this furniture? Well, yes. It's dog furniture for your car. The dog-restraint seat allows your best buddy to look out the window or curl up for a nice nap. The Joyride Pet Seat is equipped with a convenient handle and washable seat cushion. Simply place it on the front or rear vehicle seat, and secure it with the vehicle seat belt. In my opinion, it's best to place it on the back seat if you have airbags. Then attach the coupler from your dog's harness onto the handle to keep the dog in place. Lightweight, available in black, light gray, and light almond, with matching hardware and seat cushion. Seatbelts make sense for both you and the dog. A great solution for smaller dogs that like to see the view—with you!

Joyride Pet Seat,
$69.95 and up + UPS
(AZ res. add sales tax)

PPS Enterprises
P.O. Box 5418
Scottsdale, AZ 85261
(888) 229-1537

"Every dog has his day."
—Charles Kingsley

Warmable, Coolable Dog Bed

Hot or cold, this bed can handle it. Inside the cushion is a red Lava Heat Element pad that you unzip and remove. To keep the bed warm for up to 8 hours, just pop the pad into the microwave for 5 minutes. Hot summer night? Keep the bed cool by refrigerating the pad for 4–6 hours. Then simply insert it back into the cushion, zip it up, and your dog stays cool for hours! Nonelectric element pad is reusable thousands of times and contains a non-toxic, nonirritating, non-staining thermal fluid. Soft durable cover in a pleasing blue color. Two sizes: small (16″ × 20″) and large (20″ × 32″). Nice quality, great change-of-seasons idea.

LavaPet Cushion, $30 (sm.), $50 (lg.) + $5 S&H (NC res. add 6% sales tax)

Vesture Corp.
120 E. Pritchard St.
Asheboro, NC 27203
(800) 283-7887

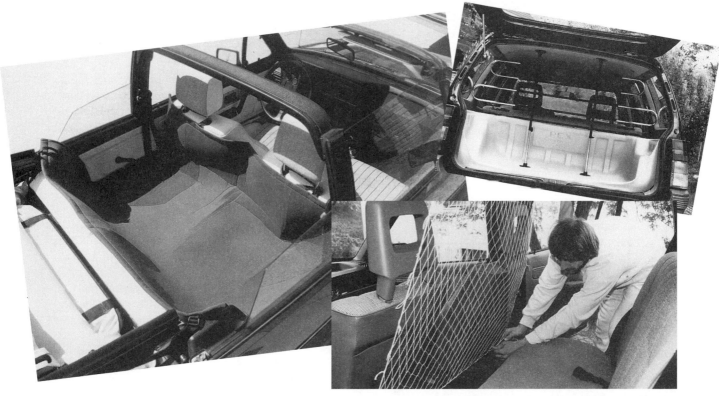

Dog Transit

Meblo's got good ideas about driving your dog around. Deluxe Travelbed is a car-seat saver. It covers the entire back seat, attracting hair, and protecting against soiling, and the hammock shape cradles your dog. Its 4 lbs. of extra-thick, padded fabric is easily installed by using straps around the headrests and seatbelt loops. Protective Car Net is great for those "dog hoppers" who just can't stay out of the front seat! Made of strong nylon netting, easy to install, stores in the glove box when not in use. Euro Car Barrier (4-bar barrier) keeps the dog in back, off the seats. It fits station wagons and hatchbacks, adjusts up to 40″ in height, has easy installation (and removal) with no drilling, features a popular European design with German craftsmanship. Polished aluminum side rods telescope in and out to fit. Screwjack system ensures a tight fit on the floor and ceiling. Two other versions, including one for Suburbans and mini-vans and other vehicles.

Deluxe Travelbed, $80
Protective Car Net, $44 (standard), $74 (extra strong)
Euro Car Barriers (4-bar), $80 (includes S&H)
(CA res. add 6.5% sales tax)

Meblo
2250 Road "E"
Redwood Valley, CA 95470
(800) 776-3256
http://www.meblo.com

Home in a Hurry

What if you're traveling or you're stuck someplace with your dog for hours? Do you keep her crammed in a carrier? Locked in the car? The Home Stretch is a patented, portable, collapsible dog shelter/enclosure. Made of water-resistant fabric, it has staking tabs for outside use and a tab to attach a dog leash. Comes with a 4′ (mini-version has 3′) screened, zippered "run"—and the whole unit fits into its own carrying case. Four sizes, from mini to large. Particularly handy if you need to shelter your dog in the event—God forbid—of an earthquake or other natural calamity. Housing a dog can be problematic if you must suddenly leave home. Take this, the leash, a few bowls, and food and water, and your dog is protected. Requires little storage space; quick setup. Smart, portable shelter.

Home Stretch, $127 (sm.), $192 (lg.) + $6.25 S&H + UPS (CA res. add 7% sales tax)

Stopgap Enterprises
1240 S. Grade Rd.
Alpine, CA 91901
(619) 445-8856

A Bed for the Road ®

On the move? Along with your favorite pillow, be sure to bring this reversible, machine-washable/dryable, stain-resistant fleece bed. Folds or rolls up for convenient storage. Warm in winter, cool in summer, a just-right bed that provides the basic comforts of home. Sizes from 15″ × 20″ to 30″ × 40″. A bed like this can provide your dog with a sense of familiarity and security while you travel.

Flexi-Fleece, $19.95–$32.95 + UPS (IL res. add sales tax)

Flexi-Mat
2244 S. Western Ave.
Chicago, IL 60608
(312) 376-5500

Pooch Buckle-Up Combo ®

You can go straight from the car to the street with this seatbelt that converts into a harness on any size dog. Just adjust to fit (3 sizes, sm., med., and lg.), then clip the end of the harness into your seatbelt holder. Push on your seatbelt holder to release. Compatible with virtually all U.S., Japanese, and Korean vehicles made since 1980. Check the chart when you buy to make sure.

Adjustable Harness and Safety Seatbelt for Dogs, $18.95 + UPS (AZ res. add sales tax)

Omaha Vaccine Pet Catalog: (800) 367-4444

Pet Affairs
691 E. 20th St.
Building 111
Tucson, AZ 85719
(800) 777-9192

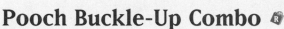

The Acarium

Picture this in your living room! It's nothing less than a sawed-off vintage Volkswagen Beetle that doubles as an aquarium and luxurious dog bed. Made by Los Angeles artist David Bailey, the entire passenger compartment is a brilliantly designed 110-gal. aquarium, while the hood doubles as a spectacular dog bed, resplendent with mauve leather tucks and rolls, reminiscent of a scallop shell. Sweet dreams for a very lucky—and very rich—dog.

**Acarium Canine Bed
with a View,** $60,000 + Shipping
(CA res. add sales tax)

Aquatecture
David Bailey
672 S. Avenue 21, Studio #6
Los Angeles, CA 90031
(213) 225-1021
E-mail: eyebeam@prime
net.com

The Personality of the Dog ®

Take this great collection of dog stories on a plane or to the beach, or just settle in for some good reading by the fireplace. Beautiful hardcover contains stories—by the likes of Virginia Woolf, Jack London, Anton Chekhov, and many others—that illustrate the personalities and eccentricities of dogs. Illustrated with paintings by Toulouse-Lautrec, Winslow Homer, Delacroix, and other fine artists. No need to hurry. The best books are meant to be savored.

Edited by Brandt Aymar and Edward Sagarin, 1995, 356 pp., $9.99 + UPS
(NJ res. add sales tax)

Wings Books
Random House Value
Publishing
40 Engelhard Ave.
Avenel, NJ 07001
(800) 793-2665

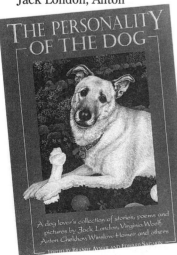

Brilliant Quotes

By luck, I stumbled upon this attractive Quilt and Pillow at a craft show. The silk-screen images are hand-painted on both new and vintage cottons. Both are multicolored, but you can specify a dominant background choice of blue, turquoise, green, or purple. The small Quilt is 22″ × 36″, the Pillow is approx. 18″ square with a cotton cover and contains a commercial pillow foam. On either, your choice of: "Every Dog Has His Day" or "Every Dog Has Her Day." Colorful, beautiful!

**Every Dog Has Her/
His Day:**
Quilt, $90
Pillow, $60 + UPS
(MA res. add sales tax)

Boss/Brown
11 Water Lane
Easthampton, MA 01027
(413) 527-9675

Photograph: John Polak

Soft Dreams ®

Fun shapes and wild designs make this unusual dog bed a big hit with hip owners. The durable, removable, washable cover protects a therapeutic cushion, for maximum comfort. Picture your dog sleeping on a raccoon, a teddy bear, a hippo, or a tiger!

Soft Sleep Dog Bed, $76.16–$126.96 + UPS (CO res. add sales tax)

Aspen Pet Products
11701 E. 53rd Ave.
Denver, CO 80239
(800) BUY-4-PET

Home Is Where the Mat Is

Whether at home or traveling, a dog feels good having a place of her own to rest. The Mutt Mat is made of heavy-weight 100% cotton, quilted with Poly-Fil. It's extremely durable, available in many attractive colors (with coordinating prints on the reverse side), and totally machine washable (just toss it in and tumble dry), and it includes a slipknot travel cord so you can roll it up for your next trip. Most importantly, it's comfortable, smells like your dog, and works just fine for floors, furniture, crates, or cars. It's home wherever you are.

Mutt Mats, $11.95 (toy, 18″ × 20″), $14.95 (med., 22″ × 28″), $17.95 (lg., 30″ × 36″), $21.95 (x-lg., 36″ × 42″) + $5.45 S&H (TN res. add 8.25% sales tax)

The Zerick Co.
837 Country Lane
Walland, TN 37886
(800) 977-1650

Your Puppy's First Home

Expecting? Your dog will need a safe, warm, quiet place to give birth and nurse her puppies. The quick-assembly, unbreakable Dura-Whelp polypropylene-plastic whelping box comes in 4 sizes with a hinged door. The entire box assembles with Velcro tabs—no tools needed. Chlorine cleansers, water, detergent, and scrub brushes won't damage the durable surface. Add a sherpa pad (sold separately) for warm, soft, new-puppy comfort. Curious about what will be happening? Prepare yourself for the big event with a 90-minute *Special Delivery* video on birth and how to take care of those new arrivals.

Dura-Whelp (34″ × 34″), $120.95
Special Delivery (VHS video tape), $34 + UPS (NJ res. add 6% sales tax)

Fawn Run Corp.
1122 Ramapo Valley Rd.
Mahwah, NJ 07430
(800) 998-3331

Enjoying the View

Riding in the car isn't all that great for small dogs. They can't see out the window, and many get carsick as a result. Solution? The Pet Car Seat provides a comfortable and secure resting place that protects both you and your dog. The safety harness keeps small dogs up to 10 lbs. in place when you stop suddenly. Machine washable. Nice view.

Pet Car Seat, $32 + 5.95 S&H (TX res. add 7.25% sales tax)

Accessory Pet
5836 Pathfinder Trail
Plano, TX 75093
(800) 558-7387

Sweeter Dreams

Look at this. The incredible deluxe bed in a rich Jacobean floral print, edged with braided cord, is the pinnacle of quality canine furniture. Tufted sides provide extra comfort. Zip-off, machine-washable cotton cover; high-density polyfoam fill. Specify burgundy or hunter; two sizes from which to choose. Elegant.

Braided Jacobean Bed,
$90 (S/M, approx. 17″ × 24″)
+ $10.95 S&H; $125
(M/L, approx. 24″ × 36″)
+ $12.95 S&H
(NY res. add sales tax)

In the Company of Dogs
P.O. Box 7071
Dover, DE 19903
(800) 924-5050

Rest Those Weary Bones

Now *there's* a big bone for dogs. Made of luxurious white sheepskin, this pillow is shaped like an oversize dog bone. Durable, tear-resistant inner sack has a Velcro opening to adjust foam filler, or add cedar chips to repel fleas. Heavy-duty zipper allows the cover to be easily removed for machine laundering.

Bone Pillow, $37 + $5.95 S&H (TX res. add 7.25% sales tax)

Accessory Pet
5836 Pathfinder Trail
Plano, TX 75093
(800) 558-7387

Communicating with Your Dog ®

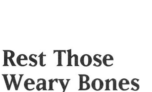

On TV or in the movies, you may have seen a shepherd waving his arms, instructing his dog to move a herd of sheep this way or that. The dog responds to the shepherd's visual and verbal commands. Now in this cool book, you can learn how to communicate 20 magic word commands and 5 hand signals to your dog. Makes sense. Dogs are always watching what we do—they know it's walk time if you head to the closet for the leash—and this great training book has color photographs to help with your lessons. It's great to watch a well-trained dog.

By Ted Baer, 1989,
144 pp., $10.95 + UPS
(NY res. add sales tax)

Barron's Educational Series
250 Wireless Blvd.
Hauppauge, NY 11788
(800) 645-3476

Simple Sofa Protection ®

This big (30″ × 60″) throw is very soft and comfortable, just right for protecting your sofa, chair, or automobile seat. Supereasy care—just toss it in the washer and dryer. Guaranteed not to shrink or fade. Available in blue, beige, or green. Dogs know it's okay—by sight and smell—to sit on this quality throw.

Pet Throw Sofa Cover, $32.99 + UPS (IL res. add sales tax)

Flexi-Mat
2244 S. Western Ave.
Chicago, IL 60608
(773) 376-5500

Packin' the Dog

This clever, adjustable backpack is perfect for backpacking Fido. Just strap it on, pop in the pup, and off you go across hill and dale. One size, bright blue, nylon mesh, holds a dog up to 20-lbs. Optional cover accessory keeps the dog's head cool and provides privacy if you want to hoof it through the mall. Great gift and leg saver for a tired pup, with tongue hanging out, giving you that "I can't take another step" look.

Dog-Gone Device Animal Carrier, $59.95
Dog-Gone Head Cover Accessory, $14.95 + $6.95 S&H (NV res. add 7% sales tax)

Sanjo
4395 S. Cameron St.
Suite D
Las Vegas, NV 89103
(800) 367-7303

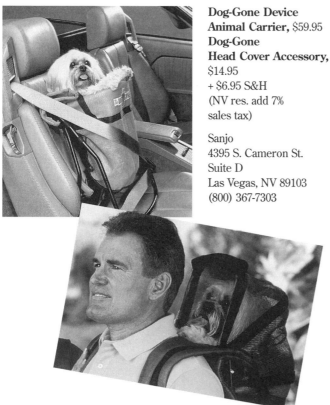

Great Dog Pillows ®

Washable Pillow Playmates measure 36″ l. × 15″ w. × 5″ d. (Dachshund is 45″ l.) and weigh 2¼ lbs. Each is stuffed with soft polyester fiberfill that really stays plumped up. Outer material is washable polyester-acrylic. No plastic or metal parts to harm a young child or pet. Made in the USA. Wonderful for a child's room or as a pack of dog pillows for your own bed. Functional fun!

Pillow Playmates, $45 + $6 S&H (CA res. add 8.25% sales tax)

Executive Accents
1547 Palos Verdes Mall, #110
Walnut Creek, CA 94596
(800) 946-0211

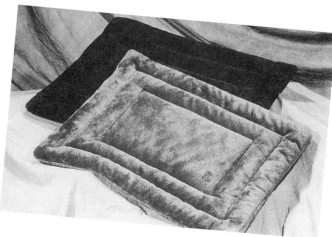

Soft Plush Comfort

Your lucky dog will appreciate this comfortable mat, quilted on one side and filled with polyester batting. Machine washable and dryable; no zipper; available in hunter green or brown. Three sizes (24″ × 30″, 30″ × 42″, 36″ × 54″) from which to choose. Cozy comfort for naps and observation around the house!

Plush Fur Mats, $21 and up + UPS
(NJ res. add 6% sales tax)

Fawn Run Corp.
1122 Ramapo Valley Rd.
Mahwah, NJ 07430
(800) 998-3331

Dog Heroes

The deeds of heroic dogs. What an amazing collection of true stories about canine heroes from around the world, ranging from the Swiss Alps to the suburbs of Tokyo. There's Tang, a burly Newfoundland who saved the lives of 92 people aboard a storm-battered ship off the coast of Canada; Nick Carter, the Kentucky Bloodhound who tracked down more than 600 criminals; Buddy, America's first seeing-eye dog; Chips, the brave World War II dog who received a hero's treatment (until he bit the hand of Gen. Dwight D. Eisenhower!); and Laika, the famous Russian space dog sent into orbit way back in 1957. Twenty incredible, goosebump stories in this hardcover.

By Tim Jones, 1995, 96 pp., $32.95 + $6 S&H
(WA res. add $2.79 sales tax)

Epicenter Press
P.O. Box 82368
Kenmore, WA 98028
(206) 485-6822

> "Animals have these advantages over man: they have no theologians to instruct them, their funerals cost them nothing, and no one starts lawsuits over their wills."
>
> – Voltaire

Dog Crossing

Live near a busy street? Need a sign for the college dorm? Big Dog Crossing Sign posts a warning to watch out for big dogs! Enamel-coated, bright yellow metal (12″ square) for indoor/outdoor use.

Big Dog Crossing Sign, $19.99 + $4.95 S&H
(CA res. add 8.25% sales tax)

Big Dog Sportswear
3112 Seaborg Ave.
Ventura, CA 93003
(800) 642-DOGS (3647)
http://www.bigdogs.com

McSpot's Hidden Spots ®

Fabulous illustrations in this hardcover book accompany a wonderful message: Looks aren't as important as they seem. That crazy McSpot is a Dalmatian who's so proud of his spots, he hides every spotted thing he can find in an old hollow tree. He eventually understands that he's a small but important part of a larger community of spotted animals.

By Laura Seeley, 1994, 32 pp., $16.95 + UPS
(GA res. add sales tax)

Peachtree Publishers
494 Armour Circle, N.E.
Atlanta, GA 30324
(800) 241-0113

CedarSack Quality ®

The nice folks at this family-run business sent me three of these beds. I kept one, gave another to Rocky, a local Wheaten Terrier "product tester," and sent the other to my mother in New England. All the dogs are happy, and why not? These are *super*-quality beds, filled with comfortable chopped foam plus aromatic cedar chips for a fresh smell (and to discourage fleas). The Jumbo Round bed has a 40″ dia. (1,256″ square of resting comfort) and sits a thick, comfortable 4″ off the floor. The Cascade Quilt is just that: quilted for extra warmth and comfort. The cover comes with a durable 100% washable nylon bottom. It's a comfortable 5″ thick and measures 29″ × 36″. The Cascade Fleece has all the warmth and softness (very smooth to the touch) of Polarfleece, with 5″ raised sides, measuring 29″ × 36″. Each bed accommodates your dog's shape and weight. I've seen more than a few dog beds, and these are right up there with the best.

CedarSack Jumbo Round, $39.99
CedarSack Cascade Quilt, $49.99
CedarSack Cascade Fleece, $59.99
+ UPS (WA res. add sales tax)

CedarSack Pet Products
17455 N.E. 67th Ct.
Suite E
Redmond, WA 98052
(800) 882-1231

Choosing and Caring for a Shelter Dog

Thank heaven there are animal shelters, especially "no kill" shelters where dogs are housed and fed until adoption. More and more of these shelters open each year. When you rescue and rehome a shelter dog, you've saved a life. But sometimes your new friend will need extra patience, caring, and understanding from you as he adapts to your lifestyle. This fabulous book specifically addresses the special needs of an adopted dog, as well as what you'll need to know in general—from training to health—to raise any dog. The author's company trains nearly 1,000 dogs a year.

By Bob Christiansen,
1996, 188 pp.,
$9.95 + $2 S&H
(CA res. add 7.75% sales tax)

Canine Learning Centers
P.O. Box 10515, Napa, CA 94581

Dinner Is Served

Tucked between those two dog sofas is the Harvest Table, a handsome dining table that makes eating easier for midsize to large dogs. The durable solid-wood top and legs are finished with a special water-resistant, nontoxic lacquer topcoat. Measures 21″ l. × 11″ w. × 12″ h. Your choice of straight (shown) or turned legs. Two 8-cup stainless steel dishes are included. After the repast, pamper your puppy with a "doggy chic" sofa bed. Stunning design has classic lines and is covered in elegant burgundy or navy floral cotton damask. Cover slips off for machine washing. Measures 32″ l. × 14″ w. × 16½″ h. Made in the USA of solid polyfoam, to insure maximum comfort and beauty.

Harvest Table, $92 + $10.95 S&H
Slipcovered Dog Sofa, $72 + $8.95 S&H
(NY res. add sales tax)

In the Company of Dogs
P.O. Box 7071
Dover, DE 19903
(800) 924-5050

The Mansion Down the Block

This impressive canine abode will be built according to your specifications of style and size. It's a true hand-hewn, braced-frame structure with mortise-and-tenon joints and stuccoed wall panels. The roof is composed of wheat straw thatch. The work, done by Irish craftsmen, is authentic in every detail. The price varies according to size and details. The house can be shipped preassembled (for the small version) or prefabricated and erected on your property—meaning they come to your house and build it! An eminently upscale dog mansion.

Doghouse with Thatched Roof, $4,500 (3′ w. × 5′ l. × 7′ h.) and up
(NY res. add sales tax)

John M. Collins
Historic Building Design
12 Prospect St.
Oyster Bay, NY 11771
(516) 624-9186

Luxury Carrier and Doghouse Mat ®

In a doghouse or in an airport crate, it's important to provide a comfortable mat for your dog. This luxurious, soft, two-sided plush really pampers your pup. It's durable, reversible, stain resistant, and easy to look after—machine washable and dryable. Nonallergenic, warm in winter, cool in summer. Sized to approximate the dimensions of most popular dog carriers and doghouses.

Dura Padd, $19.95 + UPS
(IL res. add sales tax)

Flexi-Mat
2244 S. Western Ave.
Chicago, IL 60608
(773) 376-5500

Superior Dog Pillow ®

It takes no coaxing for Fido to settle into the comfort of this fabulous, poly/cedar fill, flea-repelling bed. An elegant polished cotton print from the Country Quilt or Sporting Print collection provides lasting comfort, and the cover is fully machine washable and dryable. Sizes range from 36″ to 44″ dia.

Dognapper (Country Quilt Collection), $19.95–$39.95 + UPS

Flexi-Mat
2244 S. Western Ave.
Chicago, IL 60608
(773) 376-5500

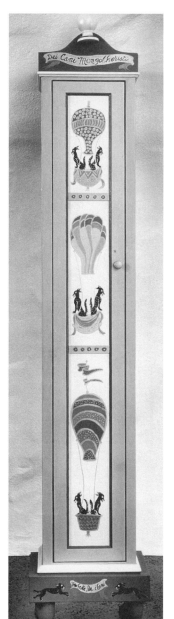

A Cupboard of Treasures

What better place to keep your treasured objects than the Doggie's Holiday Cupboard? Stands 7′1″ tall by 1½′ square, in melon, dark turquoise, lavender, or pastel colors with antiqued gold detailing. Painted dogs in hot-air balloons, with Latin expressions or with additional accents. Also available in custom colors to suit your interior. Consult the artist.

Doggie's Holiday Cupboard, $1,650 + UPS
(CA res. add 7.25% sales tax)

Whimsical Art
54 Issaquah Dock
Sausalito, CA 94965
(415) 331-7414

The Ins and Outs of Life ®

It couldn't be easier to fit this superior pet door into your sliding-glass door. When mine arrived, I took it out of the box and installed it in our glass door—with no tools—in about 2 minutes. On top of the door is a spring-activated device that adjusts to fit the vertical dimension of your door. (Call the company if you have an unusually tall door.) The Pet Eze Portable Door has flap magnets, a heavy-duty ⅝″ aluminum frame, tempered safety glass, and weather strip for the sliding-door edge. Three sizes; solid quality that you can remove in a flash. The deluxe series includes a tamper-resistant, reversible panel lock. A great company, good products, friendly customer support.

Pet Eze Portable Door (Portable 80), $119.95 (sm., 5″ × 8″ opening); $139.95 (med., 8″ × 11″ opening); $144.95 (tall, 8″ × 15″ opening) + UPS (CA res. add sales tax)

U.S. Pet Products
829 Via Alondra
Camarillo, CA 93012
(800) 843-7366
http://www.cyquest.com/petezel/pethome.htm

The Hallo-Wiener ®

All the dogs in the neighborhood make fun of Oscar the Dachshund. He's not nearly as big as the others, and his mother dresses him funny. His self-esteem is heading directly downhill. Happily, he proves his courage and has a name change from "wiener dog" to "hero sandwich." Amusing hardcover book with bright, splashy illustrations that include an important message for young children.

By Dav Pilkey, 1995, 32 pp., $12.95 + UPS
(NY res. add sales tax)

The Blue Sky Press
Scholastic
555 Broadway
New York, NY 10012

Welcome Home!

The Big Dog Welcome Mat (top) is 100-woven fiber with graphics dyed into the fabric to give each image a vibrant color. Measures 18″ × 30″. The Big Dog Printed Welcome Mat ("Get Off The Green" and "Sleeping Dog") is washable, indoor/outdoor, 20″ × 30″, fade- and mildew-resistant, with bound edges and non-skid rubber backing. Great lively colors!

Big Dog Welcome Mat, $29.99
Big Dog Printed Welcome Mat, $29.99
+ $6.95 S&H (each)
(CA res. add 8.25% sales tax)

Big Dog Sportswear
3112 Seaborg Ave.
Ventura, CA 93003
(800) 642-DOGS
http://www.bigdogs.com

The Balloon Trips

Hot-air balloons lift joyous dogs far and away to new lands in this masterwork from artist Suzanne Simpson. The 3-panel handpainted, wooden screen stands 5′ h. × 3′ w. in dark turquoise, lavender, or pastel colors with old gold detailing. Customization to match your interior is encouraged by the artist.

Ballooning Doggies,
$1,450 + UPS
(CA res. add 7.25% sales tax)

Whimsical Art
54 Issaquah Dock
Sausalito, CA 94965
(415) 331-7414

Photograph: George Post

The Cat People Who Bark!

Yes, the Cat Action Toy people of Petaluma, California, had a great revelation one night and decided to make . . . dog beds! Eleven friendly, smiling dog faces peer out on the 100% cotton fabric cover, with a beige bottom plush fabric on the bottom. Completely machine washable with a double layer of polyester fill. Comfortable, with upbeat bright colors.

Ultimate Dog Bed,
$39.95 (sm., 20″ × 30″),
$49.95 (lg., 30″ × 40″)
+ UPS
(CA res. add sales tax)

Cat Action Toys
3034 Skillman Lane
Petaluma, CA 94952
(800) 647-8777

How Good Can It Get?

Gabrielle Choo, at the request of a Danish aristocrat, once made a spectacular dog bed, using $1,200-a-yard fabric, adorned with handmade, imported tassels, and stuffed with the highest-quality goose down. $8,000 later it was finished. The aristocrat was happy. Now you can own a similar, spectacular dog bed for much, much less. The standard size is 27″ w. × 38″ h. × 16″ dia., though at your request, she'll also make one for your Great Dane. Includes two neck rolls and four tassels. Many elegant customization options available to match your decor. What would you like?

18th-Century-Style Dog Bed, $950 and up + UPS
Wood finished in gold leaf:
add $700
(CA res. add 8.5% sales tax)

Gabrielle Williams Choo
1700 Monterey Rd.
South Pasadena, CA 91030
(818) 799-6254

Chapter Three

Classy Canine Clothing and Jewelry— For You

Nice Sweater. Where'd You Get It?

You can answer the question honestly: from the dog. Here's Matt Richard wearing a sweater spun from his Samoyed, Ebenezer. See the resemblance—it's amazing! Artist Carolyn Smith will use the brushings and combings from your dog— or cat, rabbit, llama, or miniature horse—to weave a sweater. Simply brush your dog, and save the hair in brown paper bags, and when you have enough, send it to her. How much is enough? Roughly 12–16 oz.

for a sweater, 2 oz. for a cap. When she receives your dog's hair, you'll hear back from her by postcard. Then you'll both plan your sweater or other custom garment!

Custom Dog Hair Sweater,
$200–$450 + UPS
(WA res. add 8.2% sales tax)

Free Brochure (enclose SASE):
Creature Comforts/
Carolyn Smith
P.O. Box 606
Vashon, WA 98070
(206) 463-2004

Big Dog Basics

Everyone loves big dogs! Here's a variety of great sportswear: A natural for any gourmet kitchen, the white Bone Appetit Apron is made of 100% cotton twill with an adjustable strap, decorated with a classic big dog cooking up a feast. Hit the links with the Two-Color Piqué Polo Shirt that looks great on or off the course. Richly colored yarns knitted together make this collection Big Dog's best ever, with your choice of cream/charcoal, black/khaki, midnight/sea foam, midnight/cobalt, or midnight/evergreen. Beach weather? Big Kahuna T-shirt features Big Dog as the Hawaiian surfing god in cool colors. Team Big Dog and Big Dog T's are also available in extra-large sizes, from 2X–5X. Expect the best from Big Dog.

Bone Appetit Apron,
$17.99 + $4.95 S&H
Two-Color Piqué Polo Shirt,
$39.99 (M, L, XL) + $6.95 S&H
Big Kahuna T, $15.99 (M, L, XL), $16.99 (XXL) + $4.95 S&H
Team Big Dog and **Big Dog,**
$19.99 (sizes up to 5X)
+ $4.95 S&H
(CA res. add 8.25% sales tax)

Big Dog Sportswear
3112 Seaborg Ave.
Ventura, CA 93003
(800) 642-DOGS (3647)
http://www.bigdogs.com

Putting on the Dog

Now you can literally "put on the dog" with these fabulous, handpainted dog vests from Dill O'Hagan. She works in a small studio on the Rappahannock River, near Chesapeake Bay, in eastern Virginia. Specialized, vibrantly colored fabric paints (flexible to the touch) are painted on hand-washable, 100% fine cotton, which is fully lined. Each vest is titled, signed, and dated as wearable art. Custom designs are available if you furnish the photographs. "Playful Pups" (left) and "Walk" are shown. A lasting gift!

Handpainted Dog Vest
(S, M, L), $200
   (includes S&H and sales tax)

Original Works by
  Dill O'Hagan
  Rt. 2, Box 749
  Lancaster, VA 22503
  (804) 462-0227

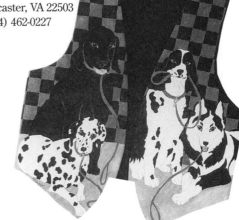

Classic Canine Rings

Superior detailing highlights these snazzy rings from Sigi's studio in California's wine country. Scottish Terriers (left) aren't always black. They come in other colors, such as grizzle, wheaten, or sandy—or in this case, gold or sterling silver. The Boston Terrier—one of the few breeds to be developed in the U.S.—is portrayed in smooth lines that embellish this intelligent, charming companion. The long schnozz and floppy ears of the Basset Hound belie his actual personality, which can be surprisingly energetic. The Rottweiler inherited his name from the German city of Rottweil in Württemberg, where it's rumored he was the favorite guard dog for butchers. Sigi's animal rings are hand-carved in wax in her Sonoma studio, then cast in precious metals. Resizing of your ring is free. Custom designs also available. New dog designs are coming, so ask for a free color catalog.

Scottish Terrier, $79.95 (sterling), $449.95 (14K gold)
Boston Terrier, $84.95 (sterling), $469.95 (14K gold)
Basset Hound, $84.95 (sterling), $469.95 (14K gold)
Rottweiler, $84.95 (sterling), $485.95 (14K gold)
+ $5.50 S&H
(CA res. add sales tax)

Sigi Designs
524 Broadway
Sonoma, CA 95476
(800) 407-SIGI (7444)

"The law is a dull dog."

—Charles Dickens

Animal Close-ups: The Wolf

Meet your dog's ancestor in this full-color photo book for young children who are curious about dogs and nature. Playing, hunting, howling, and cute puppies are just some of the highlights of this gentle introductory book.

By Christian Havard, 1994, 28 pp., $6.95 + UPS
(MA res. add sales tax)

Charlesbridge
Publishing
85 Main St.
Watertown, MA 02172
(800) 225-3214

TRUE DOG TALE

Popularity Contest

Want to know the most popular dog breeds? Based upon 1994 purebred registrations:

Labrador Retriever (126,000)
Rottweiler (102,000)
German Shepherd (78,000)
Golden Retriever (64,000)
Poodle (61,000)
Cocker Spaniel (60,000)
Beagle (59,000)
Dachshund (46,000)
Dalmatian (42,000)
Pomeranian (39,000).

Dog People Sweaters

Now you can match a beautiful sweater for your dog with a sweater for you or your children, in the same pattern and colors! Handcrafted in the village of Gilnamman in the glorious, pastoral south of Wales. Made of pure British wool and cotton yarns. Many colors and sweater choices for you and the dog. Handmade quality. You'll all look great on a cool fall day.

Harlequin Dog Sweater, $50
Child's Harlequin Sweater, $75
Adult's Harlequin Sweater,
$350
+ $5 S&H
(CA res. add 8.25% sales tax)

Petal Designs
475 Palm Dr.
Arcadia, CA 91007
(818) 447-7836

Baseball Buddies ®

Fun Play Ball T-shirt shows a brown dog and a tan dog with bright red tongues on a white baseball with blue background. Great-looking, 100% heavyweight cotton shirt for the baseball/dog lover! They just seem to go together.

Play Ball T-shirt,
$19.50 + UPS
(ID res. add sales tax)

A Tail We Could Wag
P.O. Box 3374
Ketchum, ID 83340
(208) 726-1763

Your Best Friend at Night

Diane Weiss is a leather artist. Each of her Evening Bags, measuring 5″ × 6¼″, is made of carved, hammered, and painted leather. There's a surprise inside, but I'm not telling what it is. If you don't see the breed you want, contact her— almost any breed and color is possible. These are beautiful, high-quality, small leather bags.

Dog Evening Bags, $100
(includes S&H)
(CA res. add 8.5% sales tax)

Diane Weiss
NYC on Nob Hill
1310 Jones St.
San Francisco, CA 94109
(415) 776-2696

It's Wilder in California!

Tuned-in Internet types produce this wild catalog of T-shirts with outrageous dog artwork, plus a huge catalog collection of

Chinese Shar-Peis on stone statues, magnets, bathrobes, embroidered cardigan sweaters, hats,

calendars, cooking aprons, earrings, playing cards, etc. These people are nuts about dogs, especially Shar-Peis!

Hundreds of wild products; outrageous free catalog. Call 'em.

The Rott Stuff 2-sided T-shirt (M–XXXL), $18.95
Bulldozers 2-sided T-shirt (M–XXXXL), $18.95
  + $4.95 S&H
   (CA res. add 7.75% sales tax)

Cyber-Pet
Wrinky Dinks Ink
P.O. Box 11209
Costa Mesa, CA 11209
(800) 523-PETS
http://www.cyberpet.com

Liliane's Friends

Liliane loves dogs. Her huge collection of dog T-shirts ($12.95 each), sweatshirts ($19.95 each), 9-oz. sweatshirts ($24.95 each), and tank tops ($12.95 each) are available in more than 100 breeds. Ask for her amazing catalog of dog shirts, mugs, magnets, coasters—dog everything!

Net Play T-shirt,
$12.95 + $4 S&H
(No sales tax on clothes in MA)

Liliane's Creations
P.O. Box 1004
Oak Bluffs, MA 02557
(508) 693-2515

Hope When It's Needed

HOPE is a nonprofit, "no-kill" animal care organization dedicated to the care and resocialization of lost, abused, or abandoned pets. They work as a referral service for people wanting to acquire or place a pet. They also sell some fun stuff that helps them afford to feed pets awaiting adoption. The cotton Dog Hair Everywhere T-shirt is amusing, available in black, navy, purple, red, royal, turquoise, jade, denim, moss, maroon, forest, kelly, or raspberry. Down Boy Down is a white T-shirt covered

in black pawprints. Check out the Fanny Packs (all breeds available) in 2-compartment cotton canvas, 3-compartment polyester deluxe, and 2-compartment 100% cotton. Everything you buy helps this wonderful shelter, which is staffed with volunteers.

Dog Hair Everywhere T-shirt, $14.95 (S–XL), $16.95 (XXL), $17.95 (XXX–XXXX)

Down Boy Down T-shirt,
$14.95 (S–XL), $16.95 (XXL), $17.95 (XXX–XXXX)
Fanny Pack, $9.95 (canvas), $14.95 (polyester), $10.95 (cotton)
+ $4.25 S&H
(nonprofit, no sales tax)

Free catalog with SASE:
HOPE Safehouse
1911 Taylor Ave.
Racine, WI 53403
(414) 634-4571

Dressed for Bichon

Before I knew better, I thought Bichon Frises were small, cute poodles! This upbeat, beautiful breed lends a happy image to clothing. Happy Sweatshirt, made of a 50-50 cotton/polyester blend portrays a white Bichon on your choice of forest green, burgundy, or true navy blue. The rather outrageous Bichon Vest, with fringe, is an arty choice for lovers of this wonderful breed.

Happy Sweatshirt, $35 (S–XXL) + $3 S&H
Bichon Vest, $65 (S–L) + $3 S&H
(MA res. add sales tax)

Rolande's/Talisman
68 Providence St.
Mendon, MA 01756
(508) 478-1889
E-mail:
cyberpet@ix.netcom.com
http://www.ads-online.com/
bichon.htm

Dog Fanatics

Fun, casual dog clothing for easy living. The Retriever Fever Sweatshirt, in ash or white, is a 9-oz., 50-50 blend shirt for Labrador Retriever fans. The Determined Dachshunds T-shirt features amusing art of two rather tough Dachshunds, face to face, staring out at you. Available in ash or white, 100% cotton. BBQ time for Great Dane lovers takes on new meaning with this one-size, double-pocket Greatest Danes Apron in your choice of red or white.

Retriever Fever Sweatshirt, $28 (L, XL)
Determined Dachshunds T-shirt, $18 (L, XL)
Greatest Danes Apron, $16 + $3 S&H ($5 S&H for 2 items) (PA res. add sales tax)

Up the Creek
1209 Rose Glen Rd.
Gladwyne, PA 19035
E-mail: jsmith4287@aol.com
http://home.navisoft.com/
utc/utc.htm

Cocker Spaniels ®

The advantages of owning a Cocker are extolled in this book, which thoroughly explores their history, from hunting dogs to modern-day family companions. Cocker Spaniels are highly intelligent and get along well with small children. They are beautiful in appearance, and their coats come in a variety of colors. They may look fragile, but underneath is a muscular dog with a need for regular exercise. Sold on Cockers? All the basics of what you need to parent are right here.

By Jaime J. Sucher, 1993, 80 pp., $6.95 + UPS (NY res. add sales tax)

Barron's Educational Series
250 Wireless Blvd.
Hauppauge, NY 11788
(800) 645-3476

"Any woman who does not thoroughly enjoy tramping across the country on a clear frosty morning with a good gun and a pair of dogs does not know how to enjoy life."

—Annie Oakley

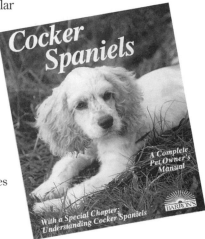

Happy Dog Dress!

Little girls look adorable in this whimsical, 100% cotton Dog Print Dress. Patterns vary depending upon availability, but they always feature dogs. Made in the USA. Machine washable and dryable. Specify size and style # DP-1-7. The best of life: kids and dogs!

Dog Print Dress for Toddlers, $32 (toddler sizes 1T–4T) + S&H (CA res. add sales tax)

Current Image
1040 Lea Dr.
San Rafael, CA 94903
(415) 492-8864

Good Owners, Great Dogs ®

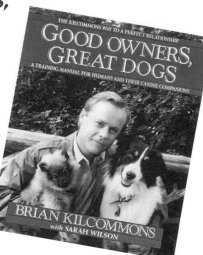

You've seen the author on ABC-TV. He's the official trainer for the PBS series *The Gentle Doctor: Veterinary Medicine,* and he's one of America's foremost dog behavior experts. His approach in this book is simple: Training should be fun, fair, and firm. You, as the owner and trainer, must give a piece of your heart and mind if training is to really work. Chapters include "Puppyhood," "Caring for and Training Your Adult Dog," and "Understanding and Solving Canine Problems." Hundreds of photos. Short of hiring a personal dog trainer, you won't do better than this.

By Brian Kilcommons with Sarah Wilson, 1992, 276 pp., $22.95 + UPS
(NY res. add sales tax)

Warner Books
1271 Ave. of the Americas
New York, NY 10020
(212) 522-7200

Dog & Keys ®

Attention to detail elevates these keychains to the level of fine jewelry. Available in most major dog breeds, cast in solid pewter or bronze heads on 2″ oval disks. American made, of 100% lead-free pewter. The hefty weight makes them harder to misplace!

Dog Breed Keychain, $15 + UPS
(CA res. add sales tax)

Dannyquest Designs
11782 Western Ave., #17
Stanton, CA 90680
(800) 215-9711

TRUE DOG TALE

Sleepless in Dreamland

Some dogs, like some people, are night owls. Why the restlessness? Some dogs—especially as their eyesight declines with age—don't like pitch-dark rooms. If your dog has this problem, install a night light, and she may sleep easier. Some dogs resent overnight guests. Solution: Have your guest spend some time with the dog before bedtime. If nothing works, and the dog is still keeping you up, put her bed in a cozy spot as far away from your bedroom as possible. She can nap during the day. You probably can't.

Puppy Feet

These are a hoot! With ears flopping as you walk (or as the kids race around!), these comfy Dalmatian Slippers look real enough to run off on their own. They have a nonskid sole pattern and slip onto your feet with ease and comfort.

Dalmatian Slippers, $12.95 (adult), $11.95 (child) + $4.99 S&H (MN res. add 6.5% sales tax)

Tails
4708 Utah Ave. North
New Hope, MN 55428
(612) 535-3055
E-mail: tailsl@ix.netcom.com

Golden Retrievers ®

I love Golden Retrievers. Here's a bit of history from this superb book. Back in 1865 Sir Dudley Marjoriebanks, the first Lord of Tweedmouth, mated a yellow, wavy-coated Retriever—all the pups in the litter were black except this one—with a female Tweed Water Spaniel. (Once known for their intelligence, this breed is now extinct.) Later he introduced more black, wavy-coated Retrievers to improve hunting ability, added a dash of Irish Setter to redden the color, then mixed in a sandy-colored Bloodhound for tracking ability and for the golden color. That's the mix—like a dog recipe—for today's Golden Retriever! This is a great book with photographs of superfriendly Goldens playing around, plus tips you'll need to raise a nice dog. Wonderful picture of ten beautiful pups peeking out of a basket. How can you resist?

By Jaime J. Sucher, 1995, 86 pp., $6.95 + UPS (NY res. add sales tax)

Barron's Educational Series
250 Wireless Blvd.
Hauppauge, NY 11788
(800) 645-3476

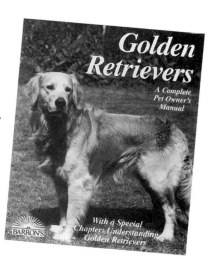

The Golden Bone Near Your Heart

Keep your dog's picture close to you—in the locket of this Dog Bone Pin, in 14K gold plate. Approx. 1¾" l. × 1½" w. Pop it open to show off the pooch. Nothing beats the look of gold.

Dog Bone Pin, $9.95 + $2 S&H (MN res. add 6.5% sales tax)

Accessories Direct
9593 Anderson Lakes Pkwy.
Suite 318
Eden Prairie, MN 55344
(800) 859-0771
E-mail: Tblons@aol.com

TRUE DOG TALE

You Can't Leave It to the Dog!

Are you leaving valuables to your dog in your will? Some people do try it. But every court throws it out. Why? The law views dogs as "property," and property can't own property. Planning ahead? Leave your dog—and money to support the dog, as specified in your will—with a trusted friend. To assure the health of your dog, work out an arrangement for pet health insurance, or reach an agreement for your vet to provide quality care—at an agreed-upon price—for the rest of your dog's life. It can be done.

Doggy Tapestry Vest

Tapestry is such beautiful, European-inspired material. You associate it right away with exquisite handwork and custom garments. Now this beautiful hand-sewn vest in a dog tapestry pattern is yours to wear on any dressy occasion. Unisex sizes, available in hunter or navy.

People Vest with Bone-Shaped Buttons
(S, M, L), $60 + $4.50 S&H
(IL res. add sales tax)

Creature Comforts
Tyler & Russell, Ltd.
357 West Erie St., 2nd Floor
Chicago, IL 60610
(312) 266-0907

The Great Dane Handbook

I love dogs, but years ago, while working for a publishing company, it always used to startle me when the office Great Dane would amble over. He'd appear silently while I pounded away on the computer, resting his enormous head on my desk, his baleful eyes staring into mine. We became friends, but I never ceased to be amazed at his size. It was like having another person around, all the time. This great book is a must-have if you own a Great Dane.

Twenty-seven chapters are devoted to everything from history to showing and training. Danes crave affection and creature comforts, and in most opinions they are too loving to be good watchdogs—despite their imposing size (up to 150 lbs. or more) and deep, resonant bark. A terrific hardcover, well illustrated, with black and white photos.

By Mary McCraken, 1995, 240 pp., $27.95 + $2.50 S&H
(AL res. add sales tax)

OTR Publications
P.O. Box 481
Centreville, AL 35042
(800) 367-2174

Putting on the Dog

Snazz it up with these Rhinestone Woof/Bone Earrings (top), Rhinestone Paw Print Earrings (center), and Golden Bone Earrings (bottom). The Rhinestone Bone and Rhinestone Paw Velvet Necklette feature Swarovski crystals in a plated 24K gold setting, with black velvet.

Rhinestone Woof/Bone Earrings, $50
Rhinestone Paw Print Earrings, $32
Golden Bone Earrings, $15

Rhinestone Bone and Rhinestone Paw Velvet Necklette
petite (7″–10″), sm. (11″–14″), med. (15″–18″), and lg. (19″–23″)
$35 + $5 S&H
(TX res. add sales tax)

Zamora's
2527 Guerrero Dr.
Carrollton, TX 75006
(214) 245-1119

Techno-Romantic Jewelry

That's the term artist Thomas Mann uses to describe his talismanic jewelry: a connection to, and separation from, technology. His pieces are designed to look *as if* they were made from found materials, like bits and pieces of metal, electronic instruments, and costume jewelry. The Small Dog Box Necklace/Pin (the 26″ chain is removable) measures 2″ × 2⅕″. Materials: nickel, brass, bronze, lucite, laminate, found objects. The Dog Box Necklace with House measures 4″ × 4½″ and is made of nickel, brass, bronze, lucite, laminate, and found objects. Mann exhibits his jewelry and sculpture in more than 200 galleries in the U.S. and around the world. His style is instantly recognizable.

Small Dog Box Necklace/Pin, $550
Dog Box Necklace With House, $1,900 + UPS
(LA res. add sales tax)

Thomas Mann Design
1810 Magazine St.
New Orleans, LA 70130
(504) 581-2111

Photographs: Will Crocker

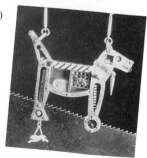

Last Days of the Dog-Men ®

"Watson's people are the wretched dreams of honorable dogs." —Barry Hannah

How is it that dogs fit so well into our complex human lives? What have we done in making this adaptable animal a partner to all of life's joy and despair? In eight stories that run the gamut from humor to darkness, this hardcover book throws new light on the meaning "best friend" in a not-always-easy read that peels back the veneer of humanity. Not too sweet.

By Brad Watson, 1996, 146 pp., $19 + UPS
(NY res. add sales tax)

W.W. Norton and Co.
500 Fifth Ave.
New York, NY 10110
(800) 233-4830

TRUE DOG TALE

Let's Get a Room, Pup

It had to happen. People traveling with pets are welcome at more and more hotels and motels across the U.S. One of the newest and brightest is American Pet Motels of Prairie View, Ill. Its $1.25 million lobby—complete with a 6,500´ square "O'Hair Port" for pet grooming—also includes an $80,000 video wall that continuously runs animal-friendly movies and cartoons to entertain children. Furry human-sized stuffed animals carry on interactive conversations, and there's a gift shop for both people and pets.

Brilliant Silk

Brilliant handpainted colors make these fabulous Dog Vests look like a rainbow. Brown dogs, yellow dogs, black and white Dalmatians on a four-button lined vest. Bright, wonderful casual wear for your next dog show or semidressy occasion.

Pure Silk Dog Vest, $69.50 + UPS
(CA res. add 7% sales tax)

Stopgap Enterprises
1240 S. Grade Rd.
Alpine, CA 91901
(619) 445-8856

Your Dog's Tag

Would you wear a beautifully finished, military-size and -shape, metal dog tag—with a picture of your dog on it? You can add in the dog's name, along with your personalized inscription on the front of the tag. Just send a photo (it will be returned) and an inscription of up to 20 characters. Includes a 24″ stainless steel beaded chain and a black rubber "silencer." The photo quality on the tag is amazingly good!

Forevergraph Dog, $14.95 + $2 S&H
(MD res. add sales tax)

I.D. Technology
117 Nelson Rd.
Baltimore, MD 21208
(410) 602-1911
http://www.abs.net/~idtech

TRUE DOG TALE

Circling Dogs

Why does a dog turn around three times before she'll lie down? Animal behaviorists think it's an ancient genetic trait. Long before domestication, dogs in forests and plains would trample down grass to check for snakes before they slept. It's so ingrained, they still do it after 12,000 years of domestication.

Fein Art

I stumbled on the art of Beth Fein while walking around the Sausalito Art Festival on a beautiful, windy fall day. Her Collage Dog Pin is made of brass, copper, and sterling silver. The incandescent Dog or Cat Necklace shimmers in sterling silver with a matching braided chain. A classy brass and sterling Bookmark is a superb gift for any dog (or cat) lover and reader. Ultramodern Collage Earrings, of brass, copper, and sterling, are chic and arty. Ask about her one-of-a-kind, Custom Dog Necklace (not shown) made of 14K gold, diamond,

sterling silver, and Chinese writing stone. This is superior jewelry she's happy to mail anywhere. Ask for her catalog.

Collage Dog Pin, $48
Dog or Cat Necklace, $110
Dog or Cat Bookmark, $18
Collage Earrings, $72
Custom Dog Necklace, $1,200
+ $5.50 UPS
(CA res. add sales tax)

fina-flor
P.O. Box 21363
Oakland, CA 94620
(510) 653-5874

> *"The old dog barks backward without getting up. I can remember when he was a pup."*
>
> —Robert Frost

Look Deep into My Eyes

It must have been those long, rainy northwestern winters that made artist Paul Alan Bennett produce this great Crazy Eyes Sterling Pin. It weighs just over an ounce and is approximately $1\frac{7}{8}'' \times 2\frac{3}{8}''$. Zany dog, smiling cat, moon and stars. Pin-on fun.

Crazy Eyes Sterling Pin,
$85 + UPS
(no sales tax in OR)

Crazy Eyes
P.O. Box 1301
Sisters, OR 97759
(541) 549-9756

Best Dog Stories ®

A veritable salute to dogs, this hardcover comprises 22 works from the world's best authors, all famous for their animal stories. The writings of James Herriott, Jack London, O. Henry, Virginia Woolf, and P.G. Wodehouse virtually guarantee that if you love dogs, you'll love this book.

Edited by Lesley O'Mara, 1990,
256 pp., $8.99 + UPS
(NJ res. add sales tax)

Wings Books
Random House Value Publishing
40 Engelhard Ave.
Avenel, NJ 07001
(800) 793-2665

TRUE DOG TALE

So Many Babies!

Is there a relationship between the size of a dog and the size of her litter? You bet. Smaller dogs typically have from 1 to 4 pups, while larger breeds (like Golden Retrievers, German Shepherds, and others) can have as many as 22. The average canine litter size is about 8 pups.

Dressy Guy

Chipp II is the only Dog Tie source you'll ever need. This company has Dog Ties in more than 75 breeds. Most are displayed on navy material, but the darker dogs (Scotties, Black Labs, and Newfies) are displayed on red material. The Suspenders are available with clips or button attachments. While you're in the giving mood, why not include a matching wallet, checkbook cover, credit card case, or belt? Chipp II will *custom-paint* a picture of your dog on almost anything they make! Just send along a good-quality color picture. Highest quality, new breeds added yearly; free catalog. A great wearable gift for a friend.

Dog Tie, $22.50
Dog Suspenders, $50
+ $4.75 S&H
(CT res. add sales tax)

Chipp II
9 Ethan Allen Lane
Stamford, CT 06903
(310) 322-4970

Joy's Dogs

Here's Joy Murray, owner of Accessory Pet, wearing her classic white cotton blouse embroidered with puppies. The blouse features a curving hem, long sleeves, and buttoned cuffs. Matching Dog Button Covers accent the design. One size fits 6–14. Machine washable.

Doggone Blouse,
$60 + $6.95 S&H
Dog Button Covers,
$18 + $4.95 S&H
(TX res. add 7.25% sales tax)

Accessory Pet
5836 Pathfinder Trail
Plano, TX 75093
(800) 558-7387

Baby Dog

Adorable Cotton Jumper for special babies is made of 100% cotton, with a black and white photo/transfer of an amusing, sweet dog. Available in your choice of cranberry, black, white, navy blue, or purple. Preshrunk, with a snap crotch for diaper changing, they are created by designer Jon Stevenson and made in Sonoma County, California, for babies and the dogs who love them.

Cotton Jumper Sizes: 0–6, 6–12, and 18–24
$24.95 + $1.50 S&H
(includes Calif. sales tax)

Trumpette
108 Kentucky St.
Petaluma, CA 94952
(707) 769-1173

Solid Gold Dogs

Hallock Coin Jewelry features a new breed of dog each year, in pure gold dog coins to wear as jewelry. The Gold Pekingese (left) is set in a 14K filigree bezel. The Gold Corgi is set in a 14K rope bezel. The Gold Collie is set in a 14K diamond cut rope bezel. Eminently wearable and collectible, these pure gold coins featuring your favorite dogs are available in the currencies of Canada, South Africa, England, the Isle of Man, Mexico, China, and Australia. The prices for the coins shown do not include the necklace and are subject to change based upon the world gold price. Superb, free color catalog.

Gold Pekingese, $199
(¹⁄₁₀ oz., with gift box)
Gold Corgi, $159
(¹⁄₂₅ oz., with gift box)
Gold Collie, $199
(¹⁄₁₀ oz., with gift box)
+ UPS (CA res. add sales tax)

Hallock Coin Jewelry
2060 W. Lincoln
Anaheim, CA 92801
(800) 854-3232

42 Dog Silhouettes

Just one of a large collection of 42 breeds, this Golden Retriever sweatshirt is available in a 50-50 cotton/poly blend, featuring a dog silhouette on ash gray material. Informative text on the back of each shirt highlights the breed, its country of origin, and its average weight and size. Also available as a T-shirt. Sizes from small to large. Wear enough of them, and you'll be a walking dog encyclopedia!

Dog Silhouette Shirts, $24
(sweatshirt, S–L), $12
(T-shirt, S–L), + $3.50 S&H
(no sales tax in NH)

Dogwild
10 Higgins St.
Manchester, NH 03102
(603) 647-1872
E-mail: dogwild2@aol.com

Golden Retriever
Great Britain
60-75 pounds
21-24 inches

A Dog Lover's Collection ®

What a fascinating story. View a canine pirate castle, with dogs in jade, malachite, and red quartz. A French petit-point sofa panel with a floral border surrounding a hunting scene. A terracotta copy of a pre-Columbian vessel decorated with two plump Mesoamerican dogs. All are part of a remarkable collection of 2,000 dog objects in the tower of Poggio Petroio, a Renaissance castle deep in the Tuscan landscape of Italy's Chianti region. This collection—the *Vanessa dei Barabba Florine*—is devoted entirely to objects created for, about, and in celebration of dogs and the life of collector Achille Alessandro Conti. This stunning hardcover features full-color photographs that document centuries of extraordinary artistic celebrations of our best friend. A magnificent obsession.

By Ptolemy Tompkins, 1995, 96 pp., $25 + UPS
(NY res. add sales tax)

M.T.Train/Scala Books
Antique Collector's Club, Ltd.
Market Street Industrial Park
Wappingers Falls, NY 12590
(914) 297-0003

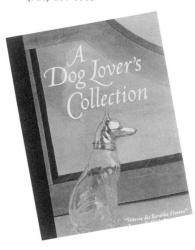

I'm Her Mom (or Pop)!

Show the world you're a proud parent! These classic white cotton caps and T-shirts from In the Company of Dogs are embroidered with "Dog Mother" or "Dog Father." Machine washable, also available in black. Specify size. Amusing, very good quality.

Dog Father/Dog Mother Cap
(S/M or M/L), $18
Dog Mother/Dog Father T-shirt
(M, L, XL, or XXL, regular cut),
$22 + $4.95 S&H
(NY res. add
sales tax)

In the Company of Dogs
P.O. Box 7071
Dover, DE 19903
(800) 924-5050

Family Look-Alike Clothes!

Dress the entire crew for your next party! Stylish Mock Turtleneck 50-50 poly-cotton T-shirt comes in wide bold stripes of green, red, yellow, and blue. Also shown in black and white with Great Outdoors prints. The 3-button Henley with hood has solid sleeves, red and white stripes, and trim with fine stripes. Since your dog is part of your family, she might as well look it.

Mock Turtleneck
(broad stripes or Great Outdoors print)
Adult (S, M, L, XL), $38
Child (7–14, S, M, L), $27
Dog Shirt, $18 (S–M), $23 (L–XL)

Henley
Adult, $40
Child, $29
Dog Shirt, $19 (S–M),
$24 (L–XL)
+ UPS (CA res. add sales tax)

Le Prot Pot
20710 S. Leapwood Ave.
Suite G
Carson, CA 90746
(800) 765-1376

Late? I'm on Dog Time!

Dogs are terrible at keeping appointments. They have absolutely no sense of time or the rat race. But *you* do—especially with one of these watches. Features a full-color drawing—your choice of over 190 AKC breeds—in a gold-plated case. Dependable quartz movement, nice leather band, sweep second hand. Men's and women's styles. Great customized watch with a picture of your own dog also available.

Dog Watch, $49.95 + $3 S&H
(MD res. add sales tax)

The Watch Works
P.O. Box 1049
Chestertown, MD 21620
(410) 778-9442
E-mail: dogwatch@friendly.net

Chapter Four

Classy Canine Clothing and Accessories— For Your Dog!

Nobody Will Dance with Me!

Says Miss Ballerina in her fabulous getup, waiting for some musky male pup to appear in her life. Not to worry. This incredible costume is enough to make any dog do a double-take. It's carefully crafted to your dog's exact measurements in your choice of fabric, with special ribbons, laces, pearls, sequins, and trims. Prices start at a very reasonable $45. Custom-designed costumes (think of the possibilities) are available. Imagine a costume custom-designed for your dog to wear to your wedding, a cool party—any outrageous occasion that includes your favorite canine.

Ballerina Costume,
$75 + $5.25 S&H
(no sales tax in OR)

Pampered Pups Extraordinaire
647 S. 44th St.
Springfield, OR 97478
(541) 746-3801
E-mail: cavlady@pond.net

Snazzy Quilted Jacket

Gorgeous, custom-made Quilted Jacket includes a snazzy 6-button display on the chest. A belt over the back helps it slip on easily. The thick fleece lining is perfect for chilly rainy weather. Available in attractive calico prints, plaids, or solids (red, dark green, navy, and denim), machine washable and dryable. Made by hand from measurements you provide. Delivery time is 1–2 weeks. It just *looks* warm.

Classic Quilted Jacket, $34.95
(sm., to 16″ l.), $54.95 (18″–24″ l.)
+ $ 3 S&H
(CA res. add sales tax)

Catalog, $2 (refundable with order)

Jazzy Jackets Co.
3852 Aborn Rd.
San Jose, CA 95135
(408) 238-8424

Cold Feet/Hot Foot ®

It's cold. It's icy. It's time for a walk. When ice and snow make for freezing-cold paws, just slip these waterproof boots on the dog. The diamond pattern on the rubber bottom is for protection and traction; all seams are double-glued and blindstitched; and each boot includes a band of highly reflective material for added visibility and protection at night. All-season (including hot summer streets), quick and easy Velcro clips.

Neo-Paws Canine Footwear
(set of 4 boots)
Sizes:
sm. (1″ w. × 3½″ h.) to
X-lg. (3″ w. × 9″ h.)
$30–$60 + $3 S&H
(includes all taxes)

Neo-Paws International
222 The Esplanade
Suite 1220
Toronto, ON
Canada M5A 4M8
(888) NEO-PAWS

Stretch Walk

Snap this nylon belt around your waist, attach it to your dog's collar, and there you are: walking the dog hands-free. Laced inside the webbing of the lead is a shock cord—a stretchable bungee—that automatically stretches without pulling on your arm. It reins the dog right in. Sewn to the belt is a strip of Scotchlite reflective material that reflects headlights at night from up to 400 yards. Adjustable length, and the leash is very lightweight—just 5 oz.

PuppyPull, $17.95 (includes S&H; no sales tax in OR)

PuppyPull Pet Products
P.O. Box 262
Hood River, OR 97031
(509) 493-4088
E-mail: docfun@gorge.net

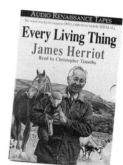

Every Living Thing ®

An absolutely superb audiotape narrated by Christopher Timothy, who starred as James Herriott in the BBC series *All Creatures Great And Small*. In this sequel to *The Lord God Made Them All,* all the characters we came to know and love in Herriott's books and TV series are packed into four highly entertaining cassette tapes, perfect for a long, leisurely drive. Fabulous animal and human interest stories for the entire family.

Every Living Thing (4 cassette tapes, approx. 6 hrs.), $22.95 + S&H
(CA res. add sales tax)

Audio Renaissance Tapes
5858 Wilshire Blvd.
Suite 205
Los Angeles, CA 90036
(800) 452-5589

Artful Collar

Have you ever seen a collar even remotely like this? Sure it's a collar, but it's also art. The Spiked Dog Collar is great for conservation-minded canines: It's handmade from used bicycle inner tubes and valves. One size fits all: Simply remove the valve sections until the collar fits comfortably around your dog's neck. Not intended for use with tags or leashes. Guaranteed to last a dog's age. Ultracool.

Spiked Dog Collar
(17″–21″),
$24 + $3 S&H
(no sales tax in OR)

Resource Revival
2130 N.W. 29th Ave.
Portland, OR 97210
(800) 866-8823

Flying Dog Sunglass Holders ®

C'mon—sunglass holder for dogs? You betcha! These are specially designed for active dogs who wear sunglasses while playing Frisbee in the park or looking cool on the beach. Sunpups include a special chin tube and head tube that hold the glasses on no matter what the dog does. They look absolutely outrageous. Just remember, they're meant to be used with supervision, or the dog might chew 'em up.

Sunpups, $4.95 + UPS
(GA res. add sales tax)

Available by mail from:
New England Serum Company: (800) NE-SERUM
Discovering the World: (714) 522-2202

Dogworks
P.O. Box 2235
Woodstock, GA 30107
(770) 592-9916

SuperDog Cape ®

Flying through the air, wings tucked under her cape, SuperDog stays warm in this attractive 100% wool and wool-blend "people quality" cape. This Winter Weight Cape is perfect for those cold, blowing days that make you want to move to Florida. Easy on-off Velcro closures provide good tummy adjustability. Nice quality. Doesn't some-one you know need a new winter coat?

Pet Threads Winter Weight Cape
Sizes: from 6″ (base of neck to start of tail) to 30″
$20 + UPS
(FL res. add sales tax)

Pedigree Perfection
7850 W. McNab Rd., #116
Tamarac, FL 33321
(305) 726-2692

Let's Go Backpacking! ®

Physical fitness and dogs are a natural combination. Most people wonder if their dog—even a smallish dog—can handle a backpack, and the answer is a resounding yes! This solid pack fastens over your dog's back and across/under the chest. Start by putting the empty pack on the dog and taking a walk. Next walk, put something light and bulky (newspapers, clothes, etc.) so he gets the feel of something bulky that sways as he walks. Next, load the pack with items that are approx. ¼ of his weight. Generally, the average dog can comfortably carry up to ⅓ of his body weight, which can take a load off your back on a long hike. Go slow and gradually accustom the dog to carrying his share.

Explorer II Dog Pack, $54 + $4 S&H
(WA res. add 7.6% sales tax)

Wenaha Dog Packs
4518 Maltby Rd.
Bothell, WA 98012
(800) 917-0707

Rough, Tough Hiking Books ®

Headed out into rough terrain? Put on your own hiking boots and a pair of Tuff Paws dog boots. They protect a dog's feet from thorns and burrs and help prevent chafing and tearing of paw pads. Constructed of super strong ballistic nylon, with genuine leather soles for added durability and strength on rugged terrain. Available in black, with a green lining.

Tuff Paws
Sizes: from tiny to extra-large
$30 + UPS
(AZ res. add sales tax)

Available by mail from:
Dog Lover's Catalog
(800) 990-9949

Cool Paw Productions
708 E. Solana Dr.
Tempe, AZ 85281
(800) 650-PAWS

TRUE DOG TALE

Goosebumps

Dogs can be afraid of anything: thunderstorms, tricycles, balloons, bags. And they generally don't outgrow their phobias, which can get worse without help. Fearful dogs can become submissive, cower, lie on their backs with their legs up, avoid eye contact, freeze in place, attack (if trapped), and generally look and feel miserable. However, these fears can be effectively treated by a professional. Two basic techniques are used: flooding and desensitization/counterconditioning. Flooding exposes the dog to a fearful situation for a long period of time—many hours—until the dog realizes the situation will not harm him. He relaxes into it. Desensitization involves exposing the dog to the fearful situation very slowly, then rewarding her with tasty treats, petting, and kind words (counterconditioning) when she starts to show reduced fear. Fears and phobias are treatable. Love your dog, but leave this stuff to the professionals and see a good animal behaviorist.

Heavy Hands Dog Walk

Smart owners can use this cool, hands-free leash with their dog if the dog is reasonably well trained—though it might get awkward with a yanker. The leash is ultrapractical, especially when your hands are full. Great for jogging, pushing a stroller, or hiking. Connects easily to any leash, using a quick-release buckle; the one-handed adjustment varies the length from 3′ to 6′. A wide soft belt provides shock absorption, so it's comfortable for you, and the slide feature prevents it from getting tangled around your legs, even if the dog sees a squirrel and decides to give chase. Smart product.

Hands-Away Leash Belt,
$19 + $3 S&H
(CO res. add 3.86% sales tax)

Woof Whirled
1705 14th St., #305
Boulder, CO 80302
(800) 471-DOGS
E-mail: weinerd@ucsub.
colorado.edu

The Sporting Dog ®

Hey! It's Saturday! Time for football, pizza, and beer. Before the game starts, dress up Rover in your favorite team's T-shirt so he can bark and run around just like you. Fun shirts; one-color art; available for all 30 NFL teams.

NFL Sportname T-shirt (M–XXXL), $14.00 + UPS (MS res. add sales tax)

Smart Dog Products
P.O. Box 1036
Picayune, MS 39466
(800) 264-DOGS

The Tibetan Spaniel: A Gift from the Roof of the World

You won't find a better book that describes everything from the history to the health of this very rare breed. When most people first see a Tibetan Spaniel, they think it's a cross between a Pekingese and another breed. Originating in the land of the Dalai Lama, some Tibbies bear a white spot on their forehead called the Buddha mark. Since their introduction into the U.S. in the late 1960s, they've become more and more popular for their dignified demeanor and intelligence. They are small dogs, easy to keep, and are so revered in Tibet they're called Prayer Dogs, from their long history of living in monasteries. This book includes an interesting sampler of Tibetan names (with English translations), in the event you choose to give your puppy a name from this mountain kingdom.

By Susan W. Miccio, 1995,
254 pp., $39.95 + $2.50 S&H
(AL res. add sales tax)

OTR Publications
P.O. Box 481
Centreville, AL 35042
(800) 367-2174

Photograph: Ed Scott

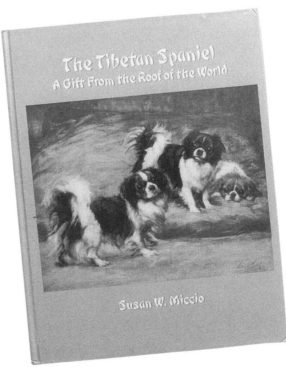

The British Way ®

Remember those chain "choke" collars that used to gag the dog? They're a thing of the distant past. The British-Style Slip Lead is a much more humane collar, combining lead and collar in one. Used for years by trainers and handlers, it's perfect for controlling, braking, and gently training your dog. It's made from top-quality, multifilament polypropylene roping that tightens briefly, • then relaxes and loosens—even in cold weather. These superb leads feature embossed leather and solid brass hardware. Available in your choice of 11 vibrant colors.

British-Style Slip Lead, $12.95 (6′ × ⁵⁄₁₆″ dia. for sm. dogs); $14.95 (6′ × ⅞″ dia. for lg. dogs) + UPS (MN res. add sales tax)

Mendota Products
1765 S. Victoria Rd.
Mendota Heights, MN 55118
(612) 452-3546

For Your Next Walk ®

Late-night walk? Definitely consider the Night Glow Safety Collar. A highly reflective tape overlay is sewn into this ⅝″ w. (12″–20″ long) and 1″ w. (18″–26″ long) red, blue, or black collar. Dramatically increases the visibility (and hence the safety) of you and the dog in automobile headlights. This company also makes a versatile and highly adjustable European Lead, which functions six different ways: as a 43″ lead, a 58″ lead, a 6′ lead, a two-dog lead, an over-the-shoulder lead, and a portable tie-out. Made of sleek leather.

Night Glow Safety Collars, $5.94 (12″–20″), $9.42 (18″–26″)
European Lead, $27.88–$32.60 (½″ and ¾″, adjustable lengths) + UPS (FL res. add sales tax)

Hamilton Products
P.O. Box 770069
Ocala, FL 34477
(352) 237-6188

The Dog Observed: Photographs 1844–1988 ®

Imagine dogs around the world, in every locale and situation: on the tar-papered porches of Harlan County, Kentucky; inside a giant redwood; doing tricks for a French girl; on the hunt with an American Indian carrying a backpack; Horst in Andy Warhol's studio; dressed as men in suits and Hawaiian shirts; William Wegman's classic *Dusted*; a stray dog in a Japanese city; a French soldier and his dog during the war in Indochina. Just a sampling from this remarkable visual record of dogs around the world.

Edited by Ruth Silverman, 1984, 160 pp., $16.95 + UPS (CA res. add sales tax)

Chronicle Books
275 Fifth Ave.
San Francisco, CA 94013
(800) 722-6657

Holiday Bells ®

It's Christmas Eve, and you hear the sound of—reindeer? Santa's sleigh? Actually, it's this very cool Jingle Bell Collar, which you can slip on Fido just in time for the party. I love the happy sound of these bells. They're affixed to an easy-slip elastic collar decorated with a plaid tartan taffeta. Another great Christmas treat is the lovely dog tapestry Jingle Bell Stocking (not shown), with a velvet cuff and three gold jingle bells. Christmas dog antics.

Jingle Bell Collar, $11 (XS, S),
$11.50 (M), $13 (L)
Jingle Bell Stocking, $26
+ $4.50 S&H each
(IL res. add sales tax)

Creature Comforts
Tyler & Russell, Ltd.
357 W. Erie St., 2nd Floor
Chicago, IL 60610
(312) 266-0907

Putting on the Dog

Taking the dog out in extreme weather? All of these products from Sylmar help you avoid problems with almost any situation you'll encounter. Talk about a total cover-up outfit: The light orange Total Protection Suit protects against burrs, foxtails, barbed wire, snakebites, and the next blizzard. It's made of 1,000-denier Cordura Plus, which allows free movement, buckles on easily, and keeps the dog toasty warm. Camouflage model available, too. The Dogpack is constructed of abrasion-resistant 1,000-denier Cordura Plus. Features four deep, roomy compartments (large and small on each side), plus D-rings for hook-ons. A vented top, for maximum air circulation, carries the weight forward on your dog's shoulders rather than on his lower back. Fast, adjustable hook-and-loop fasteners. Try these Cover-Up Boots to keep his feet and legs dry and clean, made with soft, coated, durable waterproof fabric. Adjustable elastic support strap across the back. For a hot pavement or snow, Field Boots provide protection against sharp stones, chemicals, foxtails, and snowballs that can get between your dog's toes. Keeps feet clean and dry, easy on-off. Warm, safe protection for your friend.

Total Protection Suit, $129 (med.), $139 (lg.)
Dogpack, $52 (med.), $59 (lg.)
Cover-up Boots, $34 (toy), $36 (med.) $38 (lg.), $42 (x-lg.)
Field Boots, $34 (med.), $39 (lg.), $42 (x-lg.)
+ $4 S&H each
(WA res. add 8.2% sales tax)

Sylmar Dogwear
22710 S.E. 23rd Pl.
Issaquah, WA 98027
(800) 592-6996

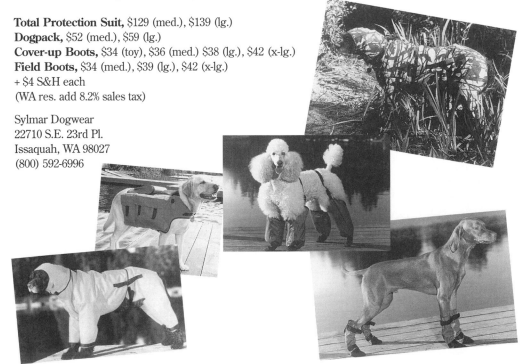

Old West/ Madison Avenue Look ®

Bandannas, like diamonds, go with anything. Any color fur, any size dog. I will pet *any* dog who's wearing a bandanna (after checking with the owner, of course). Tie a pretty Cotton Bandanna onto your small or medium dog (that's the small, pretty white pup). Or go for the tough but gentle UltraSuede Bandanna for a large dog (that's the enthusiastic guy with his mouth open). Whichever you choose, never forget: A bandanna civilizes any dog. Ask about their Groomer's Bows and the Jingle Bells Bandanna, too!

Cotton Bandanna,
$2.50 (sm., fits neck up to 15½″), $3 (med., up to 18½″)
UltraSuede Bandanna,
$10 (med., up to 18½″ neck), $11.50 (lg., up to 21½″)
+ $4 S&H each
(NC res. add 6% sales tax)

UltraMouse, Ltd.
1442 E. Park Place
Ann Arbor, MI 48104
(800) 573-8869

The Connection with Your Dog ®

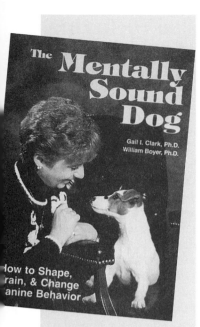

The Mentally Sound Dog

In this fascinating book two Ph.D.s share their experiences with dog behavior—the behavior you normally expect, as well as problem behavior. Every type of anxiety and aberrant behavior is explored, with specific suggestions about changing it. Bad behavior doesn't change by itself. Biting, barking, chewing, digging, house soiling, jumping, separation anxiety—the list is endless. Here's the bible on changing bad behavior into good.

By Gail Clark and William Boyer, 1995, 268 pp., $21.95 + UPS
(CO res. add sales tax)

Alpine Publications
P.O. Box 7027
Loveland, CO 80537
(800) 777-7257

Ready for some exercise with your dog? The superb, quick-fit DoubleLoop Dog Harness, combined with a BodyLeash, is *the* way to go when you're out walking the dog. The BodyLeash sensibly takes the strain off your arm by transferring the dog's energy to your body. It's just plain easier to walk with it, because you can swing your arms naturally while you walk. Hook it up to the high-quality DoubleLoop Harness, which puts the leash control over your dog's chest (instead of yanking on his neck), for a winning walking combination. Made of tough, soft, woven nylon in red, black, bright blue, or green. Reflective versions for safety at night are available in black and red. Lastly, add a TagLoop (red or black with brass ring) to your dog's harness or collar, for holding ID and vaccination tags. It's more practical and looks better than jamming them on the collar ring. Or use one for your house and car keys. Ask about their reflective collars and leashes so you can mix and match. Great dog essentials.

DoubleLoop Dog Harness (slide or snap-on version, ⅝″ and 1″), $12.50–$17

BodyLeash (1″ standard w/swivel, or ⅝″ skinny with D-ring, for sm. dog), $10.50
Reflective Collar (on black or red BodyLeash, 1″ standard), $23.50
TagLoop, $2.30
+ S&H (up to $25, add $4.95; $25.01–$50, add $5.95; 50.01–$75, add $8.95)
(CA res. add 7.25% sales tax)

Metropolitan Pet
P.O. Box 230324
Tigard, OR 97281
(800) 966-1819

Sunny Day Walks

This very cute Little Mary Sunshine Hat has a black top and yellow brim, with a sunflower on each side. A special Velcro closure system and flexible foam top ensure that the hat remains comfortably in place, whether your dog is playing or at rest. Shields your dog's eyes from the sun—great for dogs who are sensitive to bright light. Check out the cool Internet site for info on this and many other hats. Practical and amusing!

Little Mary Sunshine Hat, $14.50 (all sizes) (OH res. add sales tax)

Canine Creations
724 Maranatha Way
Loveland, OH 45140
(800) 337-7301
E-mail: lpreed@one.net
http://www.acmepet.com/doghats

Clifford Barks! ®

The happy red dog in this cute hardcover barks at almost everything. Barking means "I like you." So the dog barks at the sun, his food dish, the phone, the cat, the fish, the door, the trees. His happy enthusiasm for life rubs off on young readers. Lots of fun to read, with a push-button bark toy recessed into the front cover. Bright illustrations, thick paper for heavy usage and messy fingers. Simple dog fun for children under age 5.

By Norman Bridwell, 1996, 16 pp., $7.95 + UPS (NY res. add sales tax)

Scholastic
555 Broadway
New York, NY 10012
(800) 392-2179

How Do You Handle a Strong Dog? ®

Some dogs are so strong they can overpower you. Notice the woman's hand holding this collar? The Handler Dog Collar is specially designed to keep your dog's head close to your leg for better communication and control. Made of beautiful chestnut bridle leather and lined with soft, supple burgundy latigo for added comfort, the collar features a built-in handle with wide construction that evenly distributes pressure to humanely control your dog without choking him. Two stainless steel D-rings allow you to attach a leash when desired.

Handler Dog Collar, $70
Handler Leash, $25
+ UPS (OH res. add sales tax)

Weaver Leather
P.O. Box 68
Mt. Hope, OH 44660
(800) 932-8371

You're Taking Me Shopping?

"Putting on the dog" takes new meaning with these scrumptious, classy Tie, Tux, and Cufflinks threads. The Tie is suave silk with a vintage tie bar on a shirt collar. Just place it around your dog's neck; it looks snazzy on either a boy or a girl. The Tux includes a dashing, real tuxedo bowtie with rhinestones on a tuxedo shirt collar. It's classy, not garish. The Cufflinks feature sophisticated black onyx stones and rhinestones on a houndstooth collar, with a sterling silver pocketwatch identification locket and chain. You get the picture: superior on-the-town and party gifts for your buddy.

Tie, $51 (left, sm.), $56 (center, reg.)
Tux, $61 (top reg. only)
Cufflinks, $64 (right, sm.), $69 (reg.)
+ $6 S&H each
(MI res. add 6% sales tax)

Nutty Dog Stuff
P.O. Box 3873
Ann Arbor, MI 48106
(313) 663-5384
E-mail: nuttydogst@aol.com

Fleece for Warmth

Does your dog get cold feet? These warm outerwear fleece boots with stay-on suspenders will protect her tender paws against winter snow, ice, cold, and salt. Strictly a cold-weather boot made of fast-drying, nonpilling Polarfleece. Your choice of red, blue, or black, all with black suspenders.

Bo-Boots (sizes: sm. 10″–12″ shoulder height; med., 12″–16″; lg., 16″–20″), $19.95 + $2.50 S&H (IN res. add sales tax)

Bo-Boots for Dogs
P.O. Box 10834
Merrillville, IN 46411
(219) 942-0500

"The dog has no ambition, no self-interest, no desire for vengeance, no fear other than that of displeasing."

—Louis Leclerc Buffon

TRUE DOG TALE

Forward-March Hairs

Only two dogs in the world—the Rhodesian Ridgeback and the Thai Ridgeback—have a forward-facing ridge of hair straight down their backs. The distinctly pointed ridge looks like a spinal column. These dogs originated continents apart, and they certainly don't look like each other: one is brown (Rhodesian) and the other gray. It's a mystery why evolution chose to give this same attribute to dogs half a world apart.

Vermont Bandannas

For colorful adornment, you can't beat Pawkerchiefs, handmade in Vermont of carefully selected 100% cottons. Each is reversible, with brightly colored coordinating fabrics. All are machine washable. Drop them a note, or call for their latest color swatches. You choose the material—they make it. Beautiful accessories for your favorite canine friend.

Pawkerchiefs
Sizes: mini (**up to 10″** neck), sm. (10″–14″), med. (14″–18″), lg. (18″–24″), x-lg. (24″–32″)
$6 (mini), $7 (sm.), $8 (med.), $9 (lg.), $10 (x-lg.), + S&H $1.75
(for 1–2 Pawkerchiefs)
(VT res. add 5% sales tax)

Grande Paws
P.O. Box 711
West Rutland, VT 05777
(802) 773-0343

Hot Feet ®

On the other paw, here's the hot-weather version of the polar-climate Bo-Boots on this page. Desert climates get incredibly hot; roads can sizzle at 140°. From Heat Central in Tempe, Arizona, comes Cool Paws: special boots with insulating granules to keep your dog's feet cool. Pour water in these boots, and a cool, gel-like layer forms within the sole. Special granules in the soles reactivate again and again, never wearing out. Constructed of heavy-duty nylon with Velcro straps, available in red/black or blue/black. Cool feet on a hot, hot day.

Cool Paws (set of 4 boots)
Sizes: tiny (foot size under 1½″) to XL (3½″ to 4″)
$22 (tiny), $25 (XL) + UPS (AZ res. add sales tax)

Cool Paw Productions
708 E. Solana Dr.
Tempe, AZ 85281
(800) 650-PAWS

Dog Lover's Catalog:
(800) 990-9499

Presentable Collar

This bright collar has a friendly southwestern look, somewhat similar to colorful Central American woven goods. Unique Maya collar, with matching leash and key ring, make a great gift in this attractive 9″ × 13″ pine box, packaged with straw and shrink-wrapped. Available in four adjustable sizes: S, M, L, and XL. The look matches your dog's personality—bright, eye-catching, snappy, upbeat—and the color pattern looks especially great on outdoorsy dogs. Highly attractive packaging; one of my favorites.

Dog Gift Box, $21.99 + UPS
(NC res. add sales tax)

Color Pet Products
210 Old Dairy Rd.
Suite F
Wilmington, NC 28405
(800) 849-0276

Night Safety

Have you ever driven along at night and noticed the reflective pedals of a bike in your headlights? They catch the eye because they're moving. Same with these clever NiteSights Reflective Leg Bands for dogs. Constructed of 1″-wide highly reflective fluorescent orange material, they fit just above the dog's wrist and/or hock. Each is adjustable to fit, plus or minus ¾″. Quick on-and-off for impromptu night walks.

NiteSights Reflective Leg Bands
Adjustable sizes: sm. (5½″ l.), med. (6½″ l.) and lg. (7½″ l.)
$5.95 per pair (includes S&H)
(IN res. add sales tax)

Prints
722 Georgian Ave.
Sellersburg, IN 47172
(812) 246-2477

A Collar for Every Dog Size ®

Harnesses are the way to go for small dogs. They take pressure off the dog's neck and give you easier control. Both the Lupine Adjustable Harness (¾″) in forest gold (on the Corgi model) and the Lupine H-Style Harness, in amber wave on the small dog model, maximize control on the shoulders, not the neck. The H-style features a strap for additional strength and support. Fully adjustable on both neck and chest, these harnesses use two O-rings for greater comfort and movement. Lupine also makes a great Combo Collar (shown in redwood totem on the English Setter), which is really two collars in one. It can be used as a fully adjustable

everyday walking collar, or as a training restraint collar. The collar is only a partial choke, so the dog gets the message without risk of injury.

Lupine Adjustable Harness,
$15.80 (sm., ¾″)
Lupine H-Style Harness,
$15.80 (sm., ¾″)
Combo Collar, $9.50 (sm.)
+ UPS (no sales tax in N.H.)

Lupine
P.O. Box 1600
Conway, NH 03818
(800) 228-WOLF
E-mail: Lupineinc@aol.com

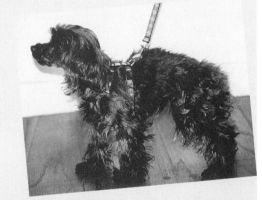

The Ultimate Rottweiler ®

The Rottweiler is an incredibly popular breed, currently ranked second in number of AKC registrations, with nearly 105,000 dogs in the U.S. alone. In this beautiful book, with more than 200 color illustrations, editor Andrew Brace heads a prominent list of international dog authorities who trace the origins and development of what used to be a native German herding dog. Includes all the basics of Rottweiler socialization (very important for this breed), basic and advanced training, a discussion of the working Rott, a major overview of breed standards in Europe and the United States, and health care and concerns specific to this highly intelligent, impressive breed.

Edited by Andrew H. Brace, 1995, 288 pp., $25.95 + UPS
(IN res. add sales tax)

Howell Book House
201 W. 103rd St.
Indianapolis, IN 46290
(800) 428-5331

Classic Faux Fur Leads

Why put a tedious, tired old collar on your dog? Where does that get you? Hep Cat faux animal skins are for the "cool cat" that's just under the surface of your canine companion. Tiger is set with cool green malachite stones, groovily finished with a feather boa. Show some *Life*! Sno Leopard has spotted leopardskin, jasper and onyx stones, stylishly edged with black velvet. Zebra—where would we be without Zebra?—is striped with blue-green azurite-malachite stones, smoothly trimmed with black velvet. Admit it. This is you.

Tiger, Sno Leopard, or Zebra Fur Lead,
$54 (sm., sizes 10 and 12),
$59 (reg. sizes 14–22)
+ $6 S&H
(MI res. add 6% sales tax)

Nutty Dog Stuff
P.O. Box 3873
Ann Arbor, MI 48106
(313) 663-5384
E-mail: nuttydogst@aol.com

Let's Go Out and Play! ®

Even in the pouring rain, no matter when you pick up the leash, you-know-who is ready to run out the door. When the raindrops fall, slip on this Doggie Rain Poncho, which includes a belt and a detachable hood. Specifically made for perky small and medium dogs in a wide array of bright, cool colors. The detachable hood is fastened with Velcro for easy conversion from poncho to city slicker coat. Let it rain and when it does, you need this. Functional and looks great.

Doggie Rain Poncho, $21 (sm.), $22 (med.),
+ $6 S&H
(MI res. add 5% sales tax)

UltraMouse, Ltd.
1442 E. Park Pl.
Ann Arbor, MI 48104
(800) 573-8869

Leash Shock Absorber ®

Here's an idea worthy of Einstein. It's a bunched-up leash that stretches as your dog pulls, saving wear and tear on your arm. Four- and six-foot lengths; comes in hot pink, hot yellow, red, or royal blue. Back and forth, in and out. Takes the pressure off your arm.

Bunchie Leash, $14.34–$16.32
+ UPS
(CO res. add sales tax)

Aspen Pet Products
11701 E. 53rd Ave.
Denver, CO 80239
(800) BUY-4-PET

Peace ®

"Shalom" is just one of the many messages your pup can wear. Dogs look so amusing in T-shirts! Dress her up for your next party or any suitable occasion. This—and many other messages—are also available in a bandanna version. Spread the word.

Shalom Dog T-shirt, $11.50
Sizes: S (10"–12", from base of neck to beginning of tail) to XXXL (26"–30")
+ UPS (MS res. add sales tax)

Smart Dog Products
P.O. Box 1036
Picayune, MS 39466
(800) 264-DOGS

Dog Heaven ®

A comforting hardcover book that shows children under age 5 what their dog is doing in Heaven. Running through endless fields, sleeping on clouds, playing with children and other dogs, returning invisibly to earth to visit and make sure everything is okay, then going back to Heaven with an angel. The focus of the text is reassurance, not religion. It helps soften a loss. Charming, happy illustrations with a simple message for a worried young child.

By Cynthia Rylant, 1995, 34 pp., $14.95 + UPS
(NY res. add sales tax)

The Blue Sky Press
Scholastic
555 Broadway
New York, NY 10012
(800) 392-2179

Heavy-Duty Dog Pack

Planning a walk-in camping trip? You'll need to equip the dog, too. Here's Kiba, the mascot of this small Oregon company, wearing their Banzai Explorer dog pack. What's in this tough equipment? Rugged black ballistic nylon brush guard panels; compression straps, to keep contents snug; two additional zippered pockets; Scotchlite reflective trim, for night safety; storm flaps over zippers; a contoured top section, to encourage an even load while providing a handy pocket; lash patches for securing extra gear; water-resistant Cordura nylon (available in 10 colors); and padded buckles with special soft Polarfleece pads. The slant design reduces restriction and wear to elbows. Just for big dogs? Nope. Sizes from tiny (toy breeds) to extra large (120+ lbs.).

Banzai Explorer,
$69.50 + $6 S&H
(no sales tax in OR)

Wolf Packs
755 Tyler Creek Rd.
Ashland, OR 97520
E-mail: traildog@wolfpacks.com
http://www.wolfpacks.com/catalog/

Button up Your Overcoat . . .

Ready for the cold white stuff? Gorgeous Polar Dog Coat is lined with Polarfleece and trimmed with a fringed collar. It's definitely an eye-catching garment. Warm and attractive for chilly days, in muted purple with hot-pink trim. Note the Polar Dog Boots (in black) with fringe to match the coat. And after the walk it's playtime with the fringed, squeaky Polarfleece bone. First class, always.

Polar Dog Coat, $50 + $6.50 S&H
Polar Dog Boots, $15 + $3.50 S&H
Polar Squeaky Bone, $14 + $3.50 S&H
(Includes MN sales tax)

L. Coffey Ltd.
4244 Linden Hills Blvd.
Minneapolis, MN 55410
(800) 448-4PET

Holiday Collars ®

Sylvan's always coming up with amusing ideas for collars. Check out these terrific ideas for every holiday or other occasion: Bright Trick-or-Treat collar, Happy Valentine's Day collar, Snow Man collar, and many more. New choices each year. Matching leashes, too!

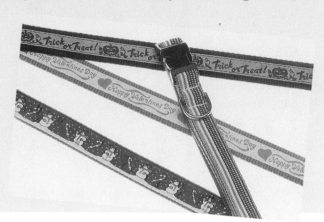

Holiday Dog Collar, $8 (sm.), $10 (med.), $12 (lg.)
Matching Leash, $16 (4' or 6')
+ $4 S&H
(FL res. add 6.5% sales tax)

Sylvan and Sons
4108 Corona St.
Tampa, FL 33629
(800) 292-6393

Tags for Her, and You

Here's the new look in dog/people tags. This attractive, anodized satin aluminum tag contains the message of your choice beneath its surface. It's lightweight, looks great, and has a clip that attaches right to your dog's collar. If you feel like it, you can order the People Adapter, a 24" steel beaded chain, so you can wear it around *your* neck, too. Big selection of messages (some risqué). You'll definitely get looks.

Dog-Gag Tag, $4.95
People Adapter Chain, $1.95
+ $2 S&H per total order
(MD res. add 25¢ sales tax per tag)

I.D. Technology
117 Nelson Rd.
Baltimore, MD 21208
(410) 602-1191
E-mail: IDTECH@ABS. NET

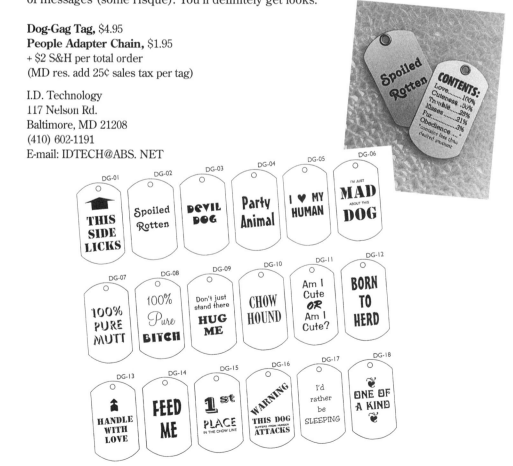

The New Chihuahua ®

The Chihuahua has an interesting history, beginning many centuries ago with the Mayans, Toltecs, and Aztecs of ancient Mexico. Americans first discovered the dog in the 1800s, prizing what were called "Mexican dogs" for their novelty and tiny size. This book includes current breed standards and information on selection, grooming, breeding, showing, and keeping Chihuahuas as family pets. Black and white photos. The energetic nature and trainability of the Chihuahua make them superb "hearing ear dogs" to alert the deaf to doorbells, telephones, and other sounds. Startle one, and you'll be in awe of the ferocious energy that comes in such a tiny package.

By E. Ruth Terry, 1990, 230 pp., $25.95 + UPS
(IN res. add sales tax)

Howell Book House
201 W. 103rd St.
Indianapolis, IN 46290
(800) 428-5331

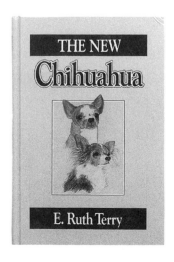

Cool-Off Bandanna ®

Rustle up some steaks and chew sticks—we're goin' Western! On a hot day, soak this bandanna in water, then fasten it around your dog's neck for a nice, long-lasting, cooling effect. Evaporation cools a hot dog. The bandanna absorbs 230 times its weight in water.

Wet Tie Cooling Bandannas, $9.50–$14 + UPS (AZ res. add sales tax)

Pet Affairs
691 E. 20th St.
Building 111
Tucson, AZ 85719
(800) 777-9192

I Can't Hear You!

Your dog will have to read your lips when she's wearing these. Ear Cozies, a famous Ear Bib design, have lightweight thermal knit material lining the ear bib, protecting delicate ears and heads from winter winds and snow. Machine wash and dry. When ordering, state your dog's breed and head diameter (at midear). Cute! and no more cold ears.

Ear Cozie, $10.95 + $2.95 S&H (No sales tax in OR)

Pampered Pups Extraordinaire
647 S. 44th St.
Springfield, OR 97478
(541) 746-3801
E-mail:
cavlady@pond.net

We're Taking a Walk? But What About My Feet? ®

When was the last time *you* walked barefoot in the snow? So why should your dog? These supple, waterproof, nonskid boots feature a warm, soft fleece interior, with easy-on, easy-off Velcro tabs that really work. Good protection against cold and mud and thorns and everything else that can hurt paws. And no more muddy feet in the car.

Paw Tectors, $27 (XS), $26 (S), $31 (M), $33 (L), $35 (XL) + UPS (FL res. add sales tax)

Pedigree Perfection
7850 W. McNab Road, #116
Tamarac, FL 33321
(305) 726-2692

Backpacking with Your Dog ®

Dreaming of long hikes through the mountains? Great fun and exercise, but there's plenty to learn first from this book before you ever strap a backpack on your dog. The basics— whether you should try it in the first place, things to consider, equipment (especially introducing your dog to a backpack), necessities, what to expect on the trail, encounters with other animals, and handling medical emergencies—are all covered. A simple primer to get you started.

By Richard Lerner, D.V.M., 1994, 46 pp., $4.95 + UPS (AL res. add sales tax)

Menasha Ridge Press
3169 Cahaba Heights Rd.
Birmingham, AL 35243
(205) 967-0566

ID Always ®

ID's are vital if your dog tends to stray. Slip this water-resistant, washable ID pouch onto your dog's collar, and rest a little easier. It includes a waterproof ID card that you complete and leave inside. The pouch uses secure metal snaps. Available in red, blue, and other colors. They also have a photo ID card.

Pet Pocket ID, $6
(includes S&H and sales tax)

Diverse Designs
139 Harper St.
Louisville, CO 80027
(800) 786-9981

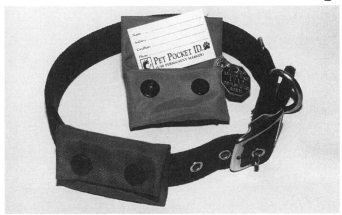

The Dog Book ®

A small, handsome, hardcover volume of interesting dog facts, amazing dog stories, and tales of dog devotion. Did you know that President Kennedy, at the height of the Cuban missile crisis, left the situation room and sat for fifteen minutes quietly stroking his dog Charlie in the Oval Office, then returned to work? Packed with interesting dog miscellany.

Edited by Mary Goodbody, 1995, 40 pp., $6.95 + UPS
(MO res. add sales tax)

Andrews & McMeil
4900 Main St.
Kansas City, MO 64112
(800) 826-4216

The Well-Heeled Look ®

Every dog deserves at least one bowtie—perhaps several—for special occasions. Parties, weddings, holidays, all deserve suitable dress-up apparel. This bright red 4″ poly-filled bow in 100% cotton (fits over your pet's collar) shows some discreet class, and it's machine washable. Three sizes. Many choices of colors and patterns, including holiday designs. Live it up!

Large Dog Bowtie
(2½″, 4″, 5″), $12.99 and $3 S+H
(CT res. add sales tax)

Z Cat & Dog Bows & Bandannas
19 Chapel St.
Greenwich, CT 06831
(203) 531-1108

Bring Me My Diamonds

Doesn't the queen of the house deserve elegance? Shimmering Austrian lead crystal gems give a classy look to this black velvet collar, with sterling silver identification locket. Queen Priscilla is modeling the Mirage Diamonds Collar, which features softly shimmering shades of rose, baby blue, and yellow, set off by sapphire rhinestones. Two sizes are available, with a matching jeweled lead in 6′ (for collar sizes 14″–22″) or 4′ (collar sizes 10″ and 12″) length. A class act. Other collars and leads include Sugarplums (royal blue and fuschia over a golden base, set off by fuschia-gold rhinestones), Smokey Topaz (gilded tones of honey and amber, set off by gold rhinestones), Royalty (regal amethyst domes with emerald base, set off by sapphire rhinestones, especially suited for longhaired dogs), and of course Diamonds (luminous crystal-clear dewdrops set off by aqua rhinestones). Snazzily packaged in a gift box.

Mirage Diamonds Collar (shown), $74 (sm.), $79 (reg.)
Mirage Diamonds Lead (shown), $39 (sm. or reg.)
+ $6 S&H each
(MI res. add 6% sales tax)

Nutty Dog Stuff
P.O. Box 3873
Ann Arbor, MI 48106
(313) 663-5384
E-mail:
nuttydogst@aol.com

A Sweater for Every Occasion ®

It's a lucky dog that has more than one of these people-quality knit sweaters for cold weather. Large variety of fashion patterns and colors. Several body shapes, including a full-length turtleneck with leg straps and a hooded dolman-sleeved sports top. Let's not forget the tube-style mock turtle blouson. Nice fit, clean design.

Pet Threads Sweaters
Sizes: 6″–30″. $19.95 and up + UPS

Pedigree Perfection
7850 W. McNab Rd., #116
Tamarac, FL 33321
(305) 726-2692

High Steppers ®

Perfect for cold weather or a hot pavement, for protecting injured feet or keeping feet clean after a rain. These genuine leather Sportster booties for toy dogs come in two colors, navy or burgundy, with matching suspenders. The X configuration of the adjustable suspenders helps prevent slipping toward hindquarters. Complete with instructions for fitting and care. Machine wash-

able. True Fifth Avenue style.

Doggie Sox
Sizes: Sportster (shown), Regular (dogs with 6″–10″ front legs), and Large (12″–15″ front legs)
$25.95–$34.95
+ UPS (WI res. add sales tax)

Doggie-Sox Mfg. Co.
P.O. Box 699
Green Lake, WI 54941
(414) 294-6719

The Basic Guide to the Chinese Shar-Pei

You've probably seen the Shar-Pei, that remarkable dog with a suit of fur three sizes too big. Now you can learn more about the breed from the collected wisdom of 63 authorities in this complete book of history, how-to, and breed standards. *Shar-Pei* is a Chinese word meaning "sandy or shark skinned." The breed can be easily traced back to 300 B.C., and it was first introduced into the U.S. in the 1960s. Everything you need to know about this intelligent, low-activity dog—ideal for modern urban life. Includes the Shar-Pei Hall of Fame, with champion breed photographs.

Edited by Michael R. Zervas, 1995, 118 pp., $9.95 + $3 S&H (VA res. add 4.5% sales tax)

Dace Publishing
P.O. Box 91
Ruckersville, VA 22968
(888) 840-DACE

TRUE DOG TALE

Puppy Sight and Sound

Puppies are born deaf and blind. Their eyes open after about two weeks, then it takes about another week before they can really focus on you. And say what you will, they can't hear a word. Puppies are deaf until about 2½ weeks, when their ear canals open.

Hold That Dog!

Many states require your dog to be secured when traveling in the back of a moving pickup truck. Use this handy, quick restraint to tie your dog to either the existing eye bolts on the sides of the truck bed, or to the tie-down rings. Black nylon, strong safety.

Pickup Truck Restraint, $19.95 + UPS (AZ res. add sales tax)

Discount Master Animal Care:
(800) 346-0749

Pet Affairs
691 E. 20th St.
Building 111
Tucson, AZ 85719
(800) 777-9192

Dog? What Dog?

Before you move into a new home, always check your landlord's lease for clauses that prohibit pets. If necessary, be prepared to convince the landlord you're a responsible dog owner. Here's how. First, arrange a meeting with the landlord. Bring your dog to the meeting on a leash, and introduce him to your landlord as you would a person. Hand the landlord a brief, written résumé about your dog: name, age, personality, special traits that endear him to you. Include your vet's name and phone number and references from past landlords who will vouch that your dog didn't damage their property. This personal approach often works, but you can also, if necessary, offer to post a modest refundable security deposit for your dog as an act of goodwill. Just make sure you protect yourself by taking pictures of the property before you move in and after you move out.

Rainy Day Fun ®

Walking in a light rain can be pleasant for both of you. Just make sure you cover Pooch up with this classy Staffordshire Raincoat. The lovely glazed chintz fabric depicts 18th-century English animals—dogs, cats, lambs, squirrels, and sheep—in a charming pattern evocative of original Staffordshire porcelains. Upscale, very arty, attractive!

Staffordshire Raincoat, $39.50 + $6.50 S&H
(includes MN sales tax)

L. Coffey Ltd.
4244 Linden
Hills Blvd.
Minneapolis,
MN 55410
(800) 448-4PET

The Illustrated Dog's Life ®

Two Cocker Spaniels smooching on the front cover set the tone for this inspiring hardcover book on how dogs live with people everywhere in the world. Chewing on a sneaker, hunting with Pygmies in the Congo, wearing a party hat, catching a Frisbee, begging at the table. It's a happy, upbeat book: an evolutionary success story showing how the 20th-century dog is part of virtually every human society on earth.

By Warren Eckstein, 1995, 128 pp., $12.99 + UPS
(NJ res. add sales tax)

Crescent Books
Random House Value Publishing
40 Engelhard Ave.
Avenel, NJ 07001
(800) 793-2665

Lights, Cameras, Hollywood!

What's all the buzz about? This fabulous canine clothing starts with a Faux Leopard Fur that simply drips decadence. If you want a less flashy look, choose the faux black Persian lamb or perhaps the rural black and white cow. Each is custom made of Eco-Fleece, composed of 87% recycled soda bottles! Low-pill, insulative windbreaking properties make this clothing durable and environmentally friendly. Not just for Dachshunds. Looking good.

Faux Leopard Fur Canine Couture, $28–$65 + $3 S&H
(OH res. add 5.75% sales tax)

Dachshund Delights
P.O. Box 712
Burton, OH 44021
(216) 834-9557
http://ourworld.compuserve.com/homepages/stemnock

The Goodger Guide to the Pug

Pug fanciers will relish this complete story of the Pug, whose history stretches back an extraordinary 2,600 years. In fact, the Pug is considered the world's second-oldest breed, after the Greyhound. After all those years, the general reaction to the Pug's scrunched-up face and turned-up tail remains the same: You either love or detest them. Not a lot of opinion in the middle. This fabulous hardcover book, illustrated with line drawings and black and white photographs, should be the first book in any Pug owner's library.

By Wilhelmina Swainston-Goodger, 1995, 240 pp., $29.95 + $2.50 S&H (includes sales tax)

OTR Publications
P.O. Box 481
Centreville, AL 35042
(800) 367-2174

Personality Change

So your beloved tail-wagging best friend turns into a very unhappy camper when visiting the vet. Growls, maybe bites. What to do? A Quick Muzzle may be in order. The adjustable Original (upper left) fits sizes from Chihuahuas to Great Danes, while the Long-Snouted version is suitable for Collies, Shelties, Greyhounds, and other long-nosed breeds. The Pug version (also works on cats) includes a quick-close control with a hook-and-loop neck tab. Fits Pekingese, Lhasa Apsos, and Boston Terriers, as well as Pugs. These look intense and can block your dog's vision, but they're humane and help calm most dogs. The padded Cozy-Standard Style, similar to the Original, includes padded fleece around the nose for comfort. All the muzzles are made of reinforced, durable, washable nylon pack cloth, for years of wear, in royal blue or red.

Quick Muzzle
Original, $8.50–$13 (10 sizes)
Long-Snouted, $9 (sm., med., or lg.)
Pug, $9 (sm. or lg.)
Cozy-Standard Style, $9.50–$13.50
(10 sizes, fleeced)
+ $2 S&H
(MN res. add 6.5% sales tax)

Four Flags over Aspen
34402 15th St.
Janesville, MN 56048
(800) 222-9263
E-mail: ffoa@ic.manka-to.mn.us

Go Cal!

Carole Stevens sells this UC Berkeley shirt for dogs, plus dog-size cotton T's personalized in school colors for 24 other universities and colleges. Send one to your son or daughter at school, so they can take the dog, dressed in the shirt, to the football game. Let's hear it for the alma mater!

Dog University T-shirt, Sizes: petite, sm., med., lg., and x-lg.
$10 (includes S&H and sales tax)

Dapper Dogwear
11611 Park Lane Circle
Los Angeles, CA 90049
(310) 476-6175

Leather and Nylon, or Spikes? ®

The Prism Accents Collar and Leash combine beautiful nylon webbing with classic chestnut bridle leather. The collar features an easy-to-use, nonrusting solid brass buckle and brass-plated D-ring for easy attachment of the matching leash. Comes in four eye-catching colors: blue, hunter green, burgundy, and purple. Superattractive quality. Special touches like precise, even stitching and smoothed, darkened leather edges make these an excellent choice. Now, if you need that macho look, the Spike's Collar features double-stitched, classic black bridle leather, with durable nickel-brass spots and spikes. A coordinated, single-ply leash to match is available.

Prism Accents Collar and Leash, $40 and up
Spike's Collar, $48
+ UPS (OH res. add sales tax)

Weaver Leather
P.O. Box 68
Mt. Hope, OH 44660
(800) 932-8371

> "It is a strange thing, love. Nothing but love has made the dog lose his wild freedom, to become the servant of man."
>
> —D. H. Lawrence

Is That a Smile, or . . . ? ®

Dog in a foul mood? Even the best dog can be upset to the point where he needs to be muzzled. An injury, a trip to the vet, that mean kid who throws rocks—any of these might necessitate use of this quick-fit, adjustable nylon muzzle available in eight sizes (from Toy Poodle to Rottweiler). Strong, soft nylon is designed to inhibit biting, chewing, and barking while allowing for panting and drinking. A plastic snap buckle makes the muzzle difficult for the dog to dislodge.

H.P. Mugz Muzzle, $9.90–$11.40 + UPS
(FL res. add sales tax)

Hamilton Products
P.O. Box 770069
Ocala, FL 34477
(352) 237-6188

Is It Time?

Convincing young children it's time for bed often takes some doing. This cute, illustrated book is about a mommy and a puppy and that age-old bedtime quandary. The puppy dutifully takes a bath, brushes his "fangs," and gets ready for bed, followed by that big moment all parents await: turning out the light. Show and tell, see and do. Sweet.

By Marilyn Janovitz, 1994, 26 pp., $5.95 + UPS (NY res. add sales tax)

North-South Books
1123 Broadway
Suite 800
New York, NY 10010
(212) 463-9736

That Southwest Look

The Santa Fe–style collar and lead evoke images of the American Southwest. Made of high-quality hand-woven cotton, backed with rugged nylon for strength. The bright, colorful material was created by the same cloth-making process used by American Indians. Each is a one-of-a-kind, unique design.

Santa Fe Collar, $13 (sm.), $14 (med.), $15 (lg.)
Santa Fe Leash, $20 (6′)
+ $4.95 S&H each
(TX res. add 7.25% sales tax)

Accessory Pet
5836 Pathfinder Trail
Plano, TX 75093

Doggie Sun Visors

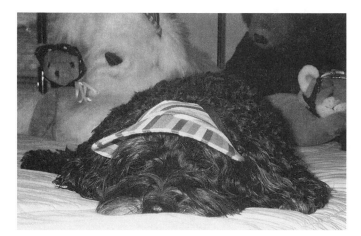

Protect your pup's eyes with this cool visor, available in five sizes. Made of a top-quality polyester-cotton fabric and high-impact polystyrene that's flexible, shapable, and resists breaking. The top of the cap is filled with foam rubber, and an adjustable hook-and-loop strap allows for a secure fit with no pressure on your dog's neck. Machine wash when necessary; just soak in water to cool down a hot pup! Wide variety of patterns and shapes, including one for cats, another for horses. More than *100,000* sold!

The Original Doggie Visor,
$9 (XS, S), $10 (M), $11 (L), $12 (XL)
+ $1 S&H
(TX res. add 8.25% sales tax)

Plano Places
5225 Mariners Dr.
Plano, TX 75093
(214) 596-8082

The Western Outdoors Look ®

Bandannas are an easy way to dress up your dog. This attractive, hemmed scarf is washable and durable, available in a wide variety of bright holiday designs and year-round patterns. It looks great on a dog, and can cool your pup down if you dampen the fabric during hot weather.

Dog Bandanna, $9.99 (12″, x-sm.), $11.99 (15″, sm.), $12.99 (22″, med.) $13.00 (29″, lg.)
+ 3 S&H
(CT res. add sales tax)

Z Cat & Dog Bows & Bandannas
19 Chapel St.
Greenwich, CT 06831
(203) 531-1108

Dog Collars and Belts! ®

This Guatemalan collar (with leash and belt to match) is made of woven cloth and features lovely, vibrant colors, backed with nylon webbing for strength, and a solid brass O-ring to prevent rusting and chipping. Cool Foolish Fish and Classic patterns. For the dog leaping into a stream or strolling the city streets. Absolutely the best.

Tail Waggin' Dog Collar
(sm.), $21
Tail Waggin' Matching Leash
(6′ l., 1″ w.), $29
Ruff Belt for Kids, $17
+ UPS (ID res. add sales tax)

A Tail We Could Wag
P.O. Box 3374
Ketchum, ID 83340
(208) 726-1763

It All Started with a Greyhound ®

Kitten the Greyhound was adopted after three years working as a race dog at the tracks for racing dogs. It's either adoption or a one-way trip to nowhere. What a brief, dreadful life. After her adoption, Kitten gladly became the mascot and model for these quality collars and leads. The Safety Choke Collar (with matching 5′ Ribbon Lead) is a simple, strong, humane collar. The Quick Release Collar just snaps apart off your dog's neck when you return home. Both shown in tapestry patterns. Nice look.

Safety Choke Collar, $15
Ribbon Lead, $17.95
Quick Release Collar, $15
+ UPS
(MA res. add sales tax)

Earth Angels
P.O. Box 775
Humarock, MA 02047
(800) 565-7700
E-mail: Eaprodx9.@aol.com

The Dogs of Our Lives ®

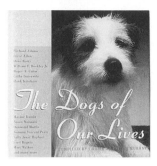

From Dave Barry to Roger Caras, nurses to cops, teachers to entrepreneurs—these are stories of the dogs these people have loved. Most are short, heartwarming reminiscences of great dogs that wandered—in one way or another, often by serendipity—into the authors' lives. A superb, warm hardcover book of beautiful moments and great dog stories.

Compiled by Louise Goodyear Murray, 362 pp., $21.95 + UPS (NY res. add sales tax)

Birch Lane Press Books
Carol Publishing Co.
122 E. 42nd St.
Suite 1601
New York, NY 10017
(212) 557-3303

On the Path ®

Packing isn't just for Saint Bernards. Almost any dog can help carry the load on your next hike or picnic. The Pooch Pack features large-capacity zippered pouches and quick-release buckles for maximum convenience, and it's fully lined with plush synthetic sheepskin on all contact points, so there's no chafing. Waterproof and durable, plus the mesh harness over the dog's back allows for good ventilation as you walk together.

Pooch Pack
Sizes: sm. (dogs up to 25 lbs.),
med. (26–50 lbs.), lg. (over 50 lbs.)
$19.95–$35.95
(CA res. add sales tax)

Lazy Pet Products
540 W. Lambert Rd., Brea, CA 92621
(800) 622-1288

Every Collar Tells a Story

What sets these collars apart is their colors—they're alive with brilliant red and pink flowers, white clouds, and intricately colored dogs. The superb ¾" or 1" Leather Collar can be inscribed with your dog's name or a quote such as "Pet Me" or "Love Me." You can also obtain a Matching Belt for yourself (1" or 1½" w.) so you're both properly attired for walks. Your choice of breed. Very high-quality, creative leather products.

Leather Collar,
$25 (¾"), $35 (1")
Matching Belt,
$65 (1"), $85 (1½")
(includes S&H)
(CA res. add 8.5% sales tax)

Diane Weiss
NYC on Nob Hill
1310 Jones St.
San Francisco, CA 94109
(415) 776-2696

Valentine's Necklace

Ready for fun? This party pet necklace with pink hearts and a black Velcro-closure collar looks very sweet for every occasion, including Valentine's Day and birthdays. It's

adjustable (just snip with scissors), reusable, ultra-lightweight, and very cute.

Deco-Pet Happy Hearts Necklace, $3 (sm.), $4 (med.), $5 (lg.) + $2 S&H
(IL res. add sales tax)

FoxStone Creations
P.O. Box 205
Mount Prospect, IL 60056
(847) 228-9080

TRUE DOG TALE

Chewy Knowledge

Dogs chew for lots of reasons: to keep their teeth and jaws healthy, for example, or to release frustration. You have lots of chewie choices for them, but try to buy beef sticks made in the USA. Beef chewsticks from other countries may contain traces of arsenic. If your dog is allergic to beef hide, try substituting natural or smoked pig ears. Good news: There's a slow but steady movement toward natural chew toys—including corn-based chew toys—as people demand healthier, more natural products that fit in with their lifestyles. Many of the new chew toys have positive dental benefits for your dog, like helping reduce tartar and freshen breath. In fact, you can include tasty dog toothpaste on some of them so the dog brushes her teeth (!) while chewing.

8

THE WHOLE DOG CATALOG

Minimalist Wardrobe ®

This delightful collar cover is simple and attractive. Machine washable, it comes in a choice of six holiday and assorted fashion designs. The decorative fabric fits over most collars (up to 30″ long). Soft and springy, pulls right over the dog's head. The bare minimum for any well-dressed dog.

Collars Cover, $4 + UPS
(OK res. add sales tax)

Just Bepaws
Laid Back Lifestyle Gifts
4020 Will Rogers Pkwy.
Suite 700
Oklahoma City, OK 73107
(800) 843-5242

Boxers ®

The endearing ability to wrinkle their foreheads has given Boxers the title, "Philosopher of the Dog World." Let's face it: They look like they're thinking! The life of the Boxer—from puppy selection to understanding this wonderful breed, gentle training approaches, grooming, nutrition, and preventive health—is thoroughly detailed in this information-packed book. Illustrations and color photos.

By Johanna Thiel, 1996, 64 pp., $6.95 + UPS (NY res. add sales tax)

Barron's Educational Series
250 Wireless Blvd.
Hauppauge, NY 11788
(800) 645-3476

Loving Life

Since 1971, Actors and Others for Animals has helped provide spay/neuter subsidies for more than 144,000 pets, humane education programs, pet-assisted therapy, cruelty intervention, disaster relief, and pet adoption programs. They also support and sponsor legislation that protects animals. As a fund-raiser for this fabulous nonprofit group, consider acquiring their Doggie Bandanna, with the paw prints of five famous K-9's, including Beethoven, Dreyfus, Lassie, Eddie, and Benji. Size is approx. 20″ × 30″—too large for small dogs. Remember: Bandannas can snag during wear, so never leave your dog alone when wearing one. Also, to help raise awareness of animals, this group is offering a new Animal Awareness Ribbon Pin that showcases the silver figures of a cat and a dog, accented by a light blue ribbon loop. It's thoughtful jewelry for you to wear, and is available for purchase at cost for fund-raising by other nonprofit groups. The accomplishments and generosity of this stellar group can be measured by the joy they have brought to more than 150,000 pet owners over the years.

Autographed Doggie Bandanna, $5.50 + $4 S&H
Animal Awareness Ribbon Pin, $5 donation (includes S&H) (CA res. add 8.25% sales tax)
Membership, $15 (regular), $10 (senior), $5 (junior, 6–12 years)

Actors and Others for Animals
P.O. Box 33473
Granada Hills, CA 91394
(818) 755-6045
E-mail: aoa@a-service.com

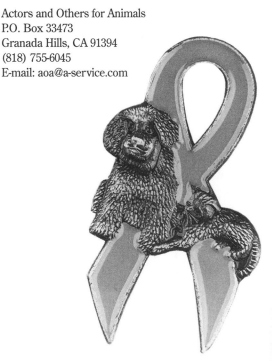

Bridle Leather Collars ®

Viva, at Hot Dogs All Dressed, uses a ruthless Boxer as a model and chief product tester of these superior leather collars, made from thick bridle leather with heavy-duty nickel hardware. Available in five widths, from ½″ to 1½″, and in lengths of 14″ to 28″. Your choice of 15 decorative styles. You can also match the collar to a 4′ or 6′ lead. Left to right: the heart collar on laced leather, daisies on 1″ collar, stars on 1¼″ collar, lion on 1¼″ collar, bone and

hydrants on ¾″ collar, and bones on ½″ collar. This leather is solid, feels good in your hands, and looks great on the dog. Extremely high quality.

Decorated Leather Dog Collar, $16–$36
Matching Leather Lead, $28–$56
+ UPS

Hot Dogs All Dressed
1751 Richardson, #6105
Montreal, Quebec
Canada H3K 1G6
(514) 933-9989

My First Puppy ®

A perfect puppy book (hardcover, includes a shrink-wrapped ID tag on the front cover) that's a joy for children to read. Complete with all the basics of puppy care, ideas for names, puppy jokes, puppy poems, and pages for children to write about nose shapes, a puppy diary, and more. A great start for a lucky puppy.

By Karla Olson, 1994, 34 pp., $9.95 + UPS (MO res. add sales tax)

Andrews & McMeil
4900 Main St.
Kansas City, MO 64112
(800) 826-4216

I'll Take Suede Any Day ®

Ready for a change? This highly unusual leash features very soft UltraSuede, which is woven through the chain links and covers the handle to create an elegant look. The adjoining collar is reinforced with nylon webbing and uses an exclusive release system to insure rugged toughness. Supercomfortable. Classy look.

UltraSuede Chain Lead, $20 (sm.) + $4 S&H; $22 (med.) or $24 (lg.) + $6 S&H
UltraSuede Collar, $10 (sm.), $14 (med.), $15 (lg.) + $4 S&H (NC res. add 6% sales tax)

UltraMouse, Ltd.
1442 E. Park Place
Ann Arbor, MI 48104
(800) 573-8869

TRUE DOG TALE

Stressed? Hug Your Dog, Not Your Spouse

When it comes to stress, researchers find that the most reassuring companion isn't your sweetheart—it's your Schnauzer. In a new study people who were put into stressful situations showed the least amount of tension when accompanied by their dogs. The stress levels were highest when the subjects were with their spouses. Oops.

Dress Up Safety ®

Bandannas look good on almost every dog, and they help with visibility near traffic. Available in assorted bright colors, the Fundanna includes important instructions for a pull-away safety knot. One size fits all dogs!

Play Safe Fundanna, $4.18 + UPS
(CO res. add sales tax)

Aspen Pet Products
11701 E. 53rd Ave.
Denver, CO 80239
(800) BUY-4-PET

Italian Leather Accessories

You'll love the look and feel of these handsome, oil-tanned, full-grain Italian leather accessories by Tanner & Dash. The collar displays custom-molded matte-gold heart ornaments and solid brass fittings. Specify red or black, neck size 10″–22″. A matching 45″ leather lead completes this beautiful, functional set.

Harlequin Heart Collar, $35 + $6.95 S&H
Leather Lead, $45 + $6.95 S&H
Set, $75 + $8.95 S&H
(NY res. add sales tax)

In the Company of Dogs
P.O. Box 7071
Dover, DE 19903
(800) 924-5050

Serious Dog Duds

In the mood to dress up your dog? There's an outfit here for every occasion. Searching for that Harley look? This outfit of Motorcycle Jacket, Chaps, Hat (in faux black suede or denim), and red Scarf/Bandanna will toughen up the appearance of even the most sensitive poodle. A dressy occasion? Tux it: His (black and white or red and white, white mock-turtle collar with bowtie and white pearl buttons) and Her (black and white or red and white collar, edged with lace, artist bow, and white pearl buttons). The Tux will stand the withering gaze of any fashion critic. You can also add a Matching Beret. Fall or winter is the time for the Venus Snowflake Sweater (lower right), heavy knit for the chill, in great colors (white-red-green, red-blue-white, or gold-white-purple), with a snowflake pattern. Pluto's four-leg

cold-weather sweater or knit snowsuit (top) gives even more warm coverage to your dog. The Confitte pink or lilac sweater (left) is soft to the touch and very feminine. Make a visible difference with a Neon Sweater in brilliant neon yellow, green, or hot, hot pink. The Matching Pom-Pom fits on top, with straps around the ears. A working dog? Forget fashion—we've got work to do! The drawing is of a bright orange Safety Vest with Armbands, the same color you see guys wearing along the highway. Includes strips of 3M Scotchlite reflective material, creating an extremely bright image for extra safety. Something for every attitude. . . .

Motorcycle Jacket, Chaps, Hat, Scarf/Bandanna, $20 each
His and Her Tux, $18 each
Matching Beret,

Venus Snowflake Sweater, Pluto's Sweater, Confitte Sweater, $15 each
Neon Sweater, $14
Matching Pom-Pom, $8
Safety Vest with Armbands, + UPS (NJ res. add sales tax)

Animal Clothiers
268 Cliffwood Ave.,
Suite 3
Cliffwood, NJ
07721
(908) 290-8100

Packin' with the Pup ♛

Headed out for a camping trip or picnic? Most dogs will take to carrying a pack if it's comfortable, not too heavy, and fits them well. Besides, it's helpful to have the dog help carry food and water when your backpack is full. This is the latest in dog portage, with a ventilated mesh back, two belly straps, and a sternum strap that keeps the pack snug. Everything's adjustable. Includes 2 large-volume compartments, 3 security straps, and a mesh back with 2 lash points. It's all made of solid, durable 500-denier Cordura Plus nylon. Your choice of evergreen, red, or meridian blue.

Eagle Creek Dog Pack, $30 + UPS
(CA res. add sales tax)

Eagle Creek Travel Gear
1740 La Costa Meadows Dr.
San Marcos, CA 92069
(800) 874-1048
http://www.eaglecreek.com

Santa Sounds and Sights ♛

A favorite in Christmas neckwear, the Jingle Dog Collar in holiday red or green will delight guests with its holiday bells. What about Christmas clothes? The terrific Santa Hat and Scarf feature a fur-rimmed hat and a yarn-fringed scarf with appliqué. Sold as a set, or you can buy just the hat. These jolly togs will put your dog—and you—in the holiday mood.

Jingle Dog Collar, $3.99 (sm.), $4.99 (med.), $5.99 (lg.)
Santa Hat, $5.99;
with **Santa Scarf,** $9.99
+ UPS (FL res. add sales tax)

Compass Marketing
115 Coastline Rd.
Sanford, FL 32771
(800) 688-9060

Riding or Walking Comfort

This is cool: a two-in-one combination Seatbelt/Walking Harness. After a safe ride in the car, you can walk down the busiest street with no worries. Made of tough white Dacron mesh that form-fits your dog, with Velcro enclosures at the neck and under the chest for adjustable comfort. The seatbelt version has an adapter for existing auto seatbelts, allowing your dog to sit or lie comfortably on the seat of the car. Unbuckle, and you have a comfortable walking harness. Black, red, blue, or pink trim—perfect for Basset Hounds, Dachshunds, and Corgis. The Dachshund harness comes with amusing "Dachshund Racing Team" patch! Custom orders also available for any breed.

Seatbelt/Walking Harness, $22.95 + $3 S&H
(OH res. add 5.75% sales tax)

Dachshund Delights
P.O. Box 712
Burton, OH 44021
(216) 834-9557
http://ourworld.compuserve.com/homepages/stemnock

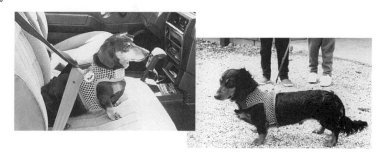

The International Encyclopedia of Dogs ®

A massive, full-color, hard-cover coffee-table guide to every breed currently recognized by the kennel clubs of the United States, Canada, England, and France. Truly encyclopedic coverage by highly respected dog authorities Anne Rogers Clark and Andrew Brace. Includes history, breed selection, and health of dogs. The real strength is the more than 400 pages of beautiful color photographs on the origin, temperament, health matters, special care and training, adaptability, and essentials of 300 dog breeds: a classic reference for every dog owner's library.

Edited by Anne Rogers Clark and Andrew H. Brace, 1995, 340 pp., $49.95 + UPS (IN res. add sales tax)

Howell Book House
A Simon & Schuster
Macmillan Co.
201 W. 103rd St.
Indianapolis, IN 46290
(317) 581-3500

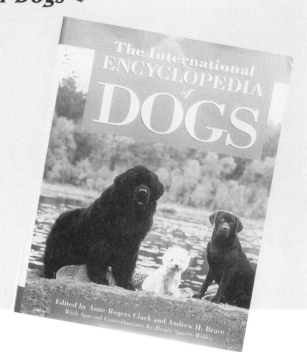

The Duke of Dogdom ®

This ensemble will get you some looks. Duke's 2-Tone Dog Shoes are cool shoes for hot dogs. Double-soled, double-toed, in 1,000-denier Cordura, with a speedy Velcro ankle fastener. Available in dozens of bright high-fashion color combinations. Warm Polar Fleece Dog Coat looks great and is odor and moisture resistant, machine washable, perfect for the next blizzard. Handy Velcro closure and practical design. Hot sun glaring down? Get some protection with this colorful Tropical Visor, and Matching Collar and Lead.

2-Tone Dog Shoes, $19.95–$22.95 (sm. to x-lg.)
Polar Fleece Dog Coat, $30.95–$40.95 (x-sm. to x-lg.)
Tropical Visor, Matching Collar, $8.95 (sm.), $10.95 (med.), $12.95 (lg.), $14.95 (x-lg.)
Matching Lead, $8.95 (½″ × 4′), $10.95 (¾″ × 4′), $12.95 (1″ × 4′) + UPS (no sales tax in OR)

Duke's Dog Fashions
6675 S.W. Imperial Dr.
Beaverton, OR 97008
(800) 880-8969

Showtime Dressing

With a set of these exquisite, finely detailed bows your dog will look beautiful for any occasion. Set includes Valentine Love Bow (with hcart), Easter Spring Bows (in Bunny Pink and Chicky Yellow), Shooting Stars Bow (4th of July, Election Day), and Jingle Bell Bows (in Christmas Red and Green). Bright, classic colors. Great, professional quality show bows—or just wow the crowd on your next stroll!

Holiday Bow Collection
(set of 6)
Sizes: med. ($1\frac{3}{4}''$ l. × $\frac{5}{8}''$ w.) or lg. ($1\frac{3}{4}''$ l. × $\frac{7}{8}''$ w.)
$29.95 + $3.95 S&H
(WA res. add 7.8% sales tax)

Fantasy Farm Products Co.
P.O. Box 1262
Bellingham, WA
(360) 734-9571
E-mail: hermann@prodigy.com

Maximum Visibility ®

Rugged electric collar flashes bright red lights at night to keep you and the dog in sight of cars, bikes, or pedestrians. Up to 70 hours of continuous operation with on-off switch. Adjustable, includes hook tag for ID, water repellent (works when wet), takes 4 type A76 batteries (included).

Flashing Collar, $19.99 + $3.95 S&H
(CA res. add 8.25% sales tax)

Protect-a-Pet
P.O. Box 7547
Beverly Hills, CA 90212
(800) 835-9899

Samurai Bulldog ®

An amusing little illustrated book about a fictional bulldog who has assumed the proportions and philosophy of a Japanese samurai warrior. Complete with chapters on the Art of War and the Art of Peace. Hilarious passages. Intellectual dog entertainment. Consider the Zen implications of The Bowl of Emptiness.

By Chibinosuke Dogizaemon, as told to Jeff Hunter, 1994, 94 pp., $9.95 + UPS (NY res. add sales tax)

Weatherhill
450 Madison Avenue, 15th Floor
New York, NY 10017
(800) 788-7323

Water Safety

All dogs can swim, but some tire easily. My dog Amber got in trouble in the water a few times, and I had to jump in, clothes and all. So I got one of these. The Dog Life Vest provides peace of mind when you're in a boat or in the water together. Made of soft white vinyl-coated foam with adjustable buckles. For best fit, measure around the dog's chest and behind the front legs.

Dog Life Vest, $22 (sm.), $24 (med.), $26 (lg.)
(TX res. add 7.25% sales tax)

Accessory Pet
5836 Pathfinder Trail
Plano, TX 75093
(800) 558-7387

Take a Walk? In This Weather?

Now you can comfortably take the dog out for a walk even in a monsoon-level downpour. The Ultrex Rain Poncho, available in bright red, yel- low, or blue, reminds me of a child's raincoat. It's made of waterproof, breathable, and wind-resistant Ultrex materials. Sizing is extra- long to hang over the dog's tail. Adjustable webbing strap at stomach, drawstring closure at hood, plus an opening for the leash at the neckline. I love the classic yellow. It reminds me of my son skipping through puddles in the rain.

Ultrex Rain Poncho, $28 (x-sm., 10", or sm., 12"–15"); $34 (med., 17"–19", lg., 20"–25", or x-lg., 27"–32") + UPS (VT res. add sales tax)

Doggie Styles
Hunger Mountain Rd.
Gaysville, VT 05746
(800) 545-1945

King and Queen Collars

Royal dog? Impressive pedigree? These impressive latigo leather collars feature oval and round medallions of semi-precious stone. Combinations vary according to size and style. Steel rivets, pewter settings, and nickel hardware. Minicollars are made of a lighter-weight, buck-finished leather that resembles suede. Rich colors include black, cordovan, green, red, or purple. Your choice of gemstones: green quartz, black onyx, brown obsidian, or Austrian crystal, with oval etched medallions. Gorgeous quality. Many choices.

Leather Collars, $29–$48 + UPS (IL res. add sales tax)

Baxter & Charming, Ltd.
11 W. Main
Carpentersville,
IL 60110
(800) 569-2761
E-mail: Baxterpets@aol.com

Dogs and the People They Own ®

Hundreds of one-liners about the attributes of dogs. Thoughts and brief comments on everything from dog food to dog-grooming salons to clothes to chasing cars. Hilarious comedy quips from one of today's funniest stand-up comics. Recognize your dog in here?

By Ed Strnad writing as Lillian Lidofsky, 1995, 130 pp., $9 + UPS (NY res. add sales tax)

Perigee Books
Berkley Publishing Group
200 Madison Ave.
New York, NY 10016
(800) 223-0510

Color in the Rain

Screamingly colorful, cute raincoat in blue, red, and yellow polka dots or black and white squares. Individually handmade and personalized for your dog. Includes a biscuit-filled pocket, which can be used later to hold mad money so a tired city dog can take the bus home. Design color is handpainted on cotton, which is covered with an acrylic varnish and then lined in nylon. Easy to clean with a damp sponge. High-quality, custom clothing.

Discuss what you'd like with Kathy James, artist/designer.

Handpainted Dog Raincoat, $45 (sm., med., or lg.) + UPS (no sales tax in NH)

James Accessories
81 Sherwood Forest, #313
Exeter, NH 03833
(603) 778-3885

Classy Gold Lamé ®

Overheard on the street as the two of you walk together: "Who was that gorgeous guy with the bowtie?" What kind of question is that? Obviously it was you and the only dog in the neighborhood wearing this very classy, gold lamé Bow Wow tie. Makes a great picture.

Bow Wow Bowtie, Gold Lamé, $15 + $3.50 S&H
(includes MN sales tax)

L. Coffey Ltd.
4244 Linden Hills Blvd.
Minneapolis, MN 55410
(800) 448-4PET

> *"A dog has no aversion to a poor family."*
> —Chinese proverb

Hands-Free Walking ®

Hands full of grocery bags? Now you can jog, walk, train, hike, or just go shopping, hands free. Polypropylene webbing leash detaches to become a conventional dog leash. Adjusts from 3′ to 5′ in length, waist belt adjusts from 28″ to 48″. Just hook it to the dog, snap it around your waist, and you're ready to go.

Includes a free matching adjustable collar.

Smokey's Hands-Free Waist Leash, $24.95–$29.95 + UPS
(NY res. add sales tax)

SWL International
286 Genesee St.
Utica, NY 13502
(315) 792-9049

TRUE DOG TALE

When's the Party Start?

You go to work. Hours later you drive home with that sinking feeling in your stomach. When you fling open the front door, the carpet is shredded, the furniture is torn, the dog has chewed up your favorite plant. Fido has gone berserk. What's going on? Generally, it's boredom. Some dogs hate to be alone, and they also get intensely frustrated if there's nothing to do but sleep. There are many solutions. Start with vigorous exercise twice a day. Next, provided your dog's not a barker, put a cushion in a window seat with a good view. He can spend hours being entertained by birds, other dogs, cats, and the mailman—life outside, coming and going. Try leaving your radio on a soothing classical music station, not too loud. TV even works for some dogs—maybe the Discovery Channel with animal shows. Try leaving the house gracefully. Hand out a new chew stick as you exit the front door. Or think about obtaining a companion dog so your pup has someone to wrestle and snooze with. What's the objective? Dogs are intelligent. They need mental stimulation. They miss your company. Provide some activity in the house while you're gone.

> *"A dog is a bond between strangers."*
> —John Steinbeck

Bright Night Walking

The Buddy Lite Illuminated Safety Leash is a 6′ leash that features a 60″ electroluminescent strip-lamp fastened to a high-quality nylon web leash. The leash lights up a 6′–12′ area around you. It's visible from 5,000 feet away—powered by a 9V battery with extra luminesence from a Scotchlite reflective stripe. Leash lamp has an expected lifetime of 20,000 hours; battery life is 12–30 hours. Very high visibility for safety on your night walks.

Buddy Lite Illuminated Safety Leash, $25.95
+ $3.95 S&H
(CA res. add sales tax)

Buddy Lite Illuminated
Safety Products
6 Calella
Laguna Niguel, CA 92677
(714) 363-1354

Serious Boots

Most dogs take a few minutes to get used to wearing boots, but the wait is generally worth it. Lewis Dog Boots protect against hot sand, burrs, rocks, cactus, ice, and snow. Supersmooth inside and out, made of the finest tire rubber, with a tread on the sole to increase traction. Takes just a few minutes to put them on. Also helpful to speed healing if your dog has an injured foot. These are the boots used by professional breeders and backwoods types. They do the job.

Lewis Dog Boots (set of four)
Five sizes available
$24 + $5.95 S&H
(OK res. add 8.5% sales tax)

Lewis Dog Boots
P.O. Box 10572
Enid, OK 73706
   (405) 237-1292

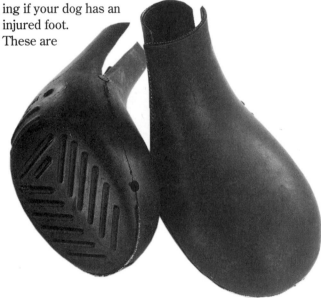

Slip-On Bandanna Art

These colorful, cool, Slip-onto-the-Collar-Bandannas do exactly that. Just remove your dog's collar, slip on your favorite design, and that's it. No tying or worry about the dog accidentally choking. A wide range of patterns and colors (two are shown) include attached jewelry that's removable for cleaning. Specially designed holiday bandannas are also available. These are unusual—even talismanic!—and they make an attractive statement.

Slip-onto-the-Collar-Bandannas, $4.95 + UPS
(AZ res. add sales tax)

Crocodile Tears
402 N. 99th St.
Mesa, AZ 85207
(602) 380-3416

The Tibetan Mastiff: Legendary Guardian of the Himalayas

Heavy on interesting mountain dog history and breed stories, this is the book to buy *before* you even consider buying a dog as intense as the Tibetan Mastiff. Bred for hundreds of years in Tibet, the dog is chained by the unlocked front door in villages during the day, then turned loose at night to patrol in packs against thieves, snow leopards, bears, anything that moves. Needless to say, nobody in the village takes midnight strolls. They are used in the United States primarily for protection, zealously maintaining a defense of their fenced perimeter and warning off intruders with deep barking that gives pause to even the most determined trespasser. The book includes fascinating stories about the history and modern life of this ancient dog, and all the the basics of caring for and owning this barely domesticated breed.

By Ann Rohrer and Cathy J. Flamholtz, 1989, 154 pp.,
$16.95 + $2.50 S&H
(AL res. add sales tax)

OTR Publications
P.O. Box 481
Centreville, AL 35042
(800) 367-2174

Luxury Leash ®

Flexi-2 Classic is an excellent, cord-retractable leash that extends up to 16′. It includes an ergonomically shaped brake button and dual locking system. Available in red, brown, blue, green, black, and purple, in three sizes for every size dog. Fashion colors (denim blue, yellow, turquoise, and bordeaux) for small and medium dogs also available. This company makes an incredible variety of retractable leashes: the Reflect (reflects light for night walks), the City (small size fits in your pocket), the Garden (for attaching your dog to garden walls and fences), and the Professional, in 5 colors and 32′ of belt leash.

Flexi-2 Classic Cord-Retractable Leash
(S, M, L), $24.99 + UPS
(OH res. add sales tax)

Flexi USA
4670 J Interstate Dr.
Cincinnati, OH 45246
(800) 543-4921

Classy Clothes This Fall ®

Le Pret Pet has been making affordable, quality dog clothing for more than 10 years. Park Avenue Coat is made of faux leopard fur with sleeves and a collar. Hound Dog is a mock-turtleneck T in houndstooth pattern, made of 100% acrylic knit, available in beige-black, red-black, or blue-black. Alpine Coat (left) has a caped look, while the Winter Coat (right) provides additional warmth for the dog's chest. Both are made of Nordic Fleece, 100% acrylic in assorted patterns. Pupsicle with Pocket comes in solid colors with a bright red pocket; made of 100% acrylic Nordic Fleece. Superior quality.

Park Avenue Coat, $30 (S–M), $48 (L–XL)
Hound Dog, $15 (S–M), $20 (L–XL)
Alpine Coat, $22 (S–M), $30 (L–XL)
Pupsicle with Pocket, $17 (S–M), $23 (L–XL)

Coat sizes: S (10″–12″), M (14″–16″), L (18″–20″), XL (22″–24″)
+ UPS (CA res. add sales tax)

Le Pret Pet
20710 S. Leapwood Ave.
Suite G
Carson, CA 90746
(800) 765-1376

Hilarious Dress Up!

What a hoot! Magic Pet Costumes include Tutu (a satin stunner with a touch of silver for your next formal), Hound Dog (satin with lamé accents and a stylish guitar), Lil Angel (with satin halo and wings), Hot Dog (a bun wrapped around the dog topped with mustard, relish, and onions), Rambark (camouflage fatigues complete with "dog tag" and attitude). Let's not forget the gorgeous Pom-Pom Pup (pleated two-tone skirt and matching pom-poms, along with a traditional design on the chest for authentic appeal). Truly a scream. Put 'em on the dog for your next party. Who thinks this stuff up?

Magic Pet Costume, $19.99
Lil Angel, $9.99
+ UPS (FL res. add 7% sales tax)

Compass Marketing
115 Coastline Rd.
Sanford, FL 32771
(800) 688-9060

Puppy Book: My Dog's Tail

A convenient illustrated journal for documenting the events in your dog's life—from your first thoughts on her day of arrival, her paw print, her pedigree, her special moments to remember, her favorite toys, games, and so on. Contains a medical record section, plus pockets for keeping all those important papers together in one place. Heavy-duty spiral-bound hardcover format. Ever try to find the vaccination certificate? Keep it here.

By Judi M. Lowrance, 1995, 50 pp., $19.95 + $3 S&H (CA res. add $1.65 sales tax)

SCT Retrievers
P.O. Box 212
Torrance, CA 90503
(310) 715-1704

Hello Dog Scarves

Betty Barcheski and her crew have their sewing needles ready, awaiting your order for an embroidered scarf (with a serged/sewn edge) that includes your dog's name. Choice of 21 fabrics—from cotton flannel plaids to typical holiday fabrics. Top quality, huge variety, quick (2-day) turnaround, great people. On your next walk people can say hello to your dog by name! Makes a thoughtful gift for your dog-owning friends.

Personalized Dog Scarf,
(S, M, L, XL), $9.24 + 90¢ S&H
(IL res. add 6.75% sales tax)

Top Drawer
860 Buttonwood Circle
Naperville, IL 60540
(800) 684-7181

Dog Co-Pilot Harness

To me there's nothing better than having my dog along in the car, cruising down the highway, headed for a vacation. She listens carefully to all my comments about life and travel, nods knowingly, and provides wonderful company. And, wearing this neat harness, she's a *safe* co-pilot. Pat Townsend will make you a great custom harness to hold your dog securely in the car. It hooks through your seatbelt. Just give Pat your dog's measurements, and she'll create a long-lasting, handmade, adjustable nylon harness in red, black, brown, or royal blue. Your best friend needs a seatbelt too.

Protect-a-Pet Harness, $28.95 (sm.), $31.95 (med.), $34.95 (lg.), $37.95 (x-lg.) + $7 S&H (Includes sales tax)

June Enterprises
Box 180
1658 Matterson Rd.
Errington, B.C.
Canada V0R 1V0
(604) 248-7345
E-mail:
ltlmtn2@nanaimo.ark.com

Chapter Five

Collectible Folk Art

Miss Lovely Pug

Beautiful 10″ Pug is just one of 30 standard and not-so-standard breeds of dogs made by Beverly Saul, who's been creating this beautiful stuffed art for more than 15 years. Hers was the prize-winning entry in a 1991 contest held by *Dog Fancy* magazine. Super quality, many breeds you'll never find in a toy store. Pug has furrowed brow, true-to-life coloring, and those big round eyes.

Stuffed Pug, $65 + $6 S&H (PA res. add 6% sales tax)

I'm Stuffed
P.O. Box 432
Richboro, PA 18954
(215) 322-8946
E-mail: 76132.1112@
compuserve.com

Photograph: Marilyn Jensen

◆ TRUE DOG TALE ◆

Oldest Haircut?

Many Great Masters paintings that include dogs show the classic grooming style called the Lion Trim. For at least 700 years, this trim has been used with various breeds, including the water dogs and Poodles, which were originally bred by hunters to be water retrievers. The Lion Trim leaves long fur on a large area of the chest in order to protect the ribs, heart, and vital organs. The legs are trimmed of fur to allow easier movement in the water. You can still see this style at any grooming shop or dog show.

Cross-Stitch Companions

Look at the nose on this Beagle! Cute. These folks will send you, for a dollar, information about their cross-stitch designs for your favorite dog breed. Or obtain their complete 180-page catalog with all breeds of dogs, horses, and cats—its cost is refundable when you order a cross-stitch design. Great counted cross-stitch patterns (including this Bernese Mountain Dog puppy) for you to complete and frame. Custom designs of your best friend, too! Mail inquiries only.

Animal Original in Cross Stitch (specify dog breed), $1 + SASE
Complete 180-page Catalog, $8 (refundable with order)

JHG Designs
3622 E. Louisiana State Dr.
Kenner, LA 70062

Porcelain Pups

Into collectibles? Here's a new way to collect your favorite dog breed. Handpainted 4"-high porcelain eggs feature marvelously detailed paintings of your favorite breeds. Display mount included. Specify your breed of choice when ordering.

Dog Eggs, $16.95 + $4.99 S&H
(MN res. add 6.5% sales tax)

Tails
4708 Utah Ave. North
New Hope, MN 55428
(612) 535-3055
E-mail: tailsl@ix.netcom.com

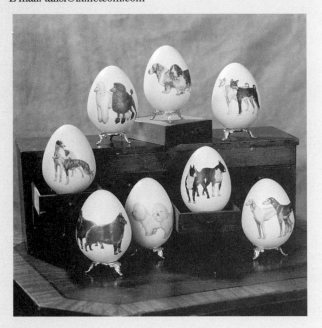

Liliane's Sculptures

Whatever your dog's breed, chances are Liliane has a sculpture of it. Each of her handcrafted figurines is meticulously handcast in resin, handpainted, and carefully researched for authenticity. Breeds come in small, medium, and large sculptures. Very affordable. Shown is the medium-sized Great Dane. Ask about your breed.

Liliane's Creations
P.O. Box 1004
Oak Bluffs, MA 02557
(508) 693-2515

Great Dane Sculpture, $18.95 + $4 S&H
(MA res. add 5% sales tax)

Go North

I've seen the watercolors of Judy North in galleries. Her expressive, brilliant use of color can truly capture the spirit and feelings of your dog companion. Locally, in California, she paints dogs after visiting and taking many pictures. But you can easily make arrangements to have photographs of your dog taken anywhere and sent to her. Her watercolor portrait of your dog alone measures 22" × 30", while a portrait of you with your pet measures a large 30" × 40". She requires a 50% deposit to proceed. Brochures and price lists upon request. Shown here are Boomer the Basset Hound, Easter Bonnet, and Rama Jean—excellent representative samples of this artist's distinguished work. Quality is always worth it.

Watercolor Portrait of Pet
(22" × 30"), $950
Watercolor Portrait of Person with Pet
(30" × 40"), $2,300
(CA res. add sales tax)

Immortal Eyes
Your Pet
Judy North
P.O. Box 306
San Geronimo, CA 94963
(415) 488-4082

Let Me Hold the Door for You

These are great! Lifelike doggie doorstops in many breeds. Handpainted on wood, with all breeds and coat colors available. A custom doorstop can be made from your photo. Wide selection (as you can see), and the Golden Retriever faithfully holds the door open. Imagine one in the likeness of your dog!

Doggie Doorstop,
$29.95 + $3 S&H
(FL res. add sales tax)

Claywood Creations
10450 S.W. 27th St.
Miami, FL 33165
(305) 551-6691
E-mail: Dogdoorstp.@aol.com

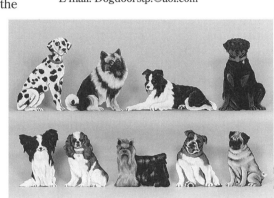

Dog Painting 1840—1940: A Social History of the Dog in Art

Author William Secord is uniquely qualified to place the emerging genre of dog painting in its historical perspective. The founding director of the Dog Museum of America, he is currently owner of a gallery in New York City specializing in 19th-century dog and animal art. This extraordinary hardcover work of 317 black and white and color photographs traces 50 of the most popular breeds as depicted by superb 19th- and 20th-century artists. From hounds and sporting dogs in the field, to Victorian portraits of pampered pets. A superior 100-year overview of dog art (including the earliest dog shows) and the importance of dogs to humanity.

By William Secord, 1992, 366 pp., $79.50 + UPS (NY res. add sales tax)

Antique Collector's Club, Ltd.
Market St.
Industrial Park
Wappingers Falls, NY 12590
(914) 297-0003

The Sterling Dog ®

Hand & Hammer Silversmiths has created 40 sterling silver pins of your favorite friend. Chip and Phil, the owners, publish a beautiful catalog of sterling silver artwork, pins, and jewelry. They begin with drawings, then transform those into three dimensions by carving in wax. The wax model is then transferred into sterling silver through the lost-wax casting technique. These are beautiful pins, and the catalog itself is a jewel. Ask for it.

Purebred Dog Pin, $20 each postpaid

Hand & Hammer Silversmiths
2610 Morse Lane
Woodbridge, VA 22192
(800) SIL-VERY
E-mail: dechip@delphi.com

Companions

These fine *life-size,* hand-painted Ceramic Dog Sculptures realistically capture the personality of any breed. Original designs by Ann Townsend, made in the USA. Golden Retriever Pup is 17½″ h. × 16″ l. × 9½″ w. Yorkshire Terrier stands 14″ h. × 11″ l. × 7″ w. Diminutive Shih Tzu is 10″ h. × 22½″ l. Dachshund and English Bulldog are also available.

Ceramic Dog Sculptures Golden Retriever Pup, $175
Yorkshire Terrier, $130
Shih Tzu, $165
+ $12.95 S&H each
(NY res. add sales tax)

In the Company of Dogs
P.O. Box 7071
Dover, DE 19903
(800) 924-5050

Susan's Dog Artistry

Susan Bahary is the creator of the nation's first monument to war dogs, a life-size Doberman entitled *Always Faithful* that was unveiled at the Pentagon and later dedicated on the island of Guam in July 1994. Here's Susan modeling the clay model, which was ultimately cast in bronze. Her sculptures—in bronze or fine acrylic, a form of Lucite—range from representational to abstract and have been featured in many publications, including *The New York Times.* Her Classic German Shepherd (shown in bronze) measures 15″ h. × 8″ w. × 13″ d. Look of the Eagles, a Doberman head study in acrylic, measures 19½″ h. × 7″ w. × 9″ d. The Classic Maltese is a life-size (12″ h.) acrylic version of this popular family companion. Her work is stunning, exhibited in many galleries nation-wide. Now you can obtain her fine sculptures by mail.

Classic German Shepherd, $8,400 (bronze or acrylic)
Look of the Eagles, $5,700 (bronze or acrylic)
Classic Maltese, $5,700 (acrylic)
+ UPS
(CA res. add 7.25% sales tax)

Susan Bahary Studios
733 Via Casitas
Greenbrae, CA 94904
(415) 925-9979

San Francisco Dog

I bought a Karen Richards pin at an art festival. Pictured here is just one of her creations: a pearl-adorned, winged noble hound made of etched brass, reflecting the golden nature of the canine heart. Measures $2'' \times 1\frac{1}{2}''$; light enough to wear even on a silk blouse. Signed by the artist. Gift boxes available. Complete strangers routinely compliment my wife on this pin.

Heavenly Hound,
$46 + $3 S&H
(Includes CA sales tax)

Karen Richards
2126 47th Ave.
San Francisco, CA 94116
(415) 242-0335

Stamp on Dogs!

Rubber stamps are popular collectibles. The Rubber Stamp Ranch down in Albuquerque has a huge catalog of all kinds of rubber stamps, including wacky dog stamps. Make your own art statement! Big free catalog.

Dog Rubber Stamp, $4–$8 + $3.50 S&H per order
(NM res. add 5% sales tax)

Rubber Stamp Ranch
3400 Anderson Ave. S.E.
Albuquerque, NM 87106
(800) 728-9762

Purebred Dog Sculptures ®

Sculptor Tony Acevedo has a well-deserved reputation for capturing our best friends in "environmentally friendly" cold-cast bronze. Tony's work is found in the best of homes and on the trophy tables at dog shows worldwide. His Standard Poodle ($11''$ l. $\times$ $11\frac{3}{4}''$ h. $\times$ $5\frac{3}{4}''$ w.) is from a limited edition of 250. Golden Retriever with Pheasant ($12''$ l. $\times$ $7\frac{1}{2}''$ h. $\times$ $3\frac{1}{2}''$ w.) is from Tony's Signature Series. Great Dane Mom and Pups measures $10''$ l. $\times 13''$ h. $\times$ $5''$ w. Lying Dane, from the Miniature Series, scales things down, measuring $6''$ l. $\times$ $4''$ h. $\times$ $3''$ w. The perky Pet Poodle ($3\frac{1}{2}''$ h. $\times$ $2''$ w.), putting on a begging show, would look fabulous on your desk or mantel, also part of Tony's Miniature Series. Many other choices available for all the popular breeds.

Standard Poodle, $250
Golden Retriever with Pheasant, $165
Great Dane Mom and Pups, $295
Lying Dane, $39
Pet Poodle, $39
+ UPS
(CA res. 8.25% sales tax)

Dannyquest Designs
11782 Western Ave., #17
Stanton, CA 90680
(800) 215-9711

Bichon Art

Carefully made, one at a time, these crafted resin sculptures are an ideal gift for any Bichon Frise owner. Whether in motion (the rocking horse), in a shoe with flowers, or wearing a rain hat, the detailed expressions of these Bichons Frises are wonderful. Each is signed and dated by the artist. Special orders (of your dog) or unique themes are welcome! Call for details.

Bichon Frise Charmer,
$25 and up + UPS
(MA res. add sales tax)

Rolande's/Talisman
68 Providence St.
Mendon, MA 01756
(508) 478-1889
E-mail: cyberpet@ix.netcom.com
http://www.ads-online.com/bichon.htm

Man and Dog ®

This is one of those mysterious books about the strange powers of dogs—their powers of survival and telepathy, "ghost dogs," canine reincarnation, and the ancient (and ongoing) spiritual connection between dogs and humans. Just to give you some idea of where the author's coming from, Brad Steiger is co-author of another work: *Strange Powers of Pets.* Along with all this book's magic there is some wonderful, comforting advice to those who are about to lose, or have lost, their best friends. It's not over....

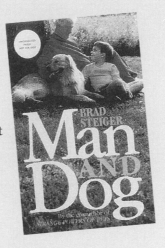

By Brad Steiger, 1995, 200 pp., $19.95 + UPS
(NY res. add sales tax)

Donald I. Fine
19 W. 21st St.
New York, NY 10010
(212) 727-9749

Cool Dog Cards ®

I put a huge effort into getting the quizzical dog you see here. Phone calls to the company. Faxes. Persistence. It was worth it. Avanti makes some of the hottest, craziest, funniest dog cards anywhere, and if you're lucky, some local retail outlet in your area has them. Expressive, intelligent, even some fairly extreme dog cards that exude personality and coolness. Worth looking for. Can't find 'em? Call Avanti yourself or check out their website.

Avanti Belated Birthday Card #00565:
Jack Russell Terrier with Cocked Head

Avanti Greeting Cards
2500 Penobscot Bldg.
Detroit, MI 48226
(313) 961-0022
http://www.avanti
press.com
© Dennis Mosner/Avanti
Press, Inc.

Dog Goddess

Are you ready for an impressive dog guardian at the entrance to—or in the garden of—your home? Suzanne Simpson's extraordinary Goddess of the Bounteous Earth clay statue stands ready to greet you, indoors or out. An impressive 20″ tall in the color of natural clay, with a deep purple and turquoise glaze. Brilliant.

Goddess of the Bounteous Earth, $495 + UPS
(CA res. add 7.25% sales tax)

Whimsical Art
54 Issaquah Dock
Sausalito, CA
94965
(415) 331-7414

Photograph:
George Post

Annie O in New England

Annie O'Leary, way up in Tilton, New Hampshire, has painted acrylic pet portraits for happy owners in all 50 states for the past 14 years. Her amazingly lifelike true-color renderings have fine brushstrokes and clear eyes and are eminently affordable. She'll also include you in the painting if you like. Annie works in a rural studio with her two companion dogs, Snoopy and Blackie, and she'll send you a nice handwritten letter to explain how she operates. (But first you need to contact her.)

Pet Portraits (of one or two pets), $62.50 (8″ × 10″), $125 (9″ × 12″–12″ × 16″), $185 (14″ × 18″ or 24″ × 30″) + UPS (no sales tax in NH)

Pet Portraits by Annie O
44 Church St.
Tilton, NH 03276
(603) 524-3778

Dog Portraiture

Karen Lisa Friedman paints quality dog portraits using a technique similar to the one used by the Old Masters, from Caravaggio to Rubens. This method of layering paint for luminosity and depth on a linen or cotton

written personality description. She'll work with you on the background setting. These are collectible paintings to pass down to future generations. The Shar-Peis in *Tucker and Truffles* live in Japan, and all the work on this 30″ × 40″ oil was done by long distance. The Greyhound portrait, *Paris and Juno,* is a 30″ × 40″ oil completed in 1995. Karen's Toned Drawings—reminiscent of silverpoint or charcoal drawings from the 15th and 16th centuries, made with pencil or conté pencil on colored paper—cost substantially less than her oil portraits but also look superb. Free catalog.

Oil Painting, $185 (5″ × 7″) to $975 (40″ × 50″)
Toned Drawing, $50 (5″ × 7″) to $165 (20″ × 24″) + UPS (no sales tax in OR)

KLF Studios
2244 S.E. Spruce
Portland, OR 97214
(800) 851-8611

TRUE DOG TALE

Hunting the Ancestor—Borzoi Tales

All dogs are descendants of wolves. Yet for centuries, the Borzoi and the Russian Wolfhound were used to *hunt* wolves. Bred for speed, two or more of these graceful, beautiful dogs would outrun a wolf and grab it behind the ears, pinning it down until the human hunters arrived.

canvas produces remarkable work. For a custom portrait of your pet, first call the artist. Send her a combination of photographs and a

The Canine Collection

Sculpted by award-winning artist Kitty Cantrell, this delightful mixed-media collection of some of America's most popular dog breeds is created in limited editions out of stunning blends of precious metals and hot-torched acid patinas. Highly realistic 5″ dog miniatures include Rottweiler (left), Dalmatian, German Shepherd, Black Lab (right), Golden Retriever, and Cocker Spaniel. Lifelike colors, superb on your mantel or desk.

Dog Miniature,
$140 + UPS
(CA res. add sales tax)

Cody
2665D Park Center Dr.
Simi Valley, CA 93065
(800) 726-9660

Crowning Christmas Dog

Enchanting Treetop Dog Angel adds a graceful, amusing, and definitely different touch to your Christmas tree. Handpainted, finely detailed head and paws of your favorite breed, in lace and satin gown. With a tiny halo. Are you ready for this?

Treetop Dog Angel, $30
+ $5.99 S&H
(MN res. add 6.5% sales tax)

Tails
4708 Utah Ave. North
New Hope, MN 55428
(612) 535-3055
E-mail: tailsl@ix.netcom.com

Exuberant Life

Celebrating each day, this wildly optimistic watercolor is just one of many artworks by Mill Valley, California, artist Sharon Searles that feature dogs. *Jubilant Restoration* is an 11″ × 14″ full-color print in rich browns, blues, and yellow. Everybody's smiling in the glow of the sun. Childlike happiness on your wall.

Jubilant Restoration, $95
(includes UPS in U.S.)
(CA res. add sales tax)

Sharon Searles Fine Art
P.O. Box 372
Mill Valley, CA 94941
(415) 381-3335

Showing Your Love ®

Sculptor/artist Tony Acevedo is noted for his unparalleled ability to accurately interpret individual dog breeds, capturing the special spark and personality that attract us to our favorite breed. Dog Heads (available in most breeds) are American made of 100% lead-free pewter, finished in your choice of pewter, bronze, or silver. Beautiful jewelry to wear on the chain of your choice.

Dog Head, $15 + UPS
(CA res. add sales tax)

Dannyquest Designs
11782 Western Ave., #17
Stanton, CA 90680
(800) 215-9711

Great Vacations for You and Your Dog, USA ®

The ideal companion book for cross-country trips and long vacations. This is a directory not of roadside motels but of actual resorts—from moderate to upscale, more than 250 in all—including rustic, wooded havens and places like the world-class Carmel Highland Doubletree Golf & Tennis Resort. New edition every two years. There's even information on a dog camp, plus all the usual rates, dog policies, deposits, and the like. Grab the book, make a phone call, put the dog in the car, and take a break!

Compiled by Martin Management Books, 1995, 226 pp., $17.95 + $2.75 S&H
(HI res. add sales tax)

Martin Management Books
2108 Kahekili Hwy.
Wailuku, HI 96793
(808) 244-4187

The Patron Saint of Animals and Pets

Most of us are familiar with the legend of Saint Francis of Assisi. He left a wealthy family, renounced all possessions, and dedicated his life to the welfare of animals. This handpainted, solid-resin statue of Assisi portrays the saint dressed in a brown robe with two dogs and cats. Standing just over 5" tall, it's an ever-present reminder of the need for compassion and kindness to all animals. What harm can possibly come to your dogs when there's a 12th-century saint protecting them? This statue sits on my desk.

Saint Francis of Assisi with Pets, $32.50
(includes S&H and sales tax)

Nova 5
4001 Rio Grande, N.W.
Albuquerque, NM 87107
(800) 628-5355

> *"I have found that when you are deeply troubled, there are things you get from the silent devoted companionship of a dog that you get from no other source."*
>
> —Doris Day

Painted Personalities

Carroll Griesedieck of Taos County, New Mexico, has a stellar reputation for her dog portraiture. Her special skill is in capturing a dog's personality in a framable monoprint. From photographs you provide, she creates a preliminary drawing. Then she makes a monoprint from multicolored inks, creating the image on a Plexiglas plate. That image is then transferred to paper on a press, from which only one image (hence the term *mono*print) can be printed from the ink on the plate. Original, one-of-a-kind framable art of your best buddy. Check out the expressions on Luca (standing, 24" × 18") and Joe with River Rocks (18" × 24"). Like anybody good, Carroll is busy. Call at least 2–3 months in advance if you'd like your painting for a special event or holiday.

Framable Monoprint,
$420–$600 + UPS
(NM res. add 6.5% sales tax)

Animal Prints
Carroll Griesedieck
P.O. Box 1346
El Prado, NM 87529
(505) 758-3226
http://taoswebb.com/nmusa/
arts/dog-art

Copper Repoussé—Your Dog in Relief

Artists Beverly Capstick and Joanne E. Kull will create a personalized, handcrafted repoussé (copper relief) sculpture from a favorite photograph of your dog. These two examples show some of the variations in the metal, antiquing, and highlights that make each a work of original art. You may also choose from their catalog of limited editions. Exceptional detail, enduring, framed or unframed. Allow 8 weeks for delivery. Makes a superb gift.

Custom Copper Repoussé, One Dog,
$250 (without frame), $275 (framed)
**Custom Copper Repoussé,
Two Dogs or a Pose,**
$300 (without frame), $325 (framed)

Limited Edition Copper Repoussé,
$60–$400
+ UPS
(MN res. add sales tax)

Lutzyn Originals
8615 Haug Ave.
Northeast
Monticello, MN
55362
(612) 295-6206

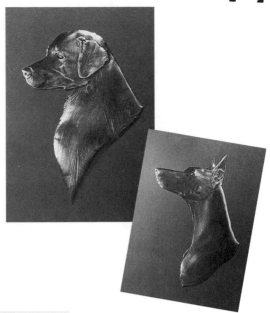

Puppies and Dogs in Cross-Stitch

Pegasus Originals offers a huge supply of over 200 different counted cross-stitch charts of dogs. Most of the designs are available in complete kits, including fabrics, floss needle, and instructions. All are viewable on the Internet, or call for their 14 books and leaflets showing designs for the creative dog lover.

Cross-Stich Chart, various prices

Pegasus Originals
129 Minnie Fallaw Rd.
Lexington, SC 29073
(805) 755-1141
http://www.pegasus.com

Favorite Dogs Coloring Book

Here's one for the kids! Forty lovely breeds for coloring, accompanied by interesting dog trivia on the bottom of every page. Includes, on the inside cover, the color of each dog, so the kids grab the right crayon—well, most of the time. Green and yellow dogs are also okay!

By John Green, 1983, 40 pp., $2.95 + $4 S&H
(NY res. add sales tax)

Dover Publications
31 E. Second St.
Mineola, NY 11501
(516) 294-7000

A Dog to Greet You

Wow! Giant, colorful resin dog statues. In fact, they're life size. Very impressive by your front door or in your home. Rottweiler (left) stands an impressive 35″ tall; Golden is 30″; Chow is 22″; Shar-Pei 21″; and Doberman is 28″. Handpainted with accurate detailing, available in most breeds. Custom commissions also accepted. (Allow 3 months for a custom statue.) The Borzoi stands 38″ tall!

Life-Size Dog Statue, $75–$595 (Yorkie to Mastiff; price varies by size of dog) + UPS (CA res. add 8.25% sales tax)

Color Critters Custom Statuary
P.O. Box 4158
West Covina, CA 91791
(818) 918-6724
http://www.cyberg8t.com/business/critters

Millicent's Art

Myra Millicent's work is brilliant. Her fabulous Cachepots and other pieces look like museum-quality collectibles. Dog Cachepot, shown (style 6,000), begins with a well-thrown terra-cotta vessel adorned with classical designs and finishes in a special patina. Siamese Shape (6″) is decorated with two rows of silk cord and French knots, with different backgrounds available. Umbrella Stand (style 15,000) is made of antique copper with 2 black rings, decorated in the "Pals" design. Either may be personalized with your dog's portrait. This is just a very small representation of the fine work from her catalog. Trust me. You will keep these forever.

Dog Cachepot, $195
Umbrella Stand, $385
+ UPS
(NJ res. add sales tax)

Millicent Cachepots
10 Leone Ct.
Glen Rock, NJ 07452
(201) 444-6098

Dogs in Motion

Check out the energy bursting from this dog portrait! Artist Carolyn Brust will paint your pet in a style reminiscent of a late-1800s "country manor" portrait: a loose, colorful painting with rich detail. She works from your photo. Kinetic art. You can practically hear the dog panting!

Carolyn Brust Dog Portrait,
$300 (10″ × 14″), $450 (12″ × 12″),
$600 (18″ × 24″) + UPS
(CA res. add 8.5% sales tax)

Carolyn Brust
1124 Hampshire St.
San Francisco, CA 94110
(415) 695-7702
E-mail: cmbrust@concentric.net

TRUE DOG TALE

Barking Lessons 101

Many owners complain about their dogs barking. It won't be a problem if you own a Basenji. They don't bark—rather, they make a muted, throaty "yodeling" sound when so inspired. This very old breed originated in Central Africa—a Basenji-like dog can be seen on Egyptian tombs from the time of the pharaohs. It's still prized today by African tribes for its silent hunting and tracking skills in the jungle.

The Toy Fox Terrier

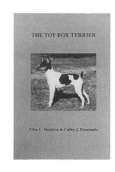

THE TOY FOX TERRIER

Eliza L. Hopkins & Cathy J. Flamholtz

Thoroughly cute, very bright and *tiny,* ranging in size from 3½ to 7 lbs., the Toy Fox Terrier has gained a major place in the hearts of Americans who enjoy a dog that can comfortably live in a small living space. This especially useful book contains more than 100 black and white photos for folks who want to know the history and breeding standards of this dog. Includes all the basics on caring for these lap-sized rascals.

By Eliza L. Hopkins and Cathy J. Flamholtz, 1988, 124 pp., $9.95 + $2 S&H (AL res. add sales tax)

OTR Publications
P.O. Box 481
Centreville, AL 35042
(800) 367-2174

Statue or Real Dog?

If you saw one of these curled up on the rug, you'd wonder. Who could resist this Beagle's big brown eyes? Made of high-quality gypsum designed for durability, trueness to color, and detail, this sculpture is just one of more than 80 show-quality breeds available. Tricolor Beagle available as a Canine Classic (measuring 7½" × 7") or a Basket Buddy (16" × 4" × 9"). Choose standard colors or—for just a bit more—you can have your statue painted to look like your own dog from color photographs you provide.

Canine Classics, $40 + $10 S&H
Basket Buddy, $50 + $10 S&H
Custom Painting, $10 additional (PA res. add 6% sales tax)

Those Dogs Accents
9 James Dr.
Denver, PA 17517
(717) 484-4872

Your Companion ®

Back in 1973, two art students began making ceramic figurines in a backyard chicken coop. Today Gary and Jeanie Clinton head United Design, one of the best sources for animal figurines to complement your home's decor. Sculpted to exacting detail, cast in hydrostone or bonded porcelain, and handpainted to capture a maximum degree of realism. Miniature Yorkies from the Stone Critters collection include Little Yorkie Pup (left, 1½" tall), Yorkie (center, 3½" tall), and Yorkie Baby (right, 2" tall). Just three of over 150 dog designs for more than 30 breeds. Curious, charming Yellow Labrador Puppy (9" × 10½") from the Animal Classics collection obviously needs a good home—perhaps yours. Scottie magnet (2½" × 2½"), from the Animal Magnetism collection, is handmade of bonded porcelain and handpainted.

More than 30 dog magnet designs are available to hold important notes on your refrigerator.

Little Yorkie Pup, $6.50
Adult Yorkie, $16
Yorkie Baby, $12
Yellow Lab Puppy, $100
Scottie Magnet, $4.90
+ UPS (OK res. add sales tax)

United Design Corp.
P.O. Box 1200
Noble, OK 73068
(800) 727-4883

Master of Fine Arts Mats

Canine Canvases for the designer dog are the latest in intelligent, functional dog art from Chia Jen Studio, among the California redwoods. These abstract Dish Mats and Sleeping Mats are screened, sponged, and painted on natural domestic cottons. Each can be purchased in three colors/designs. Treated to be water-resistant and easy to clean, the mats are perfect for your dog's sleeping or eating area. Use this exceptional, colorful abstract art as a complement to your decor. Custom colors available. Discuss your interior with Jennifer Mackey, the artist.

Canine Canvas Dish Mat, $50+ $5 S&H
Canine Canvas Sleeping Mat, $100 (sm., 36" × 48"), $120 (med., 48" × 60"), $140 (lg., 54" × 72") + $10 S&H (CA res. add 7.25% sales tax)

Jennifer Mackey
Chia Jen Studio
1961 Monument Rd.
Rio Dell, CA 95562
(707) 764-5877
E-mail: suziraz@aol.com

Crewel World

For 22 years, artist Chris Lewis Brown has transformed pictures of dogs into custom yarn portraits, rendered with a needle and fine Persian wool on Belgian linen. The yarn colors are chosen to create the texture of any coat type, the look of a wet nose, or your dog's special expression. It was Aldous Huxley who said—but you already know this—"the eyes are the doorway to the soul." Each Chris Brown portrait—using photographs provided by you—takes 3–6 weeks, beginning with a detailed pencil sketch, which is submitted for your approval. It is then enlarged to its final size and transferred to linen. When finished, the original is assembled in a natural wood and fabric frame to enhance its colors. This artist's exceptional work has been extensively reviewed in magazines and newspapers. Note the detail in the Irish Wolfhound, Doberman Pinscher, and Golden Retriever photographs. Additional choices of frames and pencil renderings are available by discussion with the artist.

Custom Yarn Dog Portrait, $1,200 (head study, finished frame size 17½″ × 21½″), $1,600 (double head study, 20″ × 24″), $2,000 (triple head study, 21″ × 25″) + UPS (OH res. add sales tax)

Custom Yarn Portraits
Chris Lewis Brown
4804 Corey Rd.
Toledo, OH 43623
(419) 885-4172

Where's Spot? ®

How many millions of tiny fingers have anticipated each page of this wonderful hardcover book for children? Here's Spot's mommy looking for him, with a handy paper flap for little children to turn on each page, expecting Spot to appear at any moment. The suspense builds. Happy ending, nothing to worry about; smiling faces and wagging tails!

By Eric Hill, 22 pp., $12.95 + UPS (NY res. add sales tax)

G.P. Putnam's Sons
200 Madison Ave.
New York, NY 10016
(800) 631-8571

Thai Woods

Native craftspeople in Thai villages handcarve each of these eclectic dogs from durable monkeypod, an acacia wood native to Thailand. Rocking Dog is an amusing rocker for children, chestnut-stained with painted black highlights on the paws, nose, and ears: 24″ length from nose to tail, 9″ wide and 14″ high, with rocker under the dog.

highlights on his feet, nose, jowls, ears, and tail, with expressive, intelligent black eyes. Sleepy Basset Hound in a pleasing brown, black, and mottled white coloration—and a painted black nose—makes an excellent companion by the hearth. Big enough to hug, measuring 19″ l. × 16″ w. × 8″ h. All have the unique hewn look of native Thai crafts.

Rocking Dog, $210
Standing Bulldog, $284
Sleepy Basset Hound, $155
+ $ 20 S&H (CA res. add 8.5% sales tax)

Horizons International Accents
904 22nd St.
San Francisco, CA 94107
(800) 933-6420
E-mail: horizonia@aol.com

Standing Bulldog, with protective stance, stretches his full 27″ length, 15″ width and height. Painted black

The Video Guide to Dogs

Great footage in this 60-minute VHS tape of more than 50 dog breeds, with step-by-step instructions for finding the best one for you. Professional narration, music, and graphics; all the basics on selecting a dog. Includes a fabulous folded chart that lists the pluses and minuses of various breeds under headings like "Good with Children," "Suitable for City/Apartment Living," etc. Great package for anyone weighing the plusses and minuses of a dog as a companion or family pet.

The Video Guide to Dogs,
(VHS videotape), $19.95
(includes S&H)
(WV res. add sales tax)

Pet Avision
P.O. Box 102
Morgantown, WV 26507
(800) 521-7898
http://www.
petlinks.com

TRUE DOG TALE

World's Briefest Haircut

The Mexican Hairless is, yes, essentially a hairless dog. He has just a tuft of hair on the tip of his tail and on the top of his head! His skin is warm to the touch. Obviously he doesn't need much brushing, but his skin does require attention in order to keep it healthy. Three varieties: standard, miniature, and toy; each gets progressively smaller. Just a little trim . . . off the top, please. Book me an appointment for the tail.

Living Watercolor

This beautiful watercolor, *Yuki, You Dawg* (22″ × 15″), was created by artist Catherine Anderson of Napa Valley, California. Her credentials are impeccable. Visiting California? She regularly holds workshops in the San Francisco Bay Area (Green Gulch Farm/Zen Center: 415/383-3134) on watercolor painting and meditation. In the words of the Buddhist Dogen: "the entire phenomenal universe and the empty sky are nothing but a painting." As with many long-distance artists, she will create a painting (oil or watercolor in any size) from the photographs you provide of your dog. Start by calling her and discussing what you would like.

Dog Portraits, $1,500–$5,000
+ UPS (CA res. add sales tax)

Catherine Anderson
P.O. Box 59
Rutherford, CA
94573
(707) 944-8736
E-mail: h2oclrz@-
aol.com

Danish Collectibles

Here's an exquisite 7½″-dia. decorator plate of the Norwegian Elkhound in the renowned Copenhagen blue underglaze finish. More than 300 designs are available to add to your collection. Ask for product sheets on the breed of your choice.

Danish Decorator Plate,
$55 + $3 S&H
(MO res. add 5.97%
sales tax)

Purple
Shamrock
P.O. Box 3595
Springfield,
MO 65808
(800) 787-7537

Claire's Inspirations

Claire's love of dogs is in each of these hand-hooked 100% wool dog rugs. Backed to prevent floor slippage, Dalmatians (26″ × 38″) shows four black and white pups with colored collars and a border of red flowers on a patchwork quilt pattern. Dachshund (22″ × 33″) features a black and tan dog with cheerful red and white flower patterns. Bright white Westie (24″ × 36″), not shown, with a red collar and a background of blues and greens, is bordered by lovely white and pink flowers. Ask for Claire's superb catalog of other dog rugs and kits.

Dalmatians,
$149 + $9.95 S&H
Dachshund,
$99 + $9.95 S&H
Westie, $149
+ $9.95 S&H
(AL and HI add $8 to
S&H)
(VT res. add sales tax)

Claire Murray Inspired Designs
ANB International
P.O. Box 390
Ascutney, VT 05030
(800) 252-4733

Wolf Slate

The world of dogs—big and small, fat and skinny—can now take their place on your mantel or desk through the artistry of Shlomo Shuval, an Israeli born craftsman and artist. He has created a new genre of animal art with these attractive slates, using a method of directly and permanently transferring images onto stone. It's a process like silk-screening, in which the image is embedded in the surface of the rock itself to create three dimensions and special effects. These are impressive and permanent artworks that include a slate stand for display. Utterly original, they almost look like Native American stone sculptures.

Wolf Slate
$30 (4″ × 5.5″)
+ $5 (slate stand) + $5 S&H
$55 (6″ × 8″) + $6 (slate stand)
+ $6 S&H
$80 (8″ × 11″) + $7 (slate stand)
+ $7 S&H
$165 (12″ × 16″) + $12 S&H
(CA res. add sales tax)

Sierra Slate Images
2124 Acton St.
Berkeley, CA 94702
(510) 845-2816
http://www.pm-connect.com/
sierra_slate

Metal Dog Sculpture

After I saw Phillip Glashoff's work at an art show, I tracked him down and insisted—nicely—that he send me photos. His commissioned sculptures are extremely popular—assemblages of found articles welded together into unique three-dimensional impressions suggestive of our familiar, everyday dogs. He will create a sculpture of any breed, from Great Dane to weenie dog. All are meant for outdoor display on a deck or pedestal, or in the garden. The sculptures weather with the elements, changing gradually to achieve their final patina. Some people keep them indoors, livening up an area in their house in need of an artistic statement. Each sculpture is created on a commission basis, with the price negotiated at the time of commission. Dog with Yellow Tail and Dog with Tongue are two fine examples.

> *"The fidelity of a dog is a precious gift."*
> —Konrad Lorenz

Phillip Glashoff Dog Sculptures, $550–$5,000
Dog with Yellow Tail (approx. 6½′ l. × 5′ h.), $3,500
Dog with Tongue (3½′ l. × 2½′ h.), $550
+ UPS (CA res. add sales tax)

Glashoff Sculptures
5402 Williams Rd.
Suisun, CA 94585
(707) 427-8060

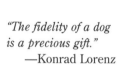

Cautrell Parables

By definition, a parable is a short story that illustrates a moral or religious truth. The Parables Series Prints are a set of black and white linoleum cuts. Linocut is a method of relief printing where the ink is rolled onto the surface of a hand-carved linoleum plate. The areas that have been cut away do not receive the ink. When the impression is taken, the ink transfers from the plate to the paper, creating a high-contrast black and white image. Used by European and Mexican artists as a form of social and political commentary, linocuts were historically one of the first artforms of "mass" production. Linos were a means of spreading the word from major cultural centers into the countryside. Artist Dan Cautrell's linocut series features 12 different prints (2 of which are shown, *Agreement # 1:Violence* and *Parable # 4: Stairs and Windows*), of black cat/white dog. There's a message in each limited-edition signed print. You'll receive a certificate of authenticity and information about the series and the artist. His work is striking, and the messages, accompanied by images of dogs and cats, ring true.

Parables Series Prints (8″ × 15″ unframed, 10″ × 17″ framed)
Per print (unframed), $60
Per print (archivally framed with pH-balanced materials for preservation, ready to hang), $150
+ UPS
(CA res. add sales tax)

Dan Cautrell
Fusion Press Studio
16894 Rainy Vale Ave.
Riverside, CA 92503
(909) 689-3205
E-mail: fusionink@aol.com

Ceramic Moments

Judy Miller moved into her first apartment at UC Berkeley in 1970. In need of dishes one day, she rolled out some clay, laid it in forms, and drew on it scenes from her life. They were an instant success. Her Menorah features an adorable dog and cat in ceramic. It's been fired in the kiln three times, with underglaze pencil and watercolor added for each firing. The Company's Coming Collectible Plate in vivid colors captures the everyday moments (complete with child and playful puppy) that we experience with our partners and our pets. Her work is excellent and widely shown in U.S. and Canadian galleries.

Menorah, $95 + $7.95 S&H
Company's Coming Collectible Plate,
$270 + $14.95 S&H
(CA res. add 8.25% sales tax)

Ceramic Art
2735 Porter St.
Soquel, CA 95073
(408) 476-9232

The Basic Guide to the Labrador Retriever

Labs are the most popular dogs in America. As far as anyone can tell, the breed traces its roots to England from dogs that originated in Newfoundland. As told in this fascinating book, these early smaller Labs were used to retrieve fish that had fallen off the boats of cod fishermen. The Lab was first mentioned in 1814, and since then this breed (yellow, black, and chocolate are all acceptable colors) has been a favorite of sportsmen and families, prized for loyalty and intelligence. Many of today's top breeders contributed to this book. A well-rounded and thorough overview of history, health, finding a breeder, the new puppy, care and training, and many breeding considerations. The Hall of Fame black and white photo gallery in the book includes contemporary champion dogs. A friendly, excellent handbook for the neophyte—or experienced—Lab lover.

Edited by Michael R. Zervas, 1995, 128 pp., $9.95 + $3 S&H (VA res. add 4.5% sales tax)

Dace Publishing
P.O. Box 91
Ruckersville, VA 22968
(888) 840-DACE

Hairy Dog Bears

What is this? A teddy bear book? Nope. Each of these Pet Hair Bears was woven from a dog's hair by artist Annie May Marshall. At your request she'll spin the brushings from your dog into soft fuzzy yarn, then knit it into an original 7" keepsake teddy bear. You'll need to save clean dog brushings and send her 5 oz., along with a good photo of your dog. Then tell her whether you want a girl or boy bear, and choose from a Basic Bear (with detailed face and claws) or a Clothed Bear (with a hand-dyed sweater on the boy bear, a lacy dress on the girl bear). She'll even weave your dog's hair into a scarf, hat, pillow, or clothing you can wear. Send her a legal-size SASE and a big handful of your dog's fur, and she'll send you a free sample of how it looks woven as yarn. Makes a nice keepsake of your furry friend.

Basic Bear, $50
Girl or Boy Bear, with hand-dyed clothing, $55
Deluxe Girl or Boy Bear, with finely detailed clothing, $60 + UPS
(CA res. add sales tax)

Annie May Marshall
Pet Hair Bears
2245 E. Colorado Blvd.
Box 104-163
Pasadena, CA 91107
(818) 793-1070
E-mail: amay tex@green heart.com

English Collectibles ®

Staffordshire dogs are much sought after by designers, antique dealers, and collectors. William Kent, a potter from a long family line of potters, established the Kent factory in 1878 in Burslem, England. His work colorfully depicted great personages, events, customs, and everyday subjects in clay. The factory ceased production in 1962, but the original molds were retained by John Kent, grandson of the founder. Now, Olde Staffordshire ware is being produced once again in England by the Bairstow Manor Pottery. All pieces carry the Kent backstamp to verify authenticity. Much effort is put into painting the ware as it was depicted so many years ago.

Staffordshire Dogs
Small pair (8½″ h.), $90
Large pair (10½″ h.), $160
+ UPS
(CA res. add sales tax)

Heirloom Editions, Ltd.
25100-B S. Normandie Ave.
Harbor City, CA 90710
(800) 433-4785

Tahoe Dogs

Friendly, amusing stuffed dogs from Michael and Laureen Tobias of Lake Tahoe make perfect gifts for a dog lover. Here's a pooch fishing with The One That Got Away Lamp. All Dogs Go to Heaven features two cute pooches with angels' wings. Get Along Little Doggies is a dog in Western getup with a vintage hankie around the neck, perfect for your country-western friend. Mary Margaret is a delightful girl dog in a dress, holding her teddy bear. Utterly unique adorable dogs, dressed in cotton/acrylic clothing, from a pleasant couple with a sense of humor, living a mile high in the scented pines of Tahoe. They like what they do. It shows.

The One That Got Away Lamp, $129 +$8 S&H
All Dogs Go to Heaven, $59.99 + $6 S&H
Get Along Little Doggies,

$49.99 + $6 S&H
Mary Margaret, $39.99 + $6 S&H
(CA res. add $3.29 sales tax)

Out of the Woods
P.O. Box 8700
S. Lake Tahoe, CA 96158
(916) 577-8026

Is It Real, or Is It Stone? ®

Seen from a distance you might wonder. This very cute Dalmatian puppy from Living Stone is sculpted and hand-painted for realism, with lifelike glass eyes. Average height is 5″, and the pup weighs about 2 lbs. The amazing Living Stone dog art includes a Golden Retriever, Dalmatian, Cocker, Schnauzer, Rottweiler, and Boxer. Virtually every breed is available as a puppy or adult in beautifully sculpted hydrostone that will last and last.

Living Stone Puppy, $11–$69 + UPS
(CA res. add sales tax)

Living Stone
P.O. Box 5476
Chula Vista, CA 91912
(800) 621-3647

From These to This

Notice the two pictures in the upper left of the photo? Those are the originals sent to artist Mary Ann Reese, who used them to create the painting you see. Given the price of portraiture these days, her work is remarkably affordable. Group portraits available. Call Mary Ann to discuss the scenic background of your choice and your pet's own personalized oil portrait.

Dog Portrait,
$55 (9″ × 12″)
to $125 (24″ × 48″)
+ UPS
(WV res. add
sales tax)

Mary Ann Reese
RD # 1
Box 524
W. Peyton Dr.
Weirton, WV 26062
(304) 748-1126

Fishing Dogs: ®

A Guide to the History, Talents, and Training of the Baildale, the Flounderhound, the Angler Dog, and Sundry Other Breeds of Aquatic Dogs (Canis piscatorius)

Fishing and lying go together like pretzels and beer: You've heard those stories of the Big One that got away! This terrific hardcover takes a satiric look at imaginary dogs—Gillie Dogs, Baildales, Already Baildales, Fish Spotter Dogs, Bilge Pups—canine companions every fisherman would want for company while foraging for dinner and seeking thrills. Outrageous fishing stories, complete with detailed dog-training tips. A hoot to every dog-loving angler with a serious hankering for tall tales.

By Raymond Coppinger, 1996, 114 pp., $12.95 + UPS
(CA res. add sales tax)

Ten Speed Press
P.O. Box 7123
Berkeley, CA 94707
(800) 841-BOOK

Everything Egyptian

Helen McCrae specializes in quality reproductions of ancient Egyptian art. Dogs were important to the Egyptians. They even had a revered dog god—Anubis—who assured Egyptians in the time of the pharaohs that they would get safely to their next life and attain eternal life. This line drawing shows McCrae's 4½″ Anubis state, reclining on a black basalt shrine, protecting the amulet and jewels inside. McCrae specializes in hundreds of Egyptian reproductions—dog and nondog—including watches, papyrus, jewelry, mugs, tote bags, wall hangings, etc. She'll inscribe your name in hieroglyphics on an authentic cartouche made to order in Egypt. Ask for her catalog.

Anubis Egyptian Statuary
(# Stat 22), $65 + $5 S&H
(CA res. add 8.25% sales tax)

Ancient Egyptian Collection
150 Inyo Ct.
San Bruno, CA 94066
(415) 873-8793

Periwinkle's Classics ®

Count on Periwinkle's Pet Gallery for the best illustrated dog art combined with amusing words on a wide variety of products. Beautifully rendered illustrations on T-shirts (including children's sizes), sweatshirts, magnets, denim golf shirts, baseball shirts, shorts, and more. These are classic drawings with just enough words for a clear message. Huge choice of superior, amusing dog artwork. Great free catalog.

Periwinkle's Pet Gallery T-shirts, $19.95 and up + UPS
(VA res. add sales tax)

Periwinkle's Pet Gallery
9691 Copeland Dr.
Manassas, VA 22110
(703) 257-9039

Chapter Six

Happy, Healthy, Trained, and Groomed

Handy Puppy Cleanup ®

Who's perfect? Everybody makes a mess once in a while. This nifty stain remover with enzymes cleans up almost any pet mess, on almost any surface, from carpet to tile, clothing, floors, and walls. Nontoxic and biodegradable, safe to use on and around your dog. Available in flip-top squirt bottles and gallons (3 sizes).

Pet Tracks, $5.25
(4 oz.), $7.50 (16 oz.),
$11.30 (32 oz.)
+ UPS (MO res. add sales tax)

Benepet Pet Care Products
P.O. Box 8111
St. Joseph, MO 64508
(800) 825-0341

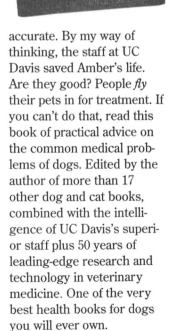

UC Davis Book of Dogs ®

This is definitely a biased review. I had a fabulous Golden Retriever I found and adopted. Only problem was, she couldn't keep down food or water. More than one vet was ready to operate after showing me X-rays of this or that. So I called the University of California at Davis, discovered they had the equivalent of an ear, nose, and throat professor for dogs, got in the car, and drove 150 miles to take Amber to this fabulous vet school. I expected to stay overnight, but the teaching professor (with 4 or 5 vet students trailing behind) told me to take a few hours for lunch and come back. On my return I got an incredible detailed explanation of what was happening—from treadmill tests to fluoroscopy. The diagnosis, at last, was

accurate. By my way of thinking, the staff at UC Davis saved Amber's life. Are they good? People *fly* their pets in for treatment. If you can't do that, read this book of practical advice on the common medical problems of dogs. Edited by the author of more than 17 other dog and cat books, combined with the intelligence of UC Davis's superior staff plus 50 years of leading-edge research and technology in veterinary medicine. One of the very best health books for dogs you will ever own.

Edited by Mordecai Siegal, 1995, 538 pp., $27.50 + UPS (N.Y. res. add sales tax)

HarperCollins Publishers
10 E. 53rd St.
New York, NY 10022
(800) 242-7737

> *"A dog teaches a boy fidelity, perseverance, and to turn around three times before lying down."*
> —Robert Benchley

Coolin' Off Romeo

Male dogs bothering the queen of the house? This 8-oz. pump spray helps eliminate odors that make female dogs in heat attractive to male dogs. While it may not work on every dog, it works on most. Simply spray it on the female's rear and leg area and where she frequently sits. Completely safe. Usually a big help in discouraging ardent males.

Lust Buster, $3.99
+ $5.99 S&H
(WI res. add 5% sales tax)

Drs. Foster & Smith
P.O. Box 100
Rhinelander, WI 54501
(800) 826-7206 (24 hours)

Flea Beacon

Fleas jump on your ankles by sensing your body heat. Incredibly, from as far as 15', they can feel a variation in temperature as small as half a degree. In no time they're jumping their way to you—or to the heat from this warm flea trap. A small 4-watt bulb provides heat and light, attracting fleas like bees to honey, gluing them onto the replaceable surface, which is specially treated to stay sticky for months. Safe, no chemicals, no smell. Uses peanuts' worth of electricity. Move it from room to room. Great idea!

The Ultimate Flea Trap, $15.95 (includes S&H)
Refills (pack of 3), $4.99
(NY res. add 6% sales tax)

Nupo
P.O. Box 2146
Queensbury, NY 12804
(800) 561-8348

Dogs for Good Owners

Okay, what would you like to know about owning, training, and raising your dog? Just pop in this CD-ROM (Mac or PC version) to view more than 300 photos, 300 audio clips, 300 canine quotes, a complete subject index with over 600 entries, video clips showing dogs in action and training techniques—all set to an original musical score with snappy art. Created by knowledgeable breeders with more than 50 years' combined experience in raising, training, and breeding dogs. Modules on the first day, training, grooming, health, and socializing, plus trivia. The subject index alone will stagger you with the sheer amount of information that can fit on a CD. You'll wind up being a walking dog encyclopedia.

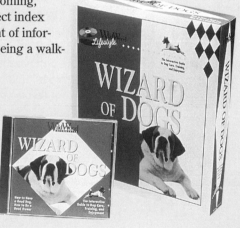

Wizard of Dogs (CD-ROM), $49.95 + UPS

Wildwood Interactive
185-911 Yates St.
Suite 408
Victoria, BC
Canada V8V 4Y9
http://www.wwood.com

Blow the Whistle on Bad Behavior!

Dog dragging you down the street? Put this on her collar, then hook it on the end of your lead. When she pulls on the lead, a whistle sound is triggered. It's not rocket science: The dog associates the whistle (and your voice) with bad behavior and corrects that behavior. Provides reliable action in all weather conditions. Safe, solid, requires no batteries, adjustable sound level. International Science Festival Award winner. Just be sure you reprimand the dog each time the whistle blows. She'll catch on.

Wonder Whistle, $24.95
+ $3.50 S&H
(CA res. add 7.75% sales tax)

Wonder
Whistle
5807 Calpine Dr.
San Jose, CA 95123
(800) 966-3370
http://www.hooked.net/users/wonder/

Light for Safety

The Mini-Safety Lite provides good nighttime, bright-blinking, red-light visibility for your dog. Comes with a hook that easily attaches to the dog's collar. One model (white disk and red light) turns on by pushing the on/off switch. The automatic model (red disk with red light) includes light and motion sensors and automatically turns itself on in the dark. Both come complete with two replaceable batteries for up to 100 hours of use.

Mini-Safety Lite (manual on/off), $5.98
Mini-Safety Lite (automatic sensors), $7.95
+ $3.95 S&H each
(CA res. add 8.25% sales tax)

Protect-a-Pet
P.O. Box 7547
Beverly Hills, CA 90212
(800) 835-9899

Brush 'Em Up! ®

It takes some getting used to, by both you and the dog, but most dogs will let you brush their teeth. They really need it, preferably twice a week. This clever, tapered toothbrush, designed by a veterinary dentist, has supersoft bristles that conform to your dog's mouth and teeth, especially along the gumline. Nonfoaming, tasty beef flavor, hydrogen peroxide toothpaste in 2.5-oz. tube helps clean teeth and fight bad breath. Terrific, essential, comes with free toothbrush. Just be thankful they don't need to rinse!

Petrodex Enzymatic Toothpaste,
$5.39 + UPS
(WA res. add sales tax)

St. Jon Laboratories
1656 W. 240th St.
Harbor City, WA 90710
(310) 326-2720

Where the Dog Doesn't Go ®

Aaah. Nothing like digging up that shady spot in the garden on a hot day. Nice, cool dirt. Shredded flowers. Your dog loves it, but you probably don't. So keep Fido from sculpting your garden with these pellets. When spread around your trees, shrubs, flowerbeds, and other outdoor areas, the taste and smell discourage dogs for up to 10 days with each application. A 1.5-lb. can should last you awhile. Keep out of reach of children.

Keep Off!, $12.99 + UPS
(NY res. add sales tax)
Four Paws Products Ltd.
50 Wireless Blvd.
Hauppauge, NY 11788
(800) 835-0909

Take A Bow Wow: Easy Tricks Any Dog Can Do!

Oh boy, tricks! Lots and lots of fun tricks, from the frivolous to the functional, to make you howl with delight! Nifty training tips make it easy to teach almost any dog to take a bow, chase his tail, play dead, ring a bell when he needs to go out, open and close doors, retrieve his leash, and more! 34-minute VHS tape includes a plastic clicker you can use for training. How have you managed to get along without this?

Take a Bow Wow: Easy Tricks Any Dog Can Do!
(VHS videotape), $24.95
(includes S&H)
(WV res. add sales tax)

Pet Avision
P.O. Box 102
Morgantown, WV 26507
(800) 521-7898

A Pleasing Scent ®

Doggy smell getting to you? Try lighting one of these Pet Candles to destroy pet odors and leave a pleasant scent in the air. Using natural citrus and wood oils to neutralize unwanted pet odors, the candle is smokeless, dripless, and long-burning (up to 60 hours), and it works. Candlelight is nice, too.

Pet Candle, $6 + UPS
(AZ res. add sales tax)

Crystal Candles
Arizona Natural Resources
2525 E. Beardsley Rd.
Phoenix, AZ 85024
(602) 569-0090

The Herbal Dog ®

What's new? Herbs have been used by people medicinally in many cultures for thousands of years. Now we're discovering the many things herbs can do for pets. This Wyoming company provides concentrated, synergistic, balanced herbal formulas for dogs, including Detoxifier, Immune System Formula, Senior Support, Skin & Hair Support, Traveler's Herbals, Vitamin & Mineral Formula, and Willow Bark Formula. The herbs also include vegetable glycerin and flower essences in 2-oz. bottles, approximately 60 doses. Skeptics should obtain Estelle Hummel's excellent free catalog explaining the benefits of natural treatments for your dog. It's an eye-opener.

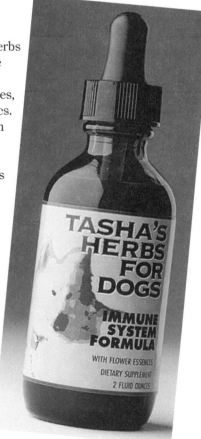

Tasha's Herbs for Dogs, $11.70 + $5 S&H
(WY res. add 6% sales tax)

Coyote Springs Co.
P.O. Box 9888
Jackson, WY 83002
(800) 315-0142

How Hot Is It?

Dogs in hot cars are prone to deadly heatstroke. Keep it from happening with this temperature-sensitive tag that hangs over the rear-view mirror in your car. It lets you know when it's too hot for the dog to enter, and it signals the approach of dangerous heat levels when you're already in the car. Anything too hot for you is way too hot for the dog. The panel begins to change color at 119° F and changes completely at 135° F.

SafeTemp, $2.50 + $1 S&H
(IN res. add sales tax)

The Burn Prevention Group
6724 Bluffridge Pkwy.
Indianapolis, IN 46278
(317) 297-1988
E-mail: erkphil@indynet.net

Health Care from Goodpet ®

Dr. Goodpet is a company with a great reputation for canine homeopathic remedies and other natural health products. These homeopathic remedies originated in Europe and provide safe and nontoxic alternatives to drugs. Digestive Enzymes, made from natural plant sources, help dogs get more nutrients from their food. Follow up the enzymes with liquid Good Breath, a safe homeopathic solution for foul breath and mouth odors. Scratch Free provides temporary relief from pain, itching, and scratching related to hot spots, dry eczema, and allergic dermatitis. Flea Relief helps relieve itching, scratching, and biting caused by fleas. Arthritis is no fun for anyone. Dr. Goodpet's Arthritis Relief is a homeopathic liquid potion you administer with just a few drops in the dog's mouth. Dog getting motion sickness in the car? Acting hyper? Calm Stress is specifically formulated to calm and relieve the stress that often causes motion sickness.

Digestive Enzymes,
$14.95 (7 oz.)
Good Breath, $8.95 (1 fl. oz.)
Scratch Free, $8.95 (1 oz.)
Flea Relief, $8.95 (1 oz.)
Arthritis Relief, $8.95 (1 oz.)
Calm Stress, $8.95 (1 oz.)
+ UPS
(CA res. add sales tax)

Dr. Goodpet Laboratories
P.O. Box 4489
Inglewood, CA 90309
(800) 222-9932

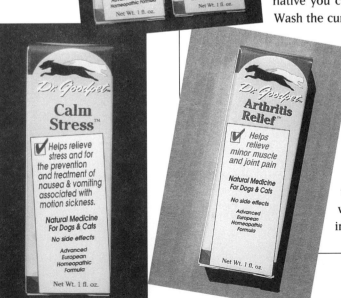

TRUE DOG TALE

When the Sneezing Starts: Tips for Allergic Owners

Aahchoo! Ever thought you might be allergic to your dog? Here are some ways to reduce allergic reactions:

The basic trick is to set aside a room or rooms that are relatively free of dander and dust—which means the dog stays out—and to remove possible sources of dander circulating through the air.

1. Keep the dog out of your bedroom. Sleeping and breathing dander all night are sure to aggravate your allergies.

2. Have someone who is not allergic brush your dog every few days. Bathe the dog every week or so to help reduce dander.

3. Vacuum every few days with a good-quality vacuum—one that includes a water filtration system to keep dander from blowing back into the house.

4. Check your furnace and air-conditioner filters. Keep them clean, replace them, and use the finest possible mesh, as recommended by the manufacturer, to keep dander from circulating in the house.

5. Consider a room air cleaner that can help eliminate dander particles from individual rooms. Keep the dog out of these rooms.

6. Upholstered furniture traps dander and dust particles. Consider an alternative you can wipe down, like leather. Wash the curtains and bedding on a regular basis to eliminate dust buildup, and consider replacing your wool blankets with combed cotton.

7. Thick wool carpeting can be a major reservoir of dander and dust. If you have a choice, replace it with a low-pile carpet or with wood or linoleum flooring.

How to Keep Your Dog Out of the Doghouse

Who's the pack leader in your home? You or the dog? This 40-minute VHS training video shows you how to rule the roost so your dog will respond to your commands. Includes instructions for teaching basic commands, such as sit, stay, and come. Includes a handy carry-along, 36-page study guide that summarizes the main points of the video, plus a laminated guide with the 10 most important tips for dog training that fits right in your pocket. More useful information on crate training and tie-down techniques. You have to be the boss.

Alon Geva Dog Training Package, $19.95 + $5 S&H (CA res. add 8.25% sales tax)

Canine Communications
6285 Bernhard Ave.
Richmond, CA 94805
(800) 364-7191

TRUE DOG TALE

4,370 Puppies?

An estimated 1,500 puppies are born every hour in the U.S. Only *one in ten* will find a good home. One unspayed female dog and her puppies can produce a mind-boggling 4,370 puppies in just seven generations! Spaying, anyone?

Pets Need Vitamins, Too! ®

Don't count on your dog getting all the vitamins she needs from packaged foods. It's smart to use supplements. These tasty, chewable tablets go down easy, providing a complete, high potency formula that's fortified with the perfect balance of essential multiple vitamins and minerals. An ideal nutritional supplement for dogs of all ages.

Nutri-Treat Chewable Vitamin/Mineral Tablets for Dogs, $6 (50 tablets), $22 (250 tablets), $45 (500 tablets) + UPS (MO res. add sales tax)

Benepet Pet Care Products
P.O. Box 8111
St. Joseph, MO 64508
(800) 825-0341

Tanned Hot Dogs

Did you know? Dogs with a light-colored or short-groomed coat can get sunburned. Protect them against the damaging rays of the sun with this SPF-15 sunblock formula specially made for canines. Provides solid 8-hour protection against cancer-causing UVA/UVB rays. Natural oils help fight the drying effects of the sun and also help prevent bleaching and discoloration of fur.

Sun Spot (8-oz. pump-spray bottle), $9.99 + UPS (MA res. add sales tax)

BioChemics
33 Third Ave.
Boston, MA 02129
(800) PETS-NOW

How to Massage Your Dog ®

Dogs, like you, thrive on attention. Your pet might reach new heights of contentment with these useful, illustrated tips for massaging any dog, from pregnant to purebred, country dog to couch potato. Using cold-pressed oils, you massage your pet with your thumbs in a French technique called *effleurage,* or stroking. Amusing, pleasing. Who can resist this?

By Jane Buckle, 1995, 82 pp., $9.95 + UPS (IN res. add sales tax)

Howell Book House
201 W. 103rd St.
Indianapolis, IN 46290
(800) 428-5331

Fine Japanese Grooming Tools

Plunked down way out in the middle of Kansas is a Japanese company called NYT Worldwide Corporation. From these headquarters they import into the United States exquisite Doggie & Kitty grooming products from Japan. Clockwise, Rake (upper left) includes Newey stainless pins from a 200-year-old Japanese metal manufacturer. Comb has 2 meshes for fine combing. Flea Catcher's

0.15mm pin spaces (top right) catches even the smallest of fleas in the clear handle. Clever. Oval Soft Slicker has rounded pins to avoid cuts, smooth to your dog's skin. Nail Clipper includes built-in file and nail collector. Grooming Scissors are made with special steel to stay sharp. Pin Grooming Brush features fine, flexible pin tips tender to your puppy's skin. All with pleasing light-blue handles.

Fine dog-grooming tools from Japan.

Rake, $7 + $3 S&H
Fine/Coarse Comb, $8 + $2.50 S&H
Flea Catcher, $13 + $2.50 S&H
Soft Slicker $7 + $3 S&H
Nail Clipper, $12 + $3 S&H
Grooming Scissors, $15 + $2.50 S&H

Pin Grooming Brush, $2 + $3 S&H (KS res. add sales tax)

Doggie & Kitty
NYT Corp.
5145 N.W. Topeka Blvd.
Topeka, KS 66617
(913) 246-0177

The Special, Older Dog

We all get older—if we're lucky. The senior years of a dog's life require special care and love. This compassionate 60-minute VHS tape shows how to provide for the needs of your aging dog. It shows real-life home visits with older dogs and their owners, an interview and demonstration with a vet about aging problems, and information on the prevention, detection, and treatment of common problems. Informative and reassuring.

Handle with Care: Caring for Your Older Dog (VHS videotape), $24.95 + UPS (NJ res. add 6% sales tax)

Fawn Run Corp.
1122 Ramapo Valley Rd.
Mahwah, NJ 07430
(800) 998-3331

Good Puppy

Noted dog behaviorist Jeanne Carlson knows a thing or two about dogs. She's a nationwide telephone consultant on problematic canine behavior. But before you call her in desperation, view her 56-minute VHS tape. It teaches humane, gentle handling of new puppies (from 7 weeks to 5 months) and covers everything from housebreaking to nipping. These are the crucial, early months of training. Doing it right, from the start, will give you and your dog

lifelong compatibility and a healthy measure of sanity. After watching the tape, if you're just plain fed up or you have an immediate problem, give Jeanne a ring.

Good Puppy (VHS videotape), $22.95 (includes S&H and sales tax)

Jeanne Carlson
Sound Dog Productions
P.O. Box 27488
Seattle, WA 98125
(206) 547-PUPS (7877)

High Power, Low Volume ®

Does your lethargic dog need a pick-me-up? Perhaps a high-calorie, high-energy supplement without a lot of volume? This 4.4-oz. tube is packed with vitamins and minerals. Good when Fido needs a lift or for a convalescing dog. Can be eaten directly or added to your dog's food. Superconcentrated nutrition when it's needed.

Nutrimalt Plus, $6.99 + UPS (WA res. add sales tax)

St. Jon Laboratories
1656 W. 240th St.
Harbor City, WA 90710
(310) 326-2720

Dog Showmanship: The Winning Edge

Thinking about showing your purebred dog? Here are all the basics: show ring movement and strategy, nutrition, conditioning and grooming, the elements of conformation show training, ring etiquette, and what the judges will be looking for. All in a user-friendly, 43-minute VHS tape. Some of America's top AKC judges answer common questions and give helpful tips to novices. Produced and directed by Bill Suchy, whose shows are seen on PBS. A good way to get started.

Dog Showmanship: The Winning Edge (VHS videotape), $29.95 + UPS (FL res. add sales tax)

Florida Films
5367 Abelia Dr.
Orlando, FL 32819
(407) 294-3456

Natural and Man-Made Hazards

Many products we use in our homes are toxic to our dogs. For example:

- **Chocolate** (especially baking chocolate) contains theobromine. It's poisonous to dogs. Your dog should never be allowed to eat chocolate. Keep those truffles out of reach.
- **Salt** can be toxic, especially to small dogs gobbling potato chips, popcorn, and other heavily salted products while watching the football game. Lay off the salted sports munchies with Mr. Fuzz.
- **Aspirin** in large quantities is toxic to dogs.
- **Rat and mice bait:** Attempting to control mice and rats, people use products containing the anticoagulant warfarin. It's poisonous to dogs, as is strychnine, also common in pesticides. If your dog eats a poisoned pest, he's poisoned.
- **Antifreeze.** Cars use antifreeze as a coolant in the radiator, year round. It's that greenish liquid you see on the garage floor. A thirsty dog will often lap it up and become desperately ill, and you won't know why. Big problem—results in kidney failure, coma, and worse. Nontoxic antifreezes are available *specifically* for this purpose. Don't let puddles form in your garage from any automotive chemical, including battery acid.

Lastly, I used to work in a beautiful office building. They sprayed the lawn with a grass retardant so it wouldn't grow so fast—hence, less expense to have it mowed. But every time it rained, worms were poisoned as the chemicals were forced deeper into the soil. Hundreds of dead worms wound up all over the sidewalk, and neighborhood birds would eat the poisoned worms. The birds would be poisoned. Stray dogs and cats would eat the birds, and continue the chain of poisoning. Everything's connected. Old expression: "What goes around, comes around." Natural solutions exist for almost everything.

Safe Grooming ®

Grooming is a great way to give your dog attention. Here's a tool with a double-faced plastic blade that's good to use with any long-haired dog. It grooms but doesn't cut hair the way some metal blades do. Comes complete with a lanyard so you can hang it, find it, and use it when you need it. Available in black or screaming-bright Day-Glo colors.

Sheds-All for Dogs,
$6.49 + UPS
(NY res. add sales tax)

Real Animal Friends
Trading Corp.
101 Albany Ave.
Freeport, NY 11520
(800) 654-PETS

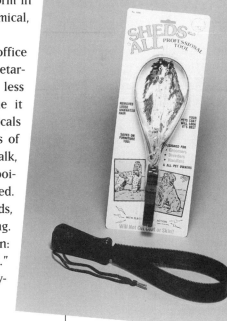

Dog-Perfect: The User-Friendly Guide to a Well-Behaved Dog

You and your dog will be together for many years. Why not have a well-trained dog that's a pleasure to be with? This book, written in plain language with commonsense advice, is purely and simply, a training guide that shows you—with easy-to-follow chapters and step-by-step programs—how to teach your dog the most basic commands, and the most complex. An exceptionally practical and useful book, written by a professional trainer who knows the ropes.

By Sarah Hodgson, 1995,
200 pp., $12.95 + UPS
(IN res. add sales tax)

Macmillan General
Reference
Howell Book House
201 W. 103rd St.
Indianapolis, IN 46290
(317) 581-3500

The Sign of Life

If—God forbid—your home is ever affected by a fire or natural disaster, it will really help to have one or two of these stickers displayed prominently in your windows. They immediately alert fire and rescue personnel that you have pets, and how many (just write the number in the box). Bright red and black lettering on 4″ × 6″ weatherproof vinyl.

Pet Emergency Rescue Stickers, $2.25 (for 1), $3.50 (for 2), $1.73 (3 or more) (includes S&H) (CA res. add sales tax)

DonMar Enterprises
1629 N. Naomi St.
Burbank, CA 91505
(818) 848-6123

TRUE DOG TALE

The Best Health Care for Dogs

Veterinarians are human. They can make mistakes. Obviously, you don't want them making a mistake with your dog. If money is no object, and you want the combined hands-on experience of many highly qualified vets and professors, let me point you in opposite geographical directions—the East and West coasts. The Animal Medical Center in New York City has been treating dogs and other pets since 1911. Open 24 hours a day, they offer advanced cancer treatment, CAT scans, acupuncture, and the combined experience of highly qualified vets, specialized in the healing arts. Their phone number: (212) 838-8100.

The Veterinary School at the University of California at Davis is also world class, treating household pets as well as zoo and theme park animals. Their Vet-Med Teaching Hospital utilizes experienced vet/professors and students. They did some extraordinary work for my dog. You can reach someone there 24 hours a day at (916) 752-1393.

Major lifesaving treatments can cost thousands of dollars. So seriously consider obtaining pet insurance from VPI (800-872-7387) or another pet insurance carrier.

Turn Down the Heat ®

Walking a female dog in heat seems to attract every male dog from miles around. But roaming Romeos lose interest fast after a quick spray of this stuff. Instantly works to eliminate bacterial heat and hormonal odors on dogs in season. 100% natural, safe to use. Leave the club at home.

Nature's Nonscents Heat Off (4 oz.), $6.95 + $4.50 S&H (IA res. add 5% sales tax)

Krueger Enterprises
5057 American Legion Rd. S.E.
Iowa City, IA 52240
(800) 942-8565

The Doctors Book of Home Remedies for Dogs and Cats ®

This excellent hardcover home-care book covers just about every medical condition you can imagine for your dog, from acne to worms But health is just part of it. The editors thoughtfully include the best music to relieve Fido's anxiety, tips on how to keep your latchkey dog from getting lonely, the easy way to eliminate fleas (without using drugs), and other compassionate, smart, natural advice. Helpful black and white illustrations accompany the text. The key benefit of this book is to help you with preliminary diagnosis of what's going on with your dog and her health. Every chapter includes a section on "When to See the Vet" that lets you know when it's time to start up the car.

By the editors of *Prevention* Magazine Health Books, 1996, 403 pp., $27.95 + UPS (PA res. add sales tax)

Rodale Books
33 E. Minor St.
Emmaus, PA 18098
(800) 678-5661

The Doctors Book of Home Remedies for Dogs and Cats

Over 1,000 Solutions to Your Pet's Problems— From Top Vets, Trainers, Breeders and Other Animal Experts

By the Editors of PREVENTION Magazine Health Books

"An owner's manual and a godsend—no four-legged home should be without it."
—Peter Mayle, *A Dog's Life* and *Toujours Provence*

Clipping Instructions ®

How do you clip a dog for the first time? You could just plunge right in and live with the comic results. Or you could pop in this 15-minute VHS cassette, see how it's done, and then do it right. You'll easily learn step-by-step clipping and bathing techniques for almost any dog—Poodles, Cocker Spaniels, mixed breeds, Schnauzers. Ready for the big moment? Start with these great clippers. The magnetic motor clipper includes four comb guides, shears, a grooming blade, a blade oil pouch, a cleaning brush, and instructions. Believe me, you can do it!

Adjustable Clipper Kit with Video, $29.99 + UPS (TN res. add sales tax)

Oster Professional Products
150 Cadillac Lane
McMinnville, TN 37110
(800) 887-6682

TRUE DOG TALE

Mosquito Warning

Plain old mosquitoes. Just an annoyance, right? Maybe to you, but not to the dog. Mosquitoes can transmit heartworm disease from one dog to another, resulting in adult worms in the large vessels of the heart, which can lead to heart failure. Good news—you can prevent heartworm disease with monthly pills like Heartgard or Interceptor or with veterinary treatment if your dog has already been exposed. Mosquitoes in the neighborhood? Have your dog checked.

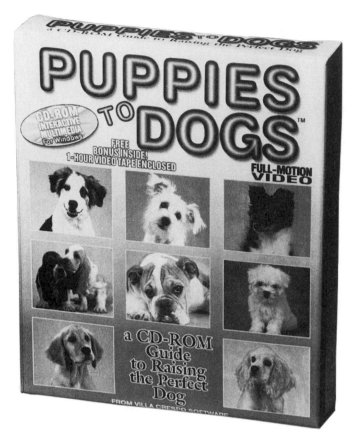

Puppies to Dogs

How much dog info can you pack onto one CD-ROM? View this and find out. You'll need a 386 chip (486 recommended) or better PC, Windows 3.1, CD-ROM drive and sound card, and VGA graphics card. Includes how to pick out a puppy, housebreaking, diet and nutrition, crate training, owners who work, solving common puppy/dog problems, grooming, socialization, health, and more. Color pictures and a detailed description of various breeds, plus a Pet Notes section to help you keep track of your dog's vaccinations, medical and breeding data, and everything else you need to remember. There are several modes by which to access the information: *Freeform* allows you to study the lessons in sequence, or you can select a specific topic from the menu. *Classroom* is perfect for 2 or more participants. Questions are asked at the end of topics, and scores for each student are automatically recorded. User-friendly, hosted by animal behaviorist Ann M. Childers.

Puppies to Dogs (CD-ROM), $39.95 + $4 S&H
(no sales tax in Ore.)

Media West Home Videos
P.O. Box 1563
Lake Grove, OR 97035
(800) 888-TAPE
E-mail: globalhv@aol.com

Shark for Dogs

Some people take shark cartilage as a supplement for aging joints. Now it's available, through your vet, for similar use with dogs. Unlike steroids, Cosequin is a true "neutraceutical," naturally harvested from sharks. It's especially useful for older dogs who are moving a little more slowly than they used to. Ask your vet if it will help.

Cosequin, price varies by veterinarian

Nutramax Laboratories
5024 Campbell Blvd.
Baltimore, MD 21236
(800) 925-5187

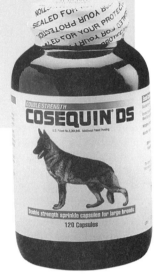

"The only creature faithful to the end."
                                    —George Crabbe

Hearts of Love ®

Garlic is a natural flea repellent. Why? When dogs eat it, garlic permeates their skin and coat, repelling fleas. These supplements contain a natural brewer's yeast treat enriched with omega-3 fatty acids, garlic, rose hips, and zinc for a healthy skin and coat. All-natural ingredients. Dogs gobble 'em down! You can provide the benefits of brewer's yeast and garlic in tablets or in a handy powder you sprinkle on Fluffy's food. Brewer's yeast and garlic: two basic, healthy products in the fight against fleas.

Love Drops (garlic), $9.95
(195 g.), $14.99 (390 g.)
Brewer's Yeast (1 lb. powder bottle or 125-tablet bottle), $16.99
+ UPS
(NY res. add sales tax)

Brewer's Yeast Specialists
P.O. Box 151
Southfields, NY 10975
(914) 351-2690

The Gift of Sound

More than 1.6 million people in the U.S. are deaf or hard of hearing and could benefit from a trained hearing dog. Imagine not being able to hear a baby crying or a knock on the door or the shrill blast of a smoke alarm. Dogs for the Deaf is a nonprofit organization that provides dogs free to people in need. DFD receives no tax dollars and instead depends upon the generosity of people like you and me. It costs, on average, $5,000 for selection of a dog, veterinary care, training, placement, and follow-up. This organization rescues many dogs from humane societies, gives them 4–6 months of intensive training, and then places them with qualified recipients nationwide.

These dogs—certified hearing dogs or working companion dogs—provide sound awareness by alerting their teammates (owners) to normal household sounds, such as the smoke alarm, doorbell, telephone, oven buzzer, a baby's crying, or alarm clock. This sound awareness enables the deaf recipient to lead a more normal, independent, and secure life.

Dogs for the Deaf can't do it without your help. Your tax-deductible contribution in any amount will bring you copies of their *Canine Listener* newsletter and opportunities to buy various gifts—from sweatshirts to tote bags and coffee mugs. You are also invited to tour their facility in Oregon.

Dogs for the Deaf
10175 Wheeler Rd.
Central Point, OR 97502
(541) 826-9220 (voice/ TDD)

TRUE DOG TALE

Ulcer Prevention

If you have a dog, you know that canine companionship helps reduce your stress. And you, in turn, can help reduce stress in your dog by providing plenty of chew toys—rawhide, tough nylon bones (which also help clean teeth), and other goodies that fill those chewing urges. Interestingly, many of the ulcers seen by vets are caused by bone fragments and pieces of wood chewed by dogs who don't have anything else to gnaw on.

Canine Acupressure: A Treatment Workbook

For 3,000 years, the Chinese have used acupressure to stimulate precise points on the surface of the body. The basic principle is that these points are related to specific internal organs and their functions, and it's possible to promote healing and well-being by changing the "chi" energy through stimulation of those points. Believe it or not, tens of millions of people depend on it. This is a competent, user-friendly, remarkably thorough overview on how to do it yourself—for your dog! Charts illustrate the canine meridian system and acupressure points and provide treatment areas for specific illnesses, including arthritis. Any method of treatment that's been around this long has some merit. Of particular interest to those concerned with alternative canine medicines and treatments.

By Nancy Zidonis and Marie K. Soderberg, 1995, 120 pp.,
$18.50 + $3 S&H
(CO res. add sales tax)

Equine Acupressure
P.O. Box 123
Parker, CO 80134
(303) 841-7211

Pills to Powder ®

Giving a pill to a dog isn't rocket science. Open his mouth, drop in the pill, keep his mouth closed with your hand, and stroke his throat. Most dogs quickly swallow the pill. Some wiseguys, however, stare up into your eyes and wait, and wait, and wait. They never swallow the pill. You open their mouth, and there it is: melted. If you have one of these characters, consider this handy device. It crushes pills into powder so you can sprinkle the medication on your dog's food. Drop in the pill, turn the canister, and the powder's in the bottom. Smart, simple.

EZ Swallow Pill Crusher & Pill Splitter, $15.95 + $4 S&H
(SD res. add sales tax)

American Medical Industries
33½ E. 3rd St.
Dell Rapids, SD 57022
(605) 428-5501

That Spot on the Carpet ®

Dogs plus carpets equals stains. This strong cleaner never "yellows" light-colored carpet and helps remove any existing yellowing or old stains. Simple to use: Just apply it, work it in, and blot it. Enzyme free, environmentally safe (no acids, alkalies, carcinogens, or solvents). Especially tough stain? Open the cap, place in microwave for 30 seconds, then apply.

Get Serious Pet Stain Remover, $9.95 (pint), $14.95 (quart) + $4 S&H (CA res. add 7.75% sales tax)

Van Charles Laboratories
633 W. Katella, Unit I
Orange, CA 92667
(714) 639-3580

Easy Mat Removal ®

Grooming a longhaired dog? You know how those hair mats seem to clump up and grow out of nowhere. Plus, it takes forever to brush out matted hair. Here's a better tool for the job. Just work it through the fur, to eliminate mats and tangles without discomfort. Mats are one thing, burrs are another. Here's a hint: You can remove burrs and seeds quickly by coating them with olive oil, then working them out with your fingers. No need to cut the fur.

Mat & Tangle Splitter,
$8.95 + UPS
(NY res. add sales tax)

Four Paws Products, Ltd.
50 Wireless Blvd.
Hauppauge, NY 11788
(800) 835-0909

Pet Therapy Is Making a Difference

It doesn't take a Ph.D. to know that people with pets live longer, happier lives. Wouldn't it be a better world if people took to dogs, not drugs, for comfort and companionship? It's so simple and so obvious. Take a look at this 20-minute videotape of residents in long-term and day-care facilities experiencing animal-assisted therapy. A great tape for anyone who wishes to volunteer for programs that involve visiting pets and improved health. Know someone who needs to be cheered up with a visit? This nonprofit organization maintains a registry of pet visitation/therapy providers. They also provide other videos to the public about human-animal-related interaction. It's all positive.

Pet Therapy Is Making a Difference (VHS videotape), $19.95 + $3 S&H (NJ res. add sales tax)

Alpha Affiliates
103 Washington St.
Suite 362
Morristown, NJ 07960
(201) 539-2770

The Delta Society

These good people need no introduction. A national nonprofit organization, they maintain programs with pets through almost 2,000 Pet Partners teams in 45 states that help an estimated 350,000 people each year. The programs include Pet Partners Program and Animal-Assisted Therapy Services (helping people heal through interactions with specially trained pets), the National Service Dog Center (assisting people with disabilities), People and Pets (teaching individuals and families how companion animals improve health and well-being), and plenty of publications, including newsletters, a quarterly magazine, and more. Joining their membership program and making a tax-deductible contribution are great ways to help—what goes around comes around.

General Member, $35
Sustaining Member, $50
President's Circle Member, $100

Delta Society
289 Perimeter Rd. East
Renton, WA 98055
(800) 869-6898

TRUE DOG TALE

Before You Plant That Garden . . .

Dogs can, and do, eat almost everything. They mosey over and take a sniff, and if it smells okay, they eat it. Take a look at this mile-long list of outdoor plants that are dangerous to dogs: Some of them might surprise you. Did you know the bark and leaves of cherry and peach trees can cause cyanide poisoning, and that spinach and rhubarb can give a dog cramps or worse? Here's a partial list of what you don't want in your yard if your puppy or dog is prone to foraging for new taste sensations. Those with an asterisk can be fatal. Also, ask your vet or nursery about toxic outdoor plants in your area.

American yew	Elderberry*	Mock orange
Angel's trumpet	English holly	Moonweed*
Apricot	English yew	Mushrooms/toadstools*
Arrowgrass*	Foxglove	Oleander
Azalea	Hemlock*	Pokeweed
Bird of paradise	Jasmine	Privit
Bittersweet (berries)*	Jimsonweed*	Rhododendron
Black locust	Larkspur	Skunk cabbage
Buttercup	Lily of the valley	Soapberry
Castor bean	Locoweed*	Tomato vine
Chinaberry*	Lupine	Wisteria
Daffodil	Mescal bean	
Delphinium	Mistletoe	

To Go or Not to Go?

What's a dog to do if you live in an apartment with no yard or are gone all day? Too many drinks of water, too much breakfast—it's sometimes hard to wait for you to get home for the evening walk. One possible solution is these thin 24″ w. × 36″ l. super-absorbent, leakproof, disposable pads. Place one on a convenient surface; your dog will use it, then you roll it up and toss it. You can train your dog to use them by placing one outdoors where your dog currently relieves himself, then moving it inside to a suitable place, like your tile bathroom floor. Excellent for late commuters. I tested it with a cup of water. The cotton surface (with blue plastic backing) didn't leak a drop. Privacy, please? Consider this white molded plastic screen with a fern design.

Pet Potty & Poop Pads,
$21 (50 pads) + $4.75 S&H;
$55 (case of 150) + $6.75 S&H
Privacy Screen,
$33 + $10 S&H
(MI res. add 6% sales tax)

The Uppity Puppy
803 Vester Ave.
Ferndale, MI 48220
(810) 543-7491

Natural Health Care for Your Pets

Alternative medicine—particularly homeopathy—seems like a mystery to some people. But it's really nothing new. Both have been practiced for hundreds of years with great effectiveness. This 18-minute video shows first-time users and the generally curious how to treat dog disorders with homeopathy. It includes a first-aid kit with the five remedies that have been found to be most effective in treating skin infections, arthritis, nervousness, and digestive disorders such as gastritis, flatulence, and hiccough. An easy approach to a confusing topic. The VHS tape is narrated by Christina Chambreau, D.V.M., a nationally known consultant and lecturer on veterinary homeopathy. Far out? Many first-class vets use homeopathy.

Natural Health Care for Your Pets (VHS videotape), $19.95 + $4 S&H (includes Homeopathic First-Aid Kit for Pets) (FL res. add 6% sales tax)

Video Remedies
P.O. Box 290866
Davie, FL 33329
(800) 733-4874

The Tellington Touch

Linda Tellington-Jones is making waves. She's an extraordinary animal trainer who combines traditional veterinary medicine with therapeutic bodywork in a unique form of animal healing and training. Her method, fully explained in this book, is a simple circular touch that can make a dramatic difference in the way an animal feels and acts, accomplishing everything from repairing a horse's injured leg to quieting a compulsively barking dog. This is amazing, very ethereal stuff, and it couldn't possibly work—but it does.

By Linda Tellington-Jones, 1992, 278 pp., $11.95 + UPS (CA res. add sales tax)

Thane Marketing International
78080 Calle Estado, 2nd Floor
La Quinta, CA 92253
(619) 777-0217
(800) 797-PETS

TRUE DOG TALE

Eau de Skunk and Tomato Juice!

Sooner or later, whether you live in suburbia or in the country, your dog is going to come home reeking to high heaven of skunk. How on earth do you get rid of the smell? There are several commercial remedies—including Critter & Litter Spray by Nature's Nonscents on page 138—to keep on hand for this eventuality. If you don't have it, use this age-old technique: Lock the dog in the yard, run to the grocery store, and grab 3–4 big cans of tomato juice. Hose off and shampoo the dog (outside if possible), and give her a tomato juice bath from head to tail. Rub it in, let it sit, then rinse it out, followed by another shampoo. Voilà! Tolerably fresh dog! Grandma was right.

Those Creaking Joints ®

You've noticed your buddy is a bit creaky getting up in the morning. It may be arthritis. You have many options other than surgery to help relieve your pet's discomfort, including this all-natural lotion. Rub it in for up to 6 hours of relief from the swelling and stiffness associated with arthritis, muscle sprains, and strains. Four-ounce bottle will last up to two months.

Arthritis Care for Dogs,
$10.99 + UPS
(Mass. res. add sales tax)

BioChemics
33 Third Ave.
Boston, MA 02129
(800) PETS-NOW

Time for a Warm-up

Both pups and adults like this wonderful warming pad. Pups gratefully lie directly on the pad, which maintains body temperature—sort of like being next to Mom—even when the weather turns cold. Eleven-foot cord is covered with a heavy protective spring (to guard against chewing) for the first 18″, but it's best to enclose the cord within a piece of 1¼″ EMT electrical conduit. Easily cleaned 18″ square fiberglass/plastic combination. Use as is. No cover required.

Temperature Maintenance Pad,
$67.99 + $7.99 S&H
(WI res. add 5% sales tax)

Drs. Foster & Smith
P.O. Box 100
Rhinelander, WI 54501
(800) 826-7206 (24 hours)

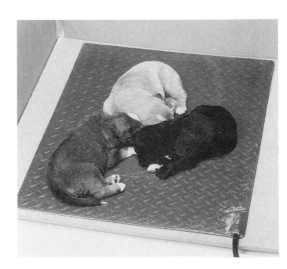

TRUE DOG TALE

The Top Nine Health Threats

Some hazards to dogs are avoidable. Here are nine of the major health dangers you can easily do something about:

1. Antifreeze

That green chemical puddle beneath your car contains ethylene glycol, which tastes great to dogs. It's a deadly poison even in tiny amounts, and tens of thousands of dogs ingest it each year. Avoid overfilling your radiator. Clean up any leakage from the radiator overflow. Don't let the dog get near it. There are also pet-safe antifreezes that work just fine.

2. Car Accidents

If you make your dog street smart, he'll know to keep away from moving vehicles. One good training tip: Have some friends cruise their cars slowly by your house. As your dog runs out to approach each moving car, have the drivers send a few well-aimed shots from water pistols into your dog's face. Eventually, Fido will come to associate moving vehicles with surprise and discomfort. Also train your dog to stay with you and respond to commands while running. Reflective gear at night is a must.

3. Heat Stroke

Dogs don't tolerate heat well. Lock a dog in a car with the windows closed in 80° weather, and you're inviting disaster as the temperature inside climbs to 120°+. Park in the shade. Leave windows cracked, or better yet, use a window screen to allow fresh air into the car. Leave the air conditioning on. Cool the dog down immediately if panting occurs. If you know you'll be stopped in hot weather—with no way to keep the dog comfortable—leave the dog at home.

4. Fleas

Fleas transmit roundworms, cause dermatitis and other diseases, and can play havoc with the well-being of your dog. Getting rid of them and preventing recurring infestations is essential.

5. Mammary Cancer

Have your female dog spayed at around 6–7 months, before she comes into heat. Spaying helps prevent mammary cancer, which is common in female dogs.

6. Heartworms

Transmitted by mosquitoes, these monsters live in the heart of your dog and are deadly. They're easily controlled with pills from your vet.

7. Ticks

Lyme disease and Rocky Mountain spotted fever are just two of the diseases caused by ticks. Check your dog daily, and remove ticks.

8. Rabies

Though encounters with rabid raccoons, skunks, rats, and squirrels are rare these days, dogs still get rabies. It's entirely preventable with a vaccine. Make sure your dog is current on her shots.

9. Obesity

More than 10 million dogs in the U.S. are overweight. Exercise and a careful diet will help prevent not only obesity but heart disease, diabetes, arthritis, and other diseases, especially in older dogs. Your dog's diet should be related to her age, lifestyle (sedentary or active), and general health. Obesity, though last on this nine-item list, plays a large (no pun intended) role in dog health. Get thee a tennis ball and a field!

The Complete Book of Flea Control

This guy Ted is a flea expert. He probably knows more about them than anybody else on earth. That's all he talks about in this book: fleas, and how to control them. If your dogs have fleas, you have fleas. All over the house. They will not go away unless you do something about them. They will get worse. For every 1 flea on your dog, another 99 are busy hatching. The book's emphasis is on natural control, though discussion of insecticides—with an eye toward maximum knockout effectiveness and minimal pet and human exposure—is included. Quite possibly the most thorough source of every known method, chemical, and technique for controlling these monsters, written by an author who's been studying the pests for years. A superior book that provides you with plenty of intelligent alternatives to dousing your dog and home with harmful chemicals.

By Ted Kuepper, 3rd ed., 1995, 78 pp., $5.95 + $2 S&H
(CA res. add sales tax)

TK Enterprises
4907 Marlin Way
Oxnard, CA 93035
(805) 985-3057

Where'd You Get That Coat?

Bright shiny dog coats start from the inside out. Put this human-grade Dream Coat supplement of six natural cold-pressed oils on your dog's food. The special formula provides a full spectrum of essential fatty acids missing from commercial, cooked, or processed dog foods. Those fatty acids are the key missing ingredient for adding a lustrous glow to your dog's coat. A shiny coat in a bottle.

Dream Coat (8 oz. bottle), $9.98 + $4.50 S&H
(FL res. add 7% sales tax)

Halo, Purely For Pets
3438 E. Lake Rd., #14
Palm Harbor, FL 34685
(800) 426-4256

Brusher or Whacker?

Your dentist has been on your case for years to make regular office visits, to brush, and to floss. What about your dog? Has he seen the dentist lately? He probably won't have to if you brush his teeth regularly. You can also use this Plaque Whacker, which is designed to remove plaque and tartar. They can get so hard in your dog's mouth, they have to be chipped off by the vet with a metal scaler. Save yourself the hassle. Use the white pad for regular cleaning, the dark pad for super cleaning with your favorite canine dentifrice.

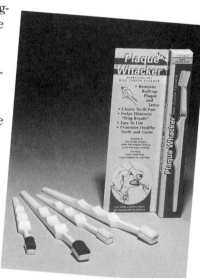

Plaque Whacker (sm. or lg.), $5.99 + UPS
(NJ res. add sales tax)

Drs. Foster & Smith Catalog:
(800) 826-7206

Branlin Enterprises
53 Lake Trail East
Morristown, NJ 07960
(201) 425-5959

Long-Lasting, Chewy Breath Strips ®

What the heck have you been *eating*? you ask the dog. Get rid of morning breath or your dog's other various taste explorations with these all-natural green beefhide strips. Each is coated with green chlorophyll and other breath-freshening ingredients. As your dog chews, the chlorophyll, mint, wintergreen, parsley oil, eucalyptol, and clove oils help sweeten up that smile!

Breath-eze Breath Strips (3.5-oz. box), $4.89 + UPS (CA res. add sales tax)

St. Jon Laboratories
1656 W. 240th St.
Harbor City, CA 90710
(310) 326-2720

The Health Law ®

Most states require you to pick up after your dog. But you don't need to carry a bulky shovel on your daily walks with Mr. Fuzzy. Dispoz-a-Scoop allows you to simply scoop waste, then press down to seal and dispose entirely of the scoop and its contents. Scoop and toss! Convenient biodegradable 5-packs are available in many pet stores, or order the 96- or 250-pack direct.

Dispoz-a-Scoop, $2.99 (5-pack), $40.95 (96-pack), $80.95 (250-pack) + UPS

PetPro Products
2651 S. Fairfax Ave.
Culver City, CA 90232
(800) 873-5957

Groom and Brush ®

Dog ready to be clipped? You can go to a professional groomer, or learn to do it yourself. These professional-quality tools make it easy. The Laube Clipper is one of the best. It's up to 15 times more powerful than the average clipper, cool-running, available in five colors, ultralight, and portable when you use the cord pack. It comes with a 2-speed motor, plus a cord pack and transformer. As you clip, be sure to fluff up your dog's coat with the Lobster Fluff Comb for easier at-home grooming. You'll be spending some money to get these quality grooming tools, but think of the money you'll save over the years. Before you go berserk with the clipper, find out how to do it. There are many dog videos that teach you how to groom your friend, including *Dog Showmanship* on page 119. View it, then do it.

Laube Clipper (Model 503), $120
Lobster Fluff Comb, $4.50
+ UPS
(CA res. add sales tax)

Kim Laube & Co.
16842 Saticoy St.
Van Nuys, CA 91406
(800) 451-1355

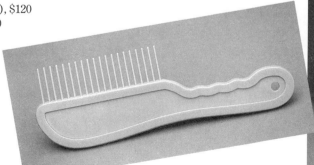

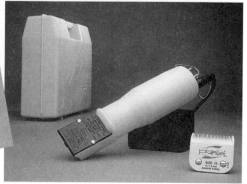

Ask Dr. Jim About Dogs

Nice guy Jim Humphries, D.V.M., is nationally known through his TV and radio programs. In this 45-minute VHS tape, he answers the most common questions from dog owners about crate training for puppies and dogs, housebreaking and controlling behavior problems, spaying and neutering, Lyme disease and its prevention, how to choose a vet, traveling with a dog, obesity, stress, frostbite and cold stress, swimming pool and home safety, socialization, and much more. Easy-to-understand information, professionally presented by the biggest media vet in the U.S. Just sit back and listen.

Ask Dr. Jim About Dogs
(VHS videotape),
$19.95 + $3.50 S&H
(TX res. add 8.25% sales tax)

St. Francis Productions
4444 Westgrove Dr.
Suite 300
Dallas, TX 75248
(214) 380-6500

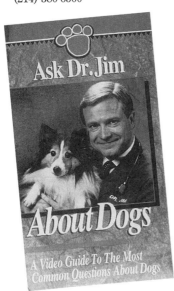

Green Treasure

Chlorophyll is a natural substance that promotes internal cleansing and proper bowel function and elimination. Chlorella combines chlorophyll with calcium (for strong bones and teeth), lecithin (for a healthy-looking coat), and Siberian ginseng, to help with stress. This isn't a drug or medicine. It's a supplement packed with the antioxidant beta-carotene. Sixty tasty green wafers for good dog health.

Pet Sun Chlorella, $29.75 + UPS
(CA res. add sales tax)

Sun Wellness
4025 Spencer St.
Suite 104
Torrance, CA 90503
(800) 829-2828
E-mail: health@interserv.com

"Not the least hard thing to bear when they go from us, these quiet friends, is that they carry away with them so many years of our own lives."

—John Galsworthy

Freshen Up That Coat! ®

Has this happened to you? You hop in the car with the dog, and all of a sudden that smell hits you. Oh boy, did he roll in something stinky. This is perfect when you don't have time to give the pup a bath. Just spray this special, nonirritating, biodegradable deodorant on the dog, carpet, or bedding, and mask the odor until you have time for a good soap and water cure.

Fresh Coat,
$8.99 + UPS
(TN res. add
sales tax)

Oster
Professional
Products
150 Cadillac Lane
McMinnville, TN
37110
(800) 887-6682

TRUE DOG TALE

The Perils of Popularity

As rising popularity of some canine breeds creates an increased demand for those dogs, some unscrupulous breeders have been churning out more and more litters—leading to the presence of hidden, inherited defects and health weaknesses. As examples: Dobermans can suffer serious heart disease, dwarfed Basset Hounds and Dachshunds have inherited defects, German Shepherds can have spinal cord problems, the expected life span of the very popular Cavalier King Charles Spaniel has been reduced by heart disease from 14 to 10 or fewer years, and hip dysplasia is common in many breeds. These health problems generally come later in life. So, before you buy a purebred puppy, ask the breeder about the last 2 generations that created the puppy in front of you. It's smart to find out now what health problems your dog might experience later on. Have any problems shown up? Ask nicely for health certificates from the breeder's veterinarian.

Doggy Smell Remover

You've sprayed and vacuumed, but that doggy odor still lingers in the room. This powerhouse purifier filters dog smells out of the air quickly and easily.

Pulling in more than 100 cubic feet per minute, it recirculates the air in an average-size room 4 times an hour. Replaceable 3M Filtrete Filter traps particles as small as 0.5 micrometers at 90% efficiency. Complete with hanging bracket for wall installation and 9′ power cord. Ultra quiet 3-speed fan/motor uses less electricity than a 100-watt light bulb.

Ultra-Aire Air Purifier, $139.95 + $12.60 S&H (IA res. add 5% sales tax)

Krueger Enterprises
5057 American Legion Rd. S.E.
Iowa City, IA 52240
(800) 942-8565

Picking Up the Pieces ®

Gingerly picking your way through the yard to avoid the land mines? Three models of the Yardmaster help you handle waste disposal. Scissor-type scoop (upper left) with rake and scoop works well on lawns and grassy areas. Yardmaster with 2 scoops (upper right) is best for pavement and hard-surface areas. Yardmaster with separate rake and scoop are best for the owner who prefers to just rake, then scoop. High-impact, tough plastic. No rust, ever!

Yardmaster, $13.99 + UPS (NY res. add sales tax)

Real Animal Friends
Trading Corp.
101 Albany Ave.
Freeport, NY 11520
(800) 654-PETS

Green Grass Supplement ®

Walk into most health food stores, and you'll find Barley Dog. Made by the same folks who make that famous Green Magma health supplement for people, it's a powdered barley grass that contains antioxidant vitamins C and E, beta-carotene, 19 amino acids, live enzymes, purifying chlorophyll, proteins, essential trace minerals, and B vitamins. The 4.8-oz. container supplies about 137 servings to a small dog weighing up to 15 lbs. Let's face it: Some wet and dry dog food is so processed that the essential digestive enzymes and nutrients are cooked out and long gone. Barley Dog puts them back.

Barley Dog, $18 (4.8 oz.) (CA res. add 8.25% sales tax)

Green Foods Corp.
23822 Hawthorne Blvd.
Suite 100
Torrance, CA 90505
(800) 222-3374
E-mail: gfc@greenfoods.com

Four Paws, Five Directions:
A Guide to Chinese Medicine for Cats and Dogs

Acupressure, food, and herbal therapy are the corner-stones of traditional Chinese medicine, used for thousands of years. This big book provides an exhaustive overview on how you can apply the theory, diagnostics, and treatments of Chinese medicine to your pet. Twenty-one chapters, assessment worksheets, diagnosis charts, 70 photographs, and straight, clear language about the working of the five elements, the meridians, the eight principles, and the vital essences. Author Cheryl Schwartz is founder of the EastWest Animal Care Center in Oakland, Calif., one of the first holistic centers of its kind in the U.S. When it comes to medical treatments for dogs, there are basically two types of people: those who want to pop a pill, and those who want to treat the disorder naturally and understand its *cause*. An important book, and a big leap in applying alternative practices to animals.

By Cheryl Schwartz, D.V.M., 1996, 406 pp., $24.95 + UPS (CA res. add sales tax)

Celestial Arts Publishing
P.O. Box 7123
Berkeley, CA 94707
(800) 841-BOOK

When the Mother's Milk Is Missing ®

(26%) protein powder is easy to mix with warm water to provide a nourishing meal. Strong pups need to be fed every 4 hours; weak or very small pups need a meal every 2 hours. Also recommended for dogs recovering from illness, when a low roughage diet is required, and for—gasp—underweight dogs. Packed with vitamins.

Lact-a-Pet, $15.45 (14-oz. jar), $98.46 (8-lb. pail) + UPS (MO res. add sales tax)

Benepet Pet Care Products
P.O. Box 8111
St. Joseph, MO 64508
(800) 825-0341

Puppies need milk. Orphaned pups, or pups whose mom isn't making enough milk, need a milk replacement. This high

No Stooping Scooper ®

Save your back. The spring action on the bottom of this scooper opens and closes metal jaws single-handedly, without your having to bend over. Made of durable plastic with a wide handle for a comfortable grip. No need to bend. Just open and close your hand to move the scooper jaws.

Allen's Spring Action Pooper Scooper, $16.95 + UPS (NY res. add sales tax)

Four Paws Products, Ltd.
50 Wireless Blvd.
Hauppauge, NY 11788
(800) 835-0909

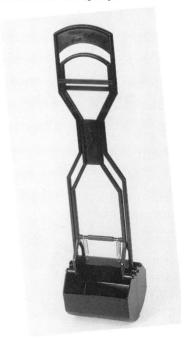

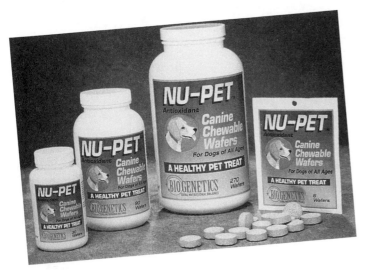

Antioxidants and Free Radicals ®

Most people who take vita-mins know about antioxi-dants. These are compounds containing vita-mins C and E and beta-carotene and selenium that help guard against disease and aging caused by free radicals—molecules with a missing electron that attack and destroy healthy cells. Antioxidants pair up with free radical molecules, thereby neutralizing their devastating effects. The principle is the same for your dog. Nu-Pet Antioxidants are chewable wafers that combine the above ingredients with bio-

guard sprouts (from wheat), beef liver (range fed, desic-cated to reduce fat, high-quality protein), and beef broth for consistent, superi-or flavor. A smart product to help you protect your dog's health. It's cheap compared to vet bills. . . .

Nu-Pet Antioxidants, $8.99 (30 wafers), $18.95 (90), $49.95 (270) + UPS
(FL res. add sales tax)

Gulf Coast Nutritionals
6166 Taylor Rd.
Suite 105
Naples, FL 34109
(800) 926-5100

A Drink for the Road ®

Traveling with a pet carrier? With lay-overs and delays a simple flight can take forever. Your dog might get very thirsty. The Lixit Dog Waterer can help him handle even the longest waits. It's an airline- and veterinarian-approved, "quick-release," locking liquid holder. The weather-resistant half-gallon bottle has a special tube tip that provides 3 times more water than portable containers.

Lixit Dog Waterer, $14.95 + UPS
(CA res. add sales tax)

Lixit Animal Care Products
P.O. Box 2580
Napa, CA 94558
(800) 358-8254

The Natural Remedy Book for Dogs and Cats

The trend in health for dogs is toward "natural" treat-ments whenever possible. The author of this book, Diane Stein, also wrote *The Natural Remedy Book for Women.* Now she applies to family pets her extensive knowledge of nutrition, vita-mins, homeopathy, miner-als, massage, and herbs. Solid advice for the holistic

dog and owner. You have many choices when attempt-ing to solve your dog's health problems, and one of the first is to read this book. Looking for a holistic vet in your area? Contact the American Holistic Veterinary Medical Association, 2214 Old Emmorton Rd., Bel Air, MD 21014, tel. (410) 569-0795.

By Diane Stein, 1995, 332 pp., $16.95 + UPS
(CA res. add sales tax)

The Crossing Press
P.O. Box 1048
Freedom, CA 95019
(800) 777-1048

TRUE DOG TALE

Reality Bites

Everybody knows this, right? Children and adults should be wary when approaching a strange dog. It seems obvious, but consider the following: In an average year more than 4 million Americans, primarily children, are bitten by dogs. The enormous physical and psychological damage from dog bites keeps the courts humming. Insurance claims alone for dog bites total more than $1 billion each year. And dog bites are among the top 10 causes of nonfatal injury in the U.S. *each and every year.* The message: Never pet a strange dog without the owner's approval, and supervise children with all dogs.

Keep the Bugs Outside

Fleas and ticks in your neighborhood? Wipe down the dog with one of these natural wipes—made of eucalyptus, citronella, Hawaiian ginger, lemongrass, and other natural oils—*before* he heads out of the house. It doesn't kill fleas and ticks, it *repels* them. Also great for skin irritations, psoriasis, and scratching problems. Pleasantly scented, safe even for puppies. Natural flea and tick avoidance. They'll wait for another ride.

K.O.S. Pet Wipes (pkg. of 25), $12.95 + $2.50 S&H
(AZ res. add 8.5% sales tax)

K.O.S. Industries
7335 E. Acoma Dr.
Suite 204
Scottsdale, AZ 85260
(708) 634-2445

Enough Barking Already!

Is your dog's barking slowly driving the neighbors crazy? Here's a solution: This techie device emits a high-pitched sound for about five seconds when your dog barks, then resets itself for the next barking attack. Dogs don't like the sound and will learn to avoid it by not barking. Use as necessary until the dog gives up the barking. Or use the device manually by pushing the button and firmly saying no when Fido starts barking. It works—some dogs get it within 2 days. A harmless solution to a very annoying problem.

Super Remote Barker Breaker, $69.95 + UPS
(CA res. add sales tax)

Amtek Pet Behavior Products
11025 Sorrento Valley Ct.
San Diego, CA 92121
(800) 762-7618
E-mail: USP@ix.netcom.com

The Eyes Have It!

Some dogs look like they've been crying for weeks, with long tear stains by the corners of their eyes. Cheer up, it's not so bad. Certain dogs, especially Boxers, Bulldogs, Cocker Spaniels, Shar-Peis, and other breeds, have a tendency to produce discharge from their eyes. No big deal: Just wipe it off with this safe, specially formulated cleaner. Also useful for cleaning between the folds of their skin.

Crystal Eye, $6.99 + UPS
(NY res. add sales tax)

Four Paws Products, Ltd.
50 Wireless Blvd.
Hauppauge, NY 11788
(800) 835-0909

Pet Allergies: Remedies for an Epidemic

Almost everyone is allergic to something. Dogs are no exception. As you might have guessed, natural products and sensible thinking may provide some solutions. It makes sense that if you eat junk foods and artificial products with poor nutritional elements, sooner or later you're going to get sick. It's very similar with your dog: If you treat her as an individual—with her own unique genetic heritage—you can carefully explore alternatives to lessen and even eliminate her allergic reactions. This interesting book, written by a vet, discusses allergy-provoking foods, the impact of improper breeding practices, and many new ideas on common dog illnesses. Seriously consider buying this book if your dog is not well, or if you are contemplating the purchase of a pedigree dog. Make an informed decision.

By Alfred Plechner, D.V.M., and Martin Zucker, 1986, 134 pp., $8 + $2 S&H (CA res. add sales tax)

Dr. Goodpet
P.O. Box 4489
Inglewood, CA 90309
(800) 222-9932

Fresh Breath, Puleeeeze ®

When Mr. Wonderful has been rooting around in the wrong food, and his breath isn't so sweet—in fact, he's burping—it's time to bring out these all-natural breath or gas-relief tablets. We've all had a weird meal or two. Same goes for the dog. Breath mints freshen breath and clean teeth, and the gas relief alleviates that uncomfortable feeling and freshens breath too. Both 2.6-oz. tubes contain 15 chewable mints. Dogs love them, so set a limit of 2 per day!

Breath-eze Breath Mints, $5.79
Breath-eze Breath & Gas Relief Tablets, $6.09
+ UPS (WA res. add sales tax)

St. Jon Laboratories
1656 W. 240th St.
Harbor City, WA 90710
(310) 326-2720

TRUE DOG TALE

Knowing What to Do

Know how to give your dog a liquid medicine? If he's been poisoned or needs a liquid prescription, here's a simple technique that works. Hold your dog's head up, tilt it slightly, and pull out the flap of the lower lip on the side of his mouth. Pour in the medicine, then let the flap fall back into place. The medicine runs between the dog's teeth and into the throat. His automatic reflexes make him swallow. It's called the "lip pocket" method. You can use this same method, if you suspect your dog has been poisoned, to administer a solution that will encourage vomiting.

Electronic De-Flea

Ultrasound is annoying to fleas. Just put this around your dog's neck instead of using all those baths and collars and powders. It's a flea collar that emits high-frequency ultrasound that can't be heard by humans or pets, causing fleas to move away from the sound and jump off your dog. The collar adjusts for fit, and the replaceable battery (included) lasts six months. Put it on, then put Fido outside so the fleas don't jump onto you!

Ultrasonic Flea Collar, $19.99 + $5.99 S&H (WI res. add 5% sales tax)

Drs. Foster & Smith
P.O. Box 100
Rhinelander, WI 54501
(800) 826-7206
(24 hours)

Hitchhiking Bugs ®

Bugs ride into the house on your dog. This natural, nontoxic spray effectively repels fleas, ticks, lice, mosquitoes, flies, gnats, and other bugs that want to make a meal out of your dog, or you. Contains only natural extracts; no insecticides; good for 8 hours of protection. Use a squirt or two before your next jaunt in the woods.

Bug Out
(8-oz. pump-spray bottle),
$9.99 + UPS
(MA res. add sales tax)

BioChemics
33 Third Ave.
Boston, MA 02129
(800) PETS-NOW

Naturally Pure ®

Espree makes simple-to-use, all-natural, effective products for your dog. Their Purity Line shampoos contain corn, coconut, and palm kernel oils that clean Pooch gently without removing the natural oils so important to a shiny coat. Tearless Hypo-Allergenic Shampoo includes aloe and ylang-ylang (flowers of flowers) from the Philippines for a fresh, clean smell. Tearless Oatmeal Shampoo (with aloe) is a natural aid in the relief of dry, itchy skin. Medicated Treatment Shampoo contains 30% aloe and a generous amount of melaeuca, which aid in the relief of flaky, dry, or irritated skin or fungus infection. Tearless Leave-In Conditioner may be applied to a damp or dry coat to revitalize skin and coat. Espree also offers two products for flea and insect control that contain neem

oil, from the Indian neem tree. Neem Shampoo with Citrus and Herbs has the pleasant aroma of citrus and herb oils. No time for a bath? Try the Neem Spray with Citrus and Herb Oils for skin problems and itchy skin. Both are good alternatives to pesticides.

Tearless Hypo-Allergenic Shampoo, $7.98
Tearless Oatmeal Shampoo, $12
Medicated Treatment Shampoo, $11.25
Tearless Leave-In Conditioner, $6.79
Neem Shampoo with Citrus and Herbs, $9.80
Neem Spray with Citrus and Herb Oils, $6.98
+ UPS
(TX res. add 8.25% sales tax)

Espree Animal Products of America
P.O. Box 167707
Irving, TX 75016
(800) 328-1317

TRUE DOG TALE

Ticks and Lyme Disease

Most researchers agree that Lyme disease is transmitted by the bite of infected ticks. New evidence suggests that it may also be passed through the saliva, blood, or urine of an infected animal. What kind of infected animal? Well, dogs. Lyme disease has been described as a "one-year case of the flu." Typical human symptoms include low energy, arthritis, a bull's-eye/concentric-circle rash around the tick bite, neurological disorders, and heart problems. Pet symptoms include lethargy, lameness, and potential heart problems. Lyme disease is treatable in both humans and pets with antibiotics. It's more common than most people realize. Keep your eyes open for ticks; keep them off your dogs; have the vet treat them if necessary. (Save any ticks you remove and show them to the vet.) Lyme disease. Contagious? Hmmmm.

Shake It and Watch

Professionals often use noise to train dogs. It's a proven method that dogs respond to noise quickly, without the negative association of physical or excessive verbal reprimand. Here's a very effective noise-training device, made to be durable and weatherproof, with a plastic case that maximizes the sound as you use it with your training. The Shaker comes with

easy instructions. Good quality, with an attractively low cost that's a good value in comparison to more expensive electronic trainers.

The Shaker, $6.95 + UPS
(CA res. add 7% sales tax)

Roger's Visionary Pet Products
4538 Saratoga Ave.
San Diego, CA 92107
(800) 364-4537
http://www.rogerspet.com

Clawful Filing ®

Long claws aren't comfortable for dog walks. While many dogs are able to wear down their claws by walking and running, sometimes you need to help by getting them clipped. Clipping is simple as long as you stay away from the quick of the nail. Start with modest claw clipping, then maintain the right length with this handy curved file. It's specially made to work with the shape of your dog's nails. Three-year guarantee against dulling.

Pet Nail File,
$6.99 + UPS
(NY res. add sales tax)

our Paws Products, Ltd.
50 Wireless Blvd.
Hauppauge, NY 11788
(800) 835-0909

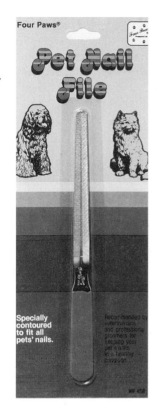

Dr. Pitcairn's Complete Guide to Natural Health for Dogs and Cats ®

Natural is best for dogs. Too many pet products are sold that are laden with chemicals, artificial colors, and preservatives—even flea-control products that use questionable poisons. This helpful book includes tips on creating a healthier environment for your dog, from special, organic diets to holistic/alternative medical treatments. Simple, practical ways to make a difference in the quality of life for both of you. A healthy lifestyle is worth a try.

By Richard Pitcairn, D.V.M., and Susan Pitcairn, 1995, 383 pp., $16.95 + UPS (PA res. add sales tax)

Rodale Books
33 E. Minor St.
Emmaus, PA 18098
(800) 441-7761

Good Dogs, Bad Habits ®

A dog that chews up your furniture, jumps on your friends, barks at the neighbors, digs up your yard, chases the cat, and drags you down the street is out of control. Fortunately, dogs can learn. But first you need to know how they think, and what works with that good brain between their ears. Jeanne Carlson is a canine behavior consultant who advises people nationwide by phone about how to solve dog problems. In this A-to-Z, easy-to-use, comprehensive primer, she provides an essential guide to understanding your dog's behavior. It will get you started.

By Jeanne Carlson with Randy Green, 1995, 252 pp., $12 + UPS (NY res. add sales tax)

Fireside Books
Simon & Schuster
1230 Ave. of the Americas
New York, NY 10020
(800) 223-2348

Feel the Field

At last! Magnetic beds for dogs! Sewn inside a quality foam pad are ceramic magnets, covered with removable, dark blue fabric. The pad is available in three sizes L small, 16″ × 16″ with 25 magnets; medium, 24″ × 32″ with 42 magnets; and large, 32″ × 36″ with 56 magnets. As your dog rests and sleeps, these magnets (according to the company) help promote blood circulation, which increases oxygen and helps reduce inflamed joints, arthritis, rheumatism, and hip dysplasia. It's called magnetic therapy. Ask your holistic vet.

Magnetic Dog Pad, $39 (sm.), $49 (med.), $69 (lrg.) + $5 S&H, additional $5 for Canadian shipments (IL res. add 6.5% sales tax)

American Health Service Magnetics
531 Bank Lane
Highland, IL 60040
(800) 544-7521

Caring for Your Older Dog

When those chin whiskers start turning white, it's time to get this book. The text begins with a discussion of aging and biology in dogs and continues on to impaired eyesight and hearing, diet, exercise, preventive health care, and elective surgery. There's no avoiding reality, but you can prepare for it. Charts, tables, and 76 full-color photographs.

By Chris C. Pinney, D.V.M., 1995, 192 pp., $8.95 + UPS (NY res. add sales tax)

Barron's Educational Series
250 Wireless Blvd.
Hauppauge, NY 11788
(800) 645-3476

Spray Everything in Sight

This 100% natural spray works on everything, everywhere. Like what? You can spray it on your dog to combat body odor, spray it on his fur to get rid of skunk odor or freshen up his bedding, or incredibly enough (according to the manufacturer), spray it in his mouth for bad breath! The possibilities are endless.

Nature's Nonscents Critter & Litter Spray
(8-oz. bottle), $6.95 + $4.50 S&H
(IA res. add 5% sales tax)

Krueger Enterprises
5057 American Legion Rd. S.E.
Iowa City, IA 52240
(800) 942-8565

The Shocking Truth! ℝ

Forget dips and shampoos and sprays. Just run this nifty electronic comb through your dog's fur. Every flea it meets gets an extremely low-voltage (1-milikolon) shock that stuns or kills the monster. The comb stops, you brush the stunned or dead flea into a bag and toss. Your dog feels nothing but a nice combing. Best on short- and medium-haired dogs, okay for puppies, too.

Flea Zapper, $49.95 + UPS
(NY res. add sales tax)

Kensington Marketing Group
145 Huguenot St.
Suite 408
New Rochelle, NY 10801
(914) 235-9300
E-mail: Kensing @soho.ios.com

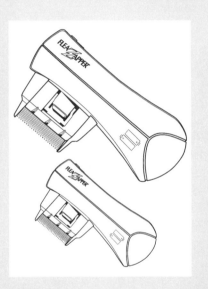

Getting Around the House

A bit slow getting around these days? It happens to the best of us. Your favorite companion may be getting older, but he still has a right to sleep on your bed, the sofa, or his favorite chair. Manufactured by WWII, Korea, Vietnam, and Desert Storm veterans in the PRIDE program, this functional ramp will help your dog get up and down to his favorite spots. It's solidly made of oak wood with stain-resistant, almond-color carpeting; 4 height settings; folds for easy storage when not in use.

Pawsway
$69 (sm. dog) + $10 S&H
$90 (med. dog) + $15 S&H
$130 (lg. dog) + $20 S&H
(IL res. add 7.75% sales tax)

Pet Care with Love
P.O. Box 764
Glenview, IL 60025
(800) 441-1765
E-mail: AMV567B@prodigy.com

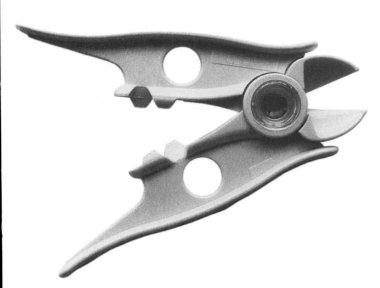

The Tick Nuisance

Ticks and the diseases they cause are a major problem in some parts of the country. You've got to get rid of them. So what makes this Tick Nipper better than tweezers? It takes about 8 lbs. of pressure to remove a firmly attached tick, but any pressure over 12 lbs. either oversqueezes the tick (which injects its fluids and any disease back into the skin) or crushes its mouth parts and leaves them behind. You want neither. This device has a self-limiting handle that gives exactly the right pressure to remove the tick, and no more. Built-in 20X microlens lets you examine the tick after removal. Small; slips easily into your pocket to take on your next hike.

Tick Nipper, $5.99 + $2 S&H
(NY res. add 6% sales tax)

Joslyn Designs
650 Union Valley Rd.
Mahopac, NY 10541
(914) 628-0364

The American Animal Hospital Association Encyclopedia of Dog Health and Care ®

Whew! Despite the imposing title, this is actually a very warm, user-friendly book. Thirteen of the 22 chapters thoroughly cover dog health, using a handy at-a-glance format to help you quickly assess symptoms. A hundred black and white illustrations accompany the text, and there's a lengthy 6-chapter discussion about caring for your dog— on basic dog care, ill dogs, caring for the older dog, and saying good-bye. Succinct overviews of each breed, including origin and history, coat and grooming requirements, compatibility with children, exercise requirements, general comments, and common ailments. A solid reference work that's good, informative reading. Not just for vets!

By the American Animal Hospital Association with Sally Bordwell, 1994, 292 pp., $25 + UPS
(NY res. add sales tax)

Hearst Books
William Morrow & Co.
1350 Ave. of the Americas
New York, NY 10019
(212) 261-6500

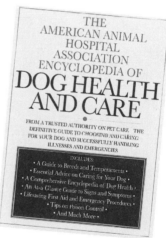

First Aid Manual for Dogs

Veterinarian Siegfried Zahn has compiled the basics of canine first aid in this modest book. He covers almost all of the intense, medical emergencies you hope never happen to your dog. Simple line art illustrates steps you should take for specific emergencies. Just the basics. Keep it in the medicine chest.

By Siegfried Zahn, D.V.M., 1984, 98 pp., $7 + $2 S&H
(CA res. add sales tax)

Univelt
P.O. Box 28130
San Diego, CA 92198
(619) 746-4005

The Valley Vet

Valley Vet Supply has a catalog packed with quality pet supplies, with a major emphasis on dog dietary supplements, wormers, topical lotions, eye care, ear care, and general health products that many vets use. And it's not all health. There's a solid selection of books and videos, plus calendars and software, ladies' dog tapestry handbags, and other gift items. Top-of-the-line grooming supplies, too!

Valley Vet Supply
P.O. Box 504
Marysville, KS 66508
(800) 360-4838

"Nature teaches beasts to know their friends."
— William Shakespeare

Vaccinations for Protection

There are plenty of weird germs out there looking to get into your dog. For protection you'll probably start with vaccinations for canine distemper, rabies, parvovirus, leptospirosis, tracheobronchitis, hepatitis, and Lyme disease. Shots start at around 8 weeks, then a second shot at 12 weeks, a third shot at 16 weeks, and yearly boosters thereafter. Ask your vet about other vaccines appropriate for where you live.

Finding Odors in the Carpet

Ugh. You know the feeling. You've just caught the scent of puppy urine, somewhere. Unless you caught her in the act or feel like crawling on your hands and knees feeling for the wet spot—or sniffing every inch of your expensive carpet—you're probably not going to find it. And if you can't find it and clean it up, the pup will probably continue to use that spot. The smell (and your aggravation) will get worse. In some instances, people throw up their hands, give up, and get rid of the pup. It might seem dopey, but actually this is a very, very important issue to many dog owners.

Pets 'n People offers a simple solution. They sell a carpet cleaner and a black light, which you can either purchase through them or rent at some pet stores. Urine shows up under black light when it won't show up under regular light. When you plug in the light (which you can also rent from a vet or pet shop), and shine it over the area you suspect, you'll see the stain. Treat it with the cleaner, and work on housebreaking the dog. Resolve the problem. Live happily ever after.

Nature's Miracle Stain and Odor Remover, $6.99 (pint), $9.95 (quart)
Black Lite, $39.95 + UPS
(CA res. add sales tax)

Pets 'n People
930 Indian Peak Rd.
Suite 215
Rolling Hills Estates, CA 90274
(310) 544-7125

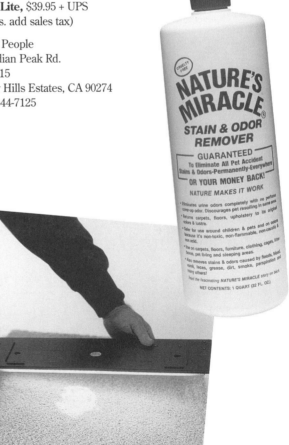

Brrrr. Let Me In!

Do you keep your dog outside in the winter? Perhaps in a nice toasty dog house with warm meals served three times a day? Well then, you certainly don't want his water to freeze. Plug in the Canine Canteen, a rust-resistant, galvanized bucket with an economical 50-watt heater. Safe, economical, works in the coldest weather, can be bolted to a wall, cordage protection against chewing, holds 2½ gallons. Makes sense for outdoor dogs in cold climates. You don't need to live in Alaska!

Canine Canteen, $89.95 + UPS
(KS res. add sales tax)

Osborne Industries
P.O. Box 388
Osborne, KS 67473
(800) 255-0316

Under the Fur

Underneath your dog's beautiful fur is pink skin that's sensitive to insect bites and irritations. This all-natural topical lotion treats hot spots, dermatitis, allergies, insect bites, callus buildup, and dry scaly skin. It provides immediate cooling relief and helps relieve your dog's urge to scratch, scratch, scratch. Two-month supply.

Skin Care for Dogs (4 oz.), $10.99 + UPS (MA res. add sales tax)

BioChemics
33 Third Ave.
Boston, MA 02129
(800) PETS-NOW

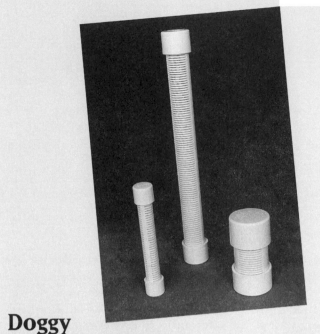

Poop Scoop

Especially handy around the yard, this backsaver lets you scoop up waste with a sturdy, long-handled tool. Simply 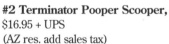 screw together the plastic handles, and you're ready to remove waste from grass or pavement. Rinse off the galvanized metal with a hose, put it away till next time.

#2 Terminator Pooper Scooper,
$16.95 + UPS
(AZ res. add sales tax)

Pet Affairs
601 E. 20th St.
Building 111
Tucson, AZ 85719
(800) 777-9192

Doggy Smell Remover

So you took the dog for a swim a week ago and the car still smells like wet dog? The De-Odor Rod contains Envirolite, a natural, volcanically charged mineral that attracts airborne doggy odors. You reactivate/recharge the rod simply by placing it in direct sunlight for one or more days. Mount one on your visor to naturally absorb wet doggy smells and all car odors.

De-Odor Rod, $10.99 (sm., 6″), $22.90 (med., 15″), $31.50 (lg., 30″) + UPS
(MD res. add sales tax)

Environmental Care Center
10214 Old Ocean City Blvd.
Berlin, MD 21811
(800) 322-1988

Understanding and Training Your Dog or Puppy

The key word here is *understanding*. The author takes you into your dog's head, so you understand how to work with your dog to instill good behaviors and correct bad ones. The physical and emotional needs of dogs are manifested in many ways. You'll learn why your dog barks, and what you can do about it. How to allergy-proof your dog. How to tell when your dog is sick or has the blues. Wonderful, sensible writing on the Heart Factor—when the heart overrules the brain—common when people pick out their puppy. Author H. Ellen Whiteley, a talented, compassionate vet, works her way from the early domestication of the dog to topics like choosing a dog, puppies, intelligence and communication, teaching, aggression and other misbehavior, sick, injured, and neurotic dogs, sex, pregnancy, and parenthood, aging, and preparing for the inevitable. Highly readable and reliable.

By H. Ellen Whiteley, D.V.M., 1996, 288 pp., $15 + UPS (NY res. add sales tax)

Crown Trade Paperbacks
201 E. 50th St.
New York, NY 10022
(212) 572-6117

Organic Flea Control

Most people would rather put a natural collar on their pet than one of those chemical monstrosities. Here's a handmade cotton collar you soak with accompanying natural flea-repelling oils. The best time to use it is when the dog doesn't have fleas because herbal collars don't kill fleas, they repel them. So first get rid of the fleas, then put this on to *keep* them away. Soak the cotton collar with the oils and put it around the dog's neck. Oil comes in a long-lasting ½-oz. bottle. Collar is fully washable. State collar size when ordering.

Flea-Free Collar and Flee! Oil, $8.95 (set) + $2.95 S&H (no sales tax in OR)

Pampered Pups Extraordinaire
647 S. 44th St.
Springfield, OR 97478
(541) 746-3801
E-mail: cavlady@pond.net

How You Can Save Your Dog's Life ®

The ideal tape for anyone who wants to know what to do in a pet emergency. Host Bernardine Cruz, D.V.M., shows you how to respond to the most common canine household emergencies: choking, fractures, heatstroke, snakebite, poisoning, drowning, frostbite, and more. Acting quickly—knowing what to do in advance—can save a dog until you get to the vet. This 45-minute VHS presentation is the best form of educational health insurance you'll ever own. Twin benefits: your dog's health and your own peace of mind. It's nice to know you can handle it, if you have to.

How You Can Save Your Dog's Life (VHS videotape), $19.95 + $3.95 S&H (CA res. add 8.25% sales tax)

Media Max Productions
9538 Brighton Way
Beverly Hills, CA 90210
(310) 285-0550

Watch My Eyes! ®

Here's a wedge-shaped slicker/brush that's ideal for grooming around sensitive areas—eyes, ears, muzzle—where a regular brush might be too stiff and hard. Constructed with an extra-soft, dense pad of wire bristles and a comfortable hardwood handle. Gentle grooming for those sensitive spots.

Sensitive Area Slicker, $6.21 + UPS (CA res. add sales tax)

Classic Products
1451 Vanguard Dr.
Oxnard, CA 93033
(800) 228-0105

Flealess Carpet ®

Fleas in your carpet are a major headache. They hide in there, hatching and hatching, waiting for you or the dog to walk by. No amount of vacuuming will ever get rid of them. This product is a nontoxic, boron-based crystal, mined from the earth. It kills fleas by dehydration, not poison. The 5-lb. canister (left) covers over 2,000′ square, the 2½ lb. over 1,000′ square. Vacuum first, then sprinkle the product on carpeting and under cushions of upholstered furniture, *not* on the dog. USDA test results document that it kills 96.7% of fleas within five days. EPA registered, guaranteed to kill fleas. No dust, no odor, no chemical poisons. Dry up those fleas.

Fleago, $19.95 (2.5 lbs.), $39.95 (5 lbs.) + UPS (FL res. add sales tax)

FleaGo Industries
3185 Van Buren Ave.
Naples, FL 33962
(941) 793-7780
http://www.fleagotj.com

Scientific Housebreaking! ®

Housebreaking a puppy used to be such a big messy deal. Now you just take advantage of your puppy's sensitive sense of smell and give a spray from this 8-oz. bottle to help spot-train her where to go. It's a smart, very simple product. Just spray, put the puppy in that area, and the training has begun. Also available in 1-oz. dropper bottle.

Puppy Housebreaking Aid (8-oz. bottle), $9.95 + UPS (NY res. add sales tax)

Four Paws Products, Ltd.
50 Wireless Blvd.
Hauppauge, NY 11788
(800) 835-0909

A Rich Dog's Shower

If money is no object, and you simply want the best grooming equipment available anywhere, look no further. The Du-Zee Hydraulic Pet Shower (top) is easy on your back—a hydraulic system raises and lowers the tub to meet your needs. Comes with either right- or left-hand plumbing ready to hook up, dog-retaining clips for bath time, a 60″ stainless supply hose, a dip reclaim system, a grate to keep paws out of the drain, and many other features. After the bath is over, blow Pooch dry on the Du-Zee Hydraulic Table (bottom), which will raise or lower to accommodate your standing, or sitting, grooming needs. Choose the

rectangular tabletop (shown) or a round or oval shape. While you're planning your grooming room, give some thought to picking up a Groomer's Chair (not shown) to make the task a bit easier. Smaller models available. Equipment the pros use for your home-grooming salon.

Du-Zee Hydraulic Pet Shower, $1,999
Du-Zee Hydraulic Table, $999
Groomer's Chair with Back, $199
+ UPS (Ohio res. add sales tax)

Du-Zee Products
309 Washington Ave.
Ravenna, OH 44266
(800) 470-4004

Puppy's First Year

Noted animal behaviorist Ann Childers helps you understand and train your pup in this 60-minute videotape. Topics include picking out your puppy, housebreaking, crating, diet, working owners, socialization, common behavior problems, grooming, and much more. Given a perfect 10-star rating by *Video Choice* magazine. Remember the first trick your dog learned? It's so gratifying to watch.

Puppy's First Year, (VHS videotape), $19.95 + $3.50 S&H (no sales tax in OR)

Media West Home Videos
P.O. Box 1563
Lake Grove, OR 97035
(800) 888-TAPE
E-mail: globalhv@aol.com

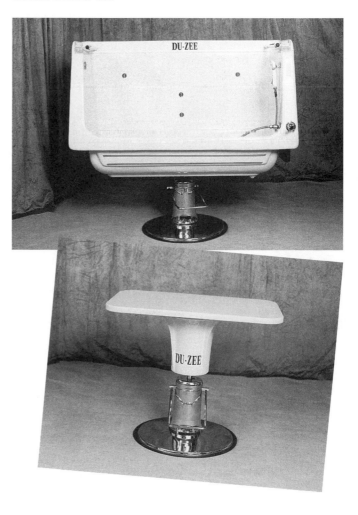

Where Do You Put the Stuff? ®

If you have a dog or two using the backyard, you have a waste-disposal problem. This product is a septic tank for dogs which works very simply. Just dig a small hole in the ground, put the unit in, drop in dog waste, and occasionally add Super Dooley Digester Powder and water. The waste is liquefied and absorbed back into the ground, below ground level, making it harmless to you, animals, lawns, and shrubs. Put it somewhere out in the corner of the yard, hidden behind a

bush. Comes with a 6-month supply of digester, uses a foot-operated lid opener, requires some very basic assembly. Unit's capacity is for one to four dogs; complete instructions included. Easy to reorder more digester, measures 17″ l. × 18.5″ w. × 4″ h. Included is the 32″ Grabber Dooley Doo Scoop, which opens with one hand to grab the stuff, has nonrusting plastic shovel blades (rinse clean with a hose), and closes automatically. Just pick it up, carry to

the Doggie Dooley, open the lid with your foot, drop it in, forget about it.

Deluxe Doggie Dooley Pet Waste Disposal System & Grabber Dooley Doo Scoop, $50.35 + UPS
(OH res. add sales tax)

Huerter Toledo
P.O. Box 346
Bellevue, OH 44811
(800) 537-1601
E-mail: dogdooley@aol.com

#2575 THE GRABBER
Dooley Doo Scoop

IMPROVED STURDIER CONSTRUCTION

IMPROVED ONE STEP ASSEMBLY

RAKE BLADE ON ONE SIDE

Owner's Guide to Better Behavior in Dogs ®

If all dogs were perfect, we wouldn't need this book. Behavior is far and away the biggest problem owners have with their pets. Here are lots of good solid suggestions—about topics from biting to barking—to make your dog less of a hassle and more of a companion. The author's easy, conversational style is accompanied by amusing illustrations about everything from how dogs think to the meaning

of their body language. Hint: Dog chewing up your favorite stuff? Dab on some Listerine (or lemon peel), but don't let him see you do it. Dogs hate the taste.

By William E. Campbell, 2nd ed., 1995, 248 pp., $16.95 + UPS
(CO res. add sales tax)

Alpine Publications
P.O. Box 7027
Loveland, CO 80537
(800) 777-7257

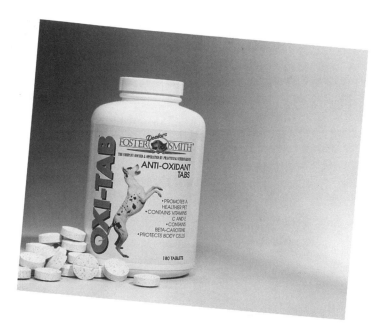

Free Radical Fighter

Free radicals are molecules with a missing electron that are linked to aging and the development of cancers, heart disease, cataracts, arthritis, and infectious diseases in living things. (Contrary to common rumor, they are not a leftist guerrilla group.) These Oxi-Tabs contain vitamins E and C and beta-carotene in amounts recommended to combat free radicals and enhance the immune system of your dog. Smart humans do the same—with vitamins—for themselves.

Oxi-Tabs, $11.99 (90 tabs), $19.99 (180 tabs) + $5.99 S&H (WI res. add 5% sales tax)

Drs. Foster & Smith
P.O. Box 100
Rhinelander, WI 54501
(800) 826-7206 (24 hours)

Dog in a Bag

Imagine washing your dog and never getting wet yourself. Sound impossible? Paul Temby of Alpha Pet has patented the system you see here. Basically, your dog stands in the tub (or outside), with the plastic liner around him. You insert your arms through special holes and give him a good washing without getting soaked. Keeps soap out of his eyes. Keeps the dog warm while you wash him. You stay absolutely dry.

Alpha Pet Doggie Wash, $29.95 + $10 S&H (CA res. add 7.75% sales tax)

Alpha Pet
4385 Shasta Pl.
Carlsbad, CA 92008
(619) 729-6543

Photograph: Julie Baker

Antifreeze? In a Dog Book?

Clear Choice Antifreeze

For some bizarre reason, dogs like the smell and sweet taste of antifreeze. It commonly drips out of radiator overflow tubes and forms that greenish liquid puddle you see on the street or garage floor. It's deadly poison to dogs; less than an ounce can kill. But nontoxic alternatives are available, such as this product, which is completely nontoxic to animals—humans and dogs—and works—according to the manufacturer—just as well as the regular stuff. The average car needs 2 gallons. Specially formulated for safety purposes, it's the smart choice for the dog, the kids, the environment.

Clear Choice Antifreeze, $9.95 (per gal.) + UPS (free UPS with 4 gals. or more) (NY res. add 8.25% sales tax)

Duratech Industries
1371-3 Church St.
Bohemia, NY 11716
(800) 322-4336

Lemon-Orange Dog ®

That's not a new hot-dog flavor. It's the clean, fresh smell of your dog after a bath with this very good citrus shampoo. Citrus cuts dirt and grease while leaving a very pleasant, orchard-fresh, lemon-orange fragrance on your dog from all-natural ingredients. Environmentally friendly—contains no phosphates. A superior dog shampoo.

Citrus Magic Pet Shampoo, $5.95 + $3 S&H (GA res. add sales tax)

Beaumont Products
1560 Big Shanty Rd.
Kennesaw, GA 30144
(800) 451-7096
http://www.citrus-magic.com

The Vet-Vax Catalog of Tonganoxie, Kansas

There are more animal products stuffed into this 140-page catalog than you could believe. Not much cute stuff, just vaccines, medications, antibiotics, a few treats, and lots of treatments. Plenty of dog stuff for the hands-on owner who wants to keep vet visits to a minimum. Vet-Vax has been doing business mail-order with steady Midwestern practicality for more than 25 years. This is a great wish book for reading by the fireplace.

Vet-Vax
P.O. Box 400
Tonganoxie, KS 66086
(800) 369-8297

Owner's Guide to Dog Health ®

A remarkably thorough overview of just about every dog illness, accompanied by useful, graphic color photographs that don't spare the details. It's intelligent and comprehensive—covering everything from diet to hip dysplasia, hearing aids to heart pacemakers, the efficacy of frozen sperm for breeding, allergic reactions, and gum disease. Of special appeal to hands-on pet owners who may need to see the actual diagnosed appearance of a canine disease.

By Lowell Ackerman, D.V.M., 1995, 432 pp., $39.95 + UPS (NJ res. add sales tax)

TFH Publications
One TFH Plaza
Third & Union Ave.
Neptune City, NJ 07753
(908) 988-8400

The Holistic Dog

Homeopathy offers your dog a health care alternative. Long recognized as a viable treatment alternative for many maladies—including anxiety, arthritis, cough, flea dermatitis, gastroenteritis, hot spot dermatitis, miliary eczema, sinusitis, skin and seborrhea, trauma, and urinary incontinence—homeopathy might help your friend. Products sold by HomeoPet originate in Ireland, are FDA registered, are cruelty free, have no chemical residue, are 100% natural, are easy to administer, are used by holistic Vets, and have no side effects. This is an interesting opportunity for you to explore treatments and educate yourself about alternative medicine for your dog. It's natural medicine. You do have a choice.

Homeopathic Dog Remedies, $14.95 each + $3.50 S&H (NY res. add sales tax)

Free brochure:
HomeoPet
P.O. Box 147
Westhampton Beach, NY 11978
(800) 555-4461

149

Grab and Toss ®

You can buy these at your favorite pet store, or you just might start to see them, free, in dispensers at thousands of parks and beaches, coast to coast. Mutt Mitts are constructed of photodegradable, biodegradable, and compostable material. When composted, the mitt degrades into humus that enriches the soil. A common-courtesy, throwaway glove that won't last a thousand years in the landfill and makes cleanup easier.

Mutt Mitt (pkg. of 10), $2.99 + UPS
(KY res. add sales tax)

Intelligent Products
P.O. Box 626
Burlington, KY 41005
(800) 697-6084

Burgers: So Near, Yet So Far . .

Underneath those burgers on the cutting board is a Scat Mat. As much as that dog would *love* to have that meat, he won't touch it. He's not willing to get shocked in the process. After a week or so of keeping a Scat Mat in place, the owner can remove it, because the dog will have learned he'll get shocked every time he jumps on the counter, or the sofa, or anywhere else you don't want him. The shock sensation is adjustable and similar to static electricity. It won't harm the dog, but it will definitely modify his behavior. Original mat is 20″ w. × 48″ l., but many sizes are available, including a semicircular design to protect your Christmas tree.

Scat Mat, $99 + $7.95 S&H
(BC res. add 7% sales tax)

Contech Electronics
P.O. Box 115
Saanichton, BC
Canada V8M 1Z5
(800) 767-8658

TRUE DOG TALE

Flea Facts II: Health Problems Caused by Fleas

Fleas are more than just an annoyance. They cause a wide range of health problems for people and dogs. In puppies, fleas can cause anemia. Adult dogs are often allergic to flea bites and may develop a nasty skin irritation called flea bite dermatitis. With dogs, a single bite can set off a highly allergic reaction with intense itching that can result in a secondary bacterial infection. Fleas that are swallowed by dogs can transmit tapeworms, which causes another set of problems. Get rid of them.

Training That Works for Your Dog

"Great men always have dogs."
—Ouida

April Frost, the highly respected New Hampshire dog trainer, gives you all the pointers necessary to teach your dog the basics: sit, stay, come, heel, wait, lie down. This 59-minute VHS tape includes great ideas on housebreaking your pup, controlling those wild emotions when friends visit, and much more. Nuts-and-bolts, plain-vanilla training that all dogs need. Wildly enthusiastic endorsement from actor Carroll O'Connor: "Right to the point. No wasted time. Dog training that really works." See for yourself.

Training That Works for Your Dog (VHS videotape), $19.95 + $4.95 S&H
(no sales tax in NH)

Lucid Media
P.O. Box 365
Etna, NH 03750
(800) 947-8236
E-mail: LucMed@aol.com

Touch for Dogs and Puppies

Linda Tellington-Jones is a gifted animal behaviorist internationally known for her abilities with animals. If your dog is driving you crazy because he barks all night, chews your shoes, chases cars, is timid or aggressive, jumps on people, is terrified of thunder or loud noises, or pulls on the leash, this is the videotape for you. Includes a super 52-page guidebook with more information and real-life stories about unique dog problems and their solutions. Highly recommended.

Deluxe Video Package (VHS videotape), $39.95 + $5.95 S&H
(CA res. add 7.75% sales tax)

Thane Marketing International
78080 Calle Estado, 2nd Floor
La Quinta, CA 92253
(800) 797-PETS
(619) 777-0217

How to Raise a Puppy You Can Live With ®

Starting out right with early training is the key to raising a good puppy into a lifetime companion. You'll find it much harder to train an older dog if you've neglected to lay a good foundation in puppyhood. So many dogs wind up in the shelters at the age of 1½ or 2 because the cuteness has worn off and the owners can't deal with adult dog behavior. How well have you done as a trainer with your new pup? Take the Puppy Tests (Come, Stroking, Following, Restraint, Retrieving, and Pinch) to predict the future. Great book for those crucial early months.

By Clarice Rutherford and David H. Neil, 1992, 170 pp., $9.95 + UPS
(CO res. add sales tax)

Alpine Publications
P.O. Box 7027
Loveland, CO 80537
(800) 777-7257

At-Home Grooming Salon ®

Using a professional groomer can be expensive. All you really need is a brush—and these fabulous, natural products—to begin grooming your dog at home. Tea Tree Spray provides soothing relief for flea bite dermatitis, hot spots, and dry skin irritations. Soothing Oatmeal Shampoo moisturizes and protects the skin, and it's perfect for itchy skin and irritations. Natural Herbal Shampoo contains eucalyptus, lavender, and horsetail for gentle, everyday cleansing and conditioning. Cedar Shampoo combines nature's most effective natural botanicals—and a strong natural flea repellent—in a cleansing shampoo. Slip on an Herbal Collar—impregnated with natural botanicals—for a fresh herbal aroma to help protect your dog before she gets fleas. Top-quality, natural care for your dog.

Tea Tree Spray, $8.95 (12 oz.)
Oatmeal Shampoo, $8.95 (12 oz.)
Herbal Shampoo, $8.95 (12 oz.)
Cedar Shampoo, $8.95 (12 oz.)
Cedar Spray, $8.95 (12 oz.)
Herbal Collar, $6.99
+ UPS (CA res. add sales tax)

Cardinal Laboratories
710 S. Ayon Ave.
Azusa, CA 91702
(800) 433-PETS
http://www.cardinalpet.com

Comb and Clip and Groom ®

Shower attention on your dog with quality grooming supplies from Oster. The Nail Trimmer has a comfortable grip and requires only light pressure to snip off those long canine nails. The red-handled Pet Comb with wide teeth helps brush out mats and tangles on longhaired dogs. The Petite Mat Comb has reversible blades for right- or left-handed users. Ideal for coarse and/or long-matted coats.

Nail Trimmer, $9.99
Pet Comb, $6.99
Petite Mat Comb, $5.99
+ UPS (TN res. add sales tax)

Oster Professional Products
150 Cadillac Lane
McMinnville, TN 37110
(800) 887-6682 (Consumer Affairs)

Training and Working Dogs

In the event you follow that sudden urge to chuck it all, leave the city or suburbia, and use your dog to raise cattle in the country, be sure to pack this book in your back pocket. Line drawings and black and white photos accompany lengthy treatises on how to "mob" (herd) cattle and perform intricate canine training methods. You know what? It's a fascinating book, even for armchair ranchers. Written by a tough, intelligent, humorous guy who spent 40 years rousting cattle on a couple hundred thousand acres outside Chinchilla, in the Australian outback. He's seen it, done it. This guy knows dogs and life.

By Scott Lithgow, 1991, 226 pp., $18.95 + UPS (no sales tax in OR)

University of Queensland Press International Specialized Book Services
5804 N.E. Hassalo St.
Portland, OR 97213
(503) 287-3093

Citrus Ugh! ®

Ever seen a dog eat an orange peel? Neither have I. They don't like citrus products, especially bitter lime. Spray this gel on furniture, wood, moldings, doorjambs—anywhere the dog has decided to chew. Effective natural deterrent.

Bitter Lime Furniture Gel, $7.95 + UPS (NY res. add sales tax)

Four Paws Products, Ltd.
50 Wireless Blvd.
Hauppauge, NY 11788
(800) 835-0909

152

Dog Camp!

You and the dog. In the mountains of California, at Lake Tahoe. Relaxing on the beach or enjoying the classes: play-training your dog for better manners, beginner- and advanced-level working clinics with trainer Patty Ruzzo, canine homeopathy and reiki "hands-on" healing techniques. Swimming, Frisbee fun, breed handling, carting, lectures, demonstrations, 32 acres of pine forest, home-cooked meals, barbecues, multiple-occupancy cabins with shared bathrooms on beautiful Lake Tahoe. A week-long summer vacation for both of you. Oh, okay, I'll struggle through it. . . .

Camp Winnaribbun,
$650 per person

Camp Winnaribbun
P.O. Box 50300
Reno, NV 89513
(702) 747-1561

Sound Control ®

I had a Beagle named Jasper as a kid, and, until his last day, at the ripe old age of 17, he would yank everybody's arm when they took him for a walk. We loved that rascal, but walks weren't much fun—he dragged us everywhere. Wish we'd had this little device back then! It slides onto your dog's leash. When he starts yanking on the leash, a loud noise blares out, startling the dog but not harming his hearing. The point? To avoid the noise, your dog will stop his out-of-control pulling and yanking and walk like a gentleman. Adjustable, weather resistant, attaches easily to almost any leash. It doesn't take forever for the dog to get the message.

The Happy Walker, $24.95 + UPS
(CA res. add sales tax)

Amtek Pet Behavior Products
11025 Sorrento Valley Ct.
San Diego, CA 92121
(800) 762-7618
E-mail: U.S.P@ix.netcom.com

The Working Airedale

The term *work* takes on new meaning in this extraordinary book about the exploits of a very popular breed that we generally think of as primarily a pet. Work? Let's talk about the Airedale as a hunting dog, livestock guardian, police dog, Alaskan trapper dog, therapy and assistance dog, and believe it or not, military dog during World Wars I and II. Dogs were used in war for thousands of years. It is said that the Roman consul Marius in the Battle of Versella was confronted by an enormous horde of war dogs. Dogs were the *deciding factor* in an ancient battle by Cyrus, king of Persia, against Alyattes, king of Lydia, in 519 B.C. So it should come as no surprise that 50,000 + Airedales assumed roles as munitions carriers, messengers, patrol dogs and most important as Red Cross or ambulance dogs in World War I, finding wounded soldiers and carrying first-aid kits. This fascinating illustrated book is probably the most extensive ever written on Airedales and other dogs in the context of work. Who would ever guess dogs had done so much for mankind?

By Bryan Cummins, 1994, 192 pp., $24.95 + $2.50 S&H (Sales tax included)

OTR Publications
P.O. Box 481
Centreville, AL 35042
(800) 367-2174

Teach Me, Please: The Basic Course

Unless you hire a professional, you're the one responsible for training your dog. It takes time, patience, and know-how. This effective, easy-to-use, 60-minute VHS dog-training program includes basic training techniques in obedience and retrieving skills, which lay the ground-work for more advanced training. This is where you start.

Teach Me, Please—The Basic Course
(VHS videotape), $19.95
(includes UPS)
(WV res. add sales tax)

Pet Avision
P.O. Box 102
Morgantown, WV 26507
(800) 521-7898

Dog Dryer

At first glance I thought this was a dehydrator for vegetables—except I noticed a dog's head peeking out the window! Maybe it's a really large hot-dog cooker? Some kind of California canine sauna? Well, it's none of the above. Here's what you do with it: Shampoo your dog, then put him inside, close the door, and he's automatically dried by warm air currents. The moist air escaping off the dog goes out the front windows, the electricity to operate the smaller unit costs about 5¢ an hour, and most important, it's impossible for the dog, or you, to be burned.

The principle behind this is a little bit of warmth and lots of air circulating all around the dog. The unit is quiet, needs no supervision, is versatile for almost any pet, and is dependable. Two-year, unlimited-use guarantee. Makes sense for multiple dog owners. How long does it take you to dry your dog with a hair dryer?

The Pet Dryer, $650 (sm., model SP-5), $950 (lg., model LS-1), $1,800 (double unit, lg., model DXL-2) + freight collect (CA res. add 7.75% sales tax)

Doggie Products of America
P.O. Box 2302
Palm Springs, CA 92263
(619) 321-7202

Wild Abandon

It exists in the heart of every dog: the urge to let fly, run far and wide, cover territory, chase everything in sight. It's natural, and it's dangerous for all dogs: city, suburban, and rural. Here are three methods of administering a mild shock to the dog when he's out of control. Home Free works with a training collar, a hand-activated trainer, and lots of wire. Put the wire around the perimeter of your house or yard, and the dog doesn't go beyond it. Models cover yard sizes from 5 to 25 acres. To combat constant barking, the small (2½-oz.) Bark Inhibitor training collar picks up vibrations from a dog's vocal cords and allows her to bark but not incessantly. Seven levels of correction—you choose how much. Works indoors or out, can be left on while you're away. The Basic Trainer is for correcting problem behavior and reinforcing basic obedience. Three stimulation levels, 50-yard range. No external antenna on handheld transmitter or receiver. Made in the USA, high quality from a very good company.

Home Free Pet Containment System
Model 200 (up to 60 lbs., 5 acres), $229 + $9.25 S&H
Model 201 (up to 200 lbs., 25 acres), $298.95 + $9.95 S&H
Bark Inhibitor
Model BC-50, $89.95 + $7.55 S&H
Model BC-100 (rechargeable), $119.95 + $8.55 S&H
Basic Trainer, $128.95 + $8.55 S&H
(IN res. add 5% sales tax)

Innotek Pet Products
One Innoway
Garrett, IN 46738
(800) 826-5527
http://www.pet-products.com

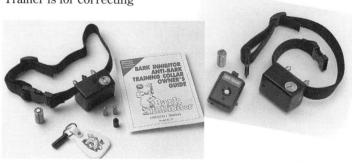

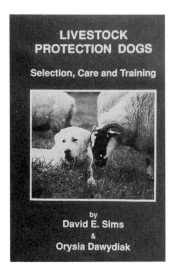

Livestock Protection Dogs

Some dogs have an amazing, innate ability to care for other animals. Consider the Komondor from Hungary, with his trademark dreadlocked coat. The Kangal, Anatolian, and Akbash dogs from Turkey, who wear iron collars with spikes for protection during combat with predators. The Castro Loboreiro from Portugal, who has been used for more than 1,000 years by shepherds. The Hungarian Kuvasz, who since A.D. 1400 has guarded man and his possessions. Well written and amply illustrated with many photographs, this book provides an impressive perspective for modern dog owners who consider their best friends to be "pets." In most parts of the world, dogs have *jobs*.

By David E. Sims, Ph.D., and Orysia Dawdiak, 1990, 128 pp., $9.95 + $2 S&H (Ala. res. add sales tax)

OTR Publications
P.O. Box 481
Centreville, AL 35042
(800) 367-2174

Please. Not So Close. ®

Doggie breath not so sweet this morning? Reach over in bed, grab the can, and give a spray from this dispenser to freshen up that breath with no fuss, muss, or chewing. Now you can show me those pearly whites. . . .

Pet Dental Breath Spray (4 oz.), $8.95 + UPS (NY res. add sales tax)

Four Paws Products, Ltd.
50 Wireless Blvd.
Hauppauge, NY 11788
(800) 835-0909

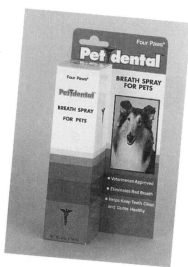

Puppy Preschool ®

According to the authors, about 8 weeks of age is the time to begin educating and disciplining your new dog. Plenty of good information on selecting the right breed of dog for your lifestyle, controlling and redirecting those puppy chewing urges, the right way to use your puppy's name (only in a positive way), selection of the bathroom spot (the first place your puppy will visit immediately upon arrival), plus suggestions on essential equipment and fun toys and, yes, how to make a special guttural, doglike growl to stop unwanted behavior. Just puppies and pictures and good information you'll use!

By John Ross and Barbara McKinney, 1996, 260 pp., $22.95 + UPS (NY res. add sales tax)

St. Martin's Press
175 Fifth Ave.
New York, NY 10010
(800) 221-7945

Safety on the Trail

Pop one of these dog first-aid kits in your backpack before your next hike with the dog. Includes triple antibiotic ointment, vet eyewash, styptic pencil, Hartman mosquito forceps, scissors, thumb forceps, self-adherent bandage, gauze bandages, gauze pads, and adhesive tape. All in a 6″ × 4″ × 2″ water-repellent, camo Cordura pouch. Remember the Boy Scout motto: Be prepared.

Camo Dog First-Aid Kit, $29.95 + $5.95 S&H (MN res. add 6.5% sales tax)

Outdoor Safety
P.O. Box 103
Winona, MN 55987
(800) 348-7602

Natural Healing for Dogs and Cats

"Natural" is the key word in this virtual encyclopedia of alternative remedies that are each and every day moving into mainstream health practice. The book explores almost every conceivable natural and alternative therapy to keep your dog healthy, from massage to herbal remedies, acupressure, nutrition, vitamins and minerals, psychic healing, homeopathy, acupuncture, flower essences, and muscle testing. Sensitive, loving, highly informed text, recommended for open-minded canine fanciers with an interest in holistic healing methods.

By Diane Stein, 1993, 186 pp., $16.95 + UPS
(CA res. add sales tax)

The Crossing Press
P.O. Box 1048
Freedom, CA 95019
(800) 777-1048

TRUE DOG TALE

Flea Facts III: Fleas, Boarding, and Health

From personal experience, I can tell you one key tip for avoiding fleas: *Be extremely careful where you board your dog.*

Fleas don't come out of thin air. Too often a dog will come back from boarding with a flea problem, simply because so many dogs that are boarded do have fleas. Taking your dog into most (but not all) boarding environments can be asking for it.

And think about this: If you're in a crowded movie theater, and somebody behind you has the flu, and they're coughing, there's a chance you might get the flu. Makes sense, right? Some dog diseases are also contagious. Is it a good idea to put your dog into a packed, dense boarding situation near other potentially unhealthy dogs?

Why not try a pet sitting service instead? Many pet sitters are bonded. They come to your house, feed and walk the dog, and give her some nice attention. This keeps her away from a big source of fleas: other dogs. And it's much easier psychologically on your dog. She stays at home in her own environment, not in a cage in a prison, where she sits awaiting your return.

To find a sitter whom you can trust, ask friends who they use. Check local listings in the Yellow Pages and local bulletin boards. It's reasonable to ask a prospective pet sitter to come to your house and meet the dog, kind of like an interview. Most will do it for no charge.

Incidentally, the cost of pet sitting is comparable to boarding your dog—often less.

Get Wet Basics!

Bath time again—already? Sure. Your dog will smell so clean and sweet after a Just Bepaws bath, you'll start looking forward to them. Start with a squirt of Eucalyptus & Peppermint Shampoo (smells good and helps discourage fleas), or rub in just a dab of Extra Gentle Shampoo. Dry your pooch with the thick terry-cloth Love My Dog Towel. Then, for a nice shiny coat of beautiful fur, work in some Coat Enhancer. Every step of the way, you're using environmentally friendly, biodegradable products with no phosphates. Great for the dog, nice for your nose.

Earthbath Eucalyptus & Peppermint Shampoo, $7.50
Earthbath Extra Gentle Shampoo, $7.50
Love My Dog Towel, $16.50
Earthbath Coat Enhancer, $7.50
+ UPS (OK res. add sales tax)

Just Bepaws
Laid Back Lifestyle Gifts
4020 Will Rogers Pkwy.
Suite 700
Oklahoma City, OK 73107
(800) 843-5242

Easy Dog Shower ®

This is one of the best systems I've ever seen for giving a dog a bath/shower/ rinse-off. Unlike those cheap versions that can blow off the faucet when you increase the water flow, the Rinse Ace installs with no tools between the shower head and the ½″ shower pipe. Just screw it on, like one of those shave-in-the-shower mirrors. Then attach the removable 6′ hose, put the dog in the tub, turn the water on, press the lever on the hose handle, and you're in business. Saves water—it flows only when the lever is pressed. A quick, easy, and intelligent system. When you're finished, remove the hose (the valve is permanently installed and does not affect normal shower operation) and store it out of sight until next bath day. Valves are sold separately for additional shower heads. Some people keep it in their shower for bathing the kids, watering indoor plants, rinsing while shaving, etc. Good quality. Giving the dog a bath can be so easy.

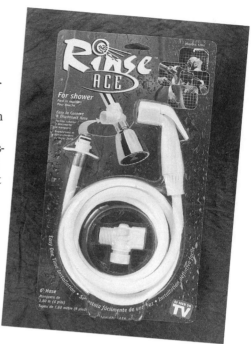

Rinse Ace, $19.95 + $4.95 S&H
(WI res. add 5.1% sales tax)

Idea Factory
W. 140 N5080 Lilly Rd.
Menomonee Falls, WI 53051
(800) TO-RINSE

Easy Paper Training ®

No paper involved! That old method of putting down newspapers to housebreak a puppy just got much, much easier and faster. How's it work? Place a training pad in the area where the puppy is normally kept. A special scent-attractant will encourage the puppy to relieve herself on the pad. Keep that up for 3 or 4 days. Next, take the puppy (and a pad) outdoors and let her use the pad outside. Keep that up for 3 or 4 days. You are now well on the way to having a beautiful puppy that will go outside. Brilliant!

No Accident Puppy Training Pads (30 to a bag), $14.99 + UPS
(NY res. add sales tax)

Real Animal Friends Trading Corp.
101 Albany Ave.
Freeport, NY 11520
(800) 654-PETS

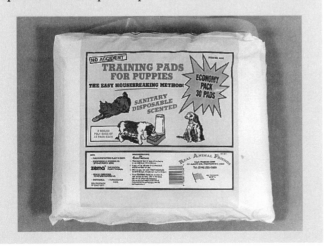

Biodegradable Cleanup

It's the law in most states—as well as plain common courtesy—to pick up after your dog. These patented, double-insulated mitts have a specially designed gusset for easy disposal of dog waste. Put on a mitt, pick up the waste, then turn the mitt inside out. Throw away both mitt and waste, and you never touch a thing. Unlike some gloves, these are bio-, photo-, and oxygen-degradable. A nice plus for the environment.

Pooch Pick-Up Mitt,
$10.25 (50) + $3.95 S&H;
$18.95 (100) + $5.25 S&H
(AZ res. add 8.5% sales tax)

K.O.S. Industries
7335 E. Acoma Dr.
Suite 204
Scottsdale, AZ 85260
(602) 905-0080

Dr. Jim's Animal Clinic for Dogs ®

Jim Humphries, D.V.M., needs no introduction. You can hear him on the radio, see him on TV, or explore his St. Francis Productions Internet site. He knows dogs and doesn't use a lot of medical jargon. In this book he provides just the facts on how to select a pet, grooming, training and behavior problems, nutrition and exercise, fleas and parasites, medicine and disease. Straight-up, friendly advice from the best media vet in the business.

By Dr. Jim Humphries, D.V.M., 1994, 286 pp., $15 + UPS
(IN res. add sales tax)

Howell Book House
Macmillan Publishing USA
201 W. 103rd St.
Indianapolis, IN 46290
(800) 858-7674

Let's Shake on It!

Bath time already? This glove's poly-grass surface works like a combination brush and sponge. Dip it into diluted shampoo, lather up the dog, then rinse. Holds lots of water while gently separating fur to clean and remove dead skin and hair. Shake to remove excess water from the glove, and hang to dry. Or machine-wash and toss it into the dryer.

Blue Grass Bath Glove,
$4.49 + $5.99 S&H
(WI res. add 5% sales tax)

Drs. Foster & Smith
P.O. Box 100
Rhinelander, WI 54501
  (800) 826-7206
   (24 hours)

TRUE DOG TALE

The Greyhound

A delightfully calm, intelligent companion that can reach speeds of nearly 40 mph, the Greyhound is an ancient breed whose likeness is found chiseled in the rock of 4,000-year-old Egyptian tombs. In some states they are wagered upon in races that use a mechanical rabbit on a circular course. The awful part of this is that after a few years at the track—and one too many second-place finishes—an appalling 50,000 Greyhounds a year are euthanized because they're not making money. It's a barbaric practice, straight out of the Middle Ages, which concerned dog lovers, shelters, and breed rescue centers are attempting to eliminate. The life of a racing Greyhound is very brief, but these wonderful companion dogs can easily live 12 years in a good home. Thankfully, some superb organizations now offer retired racing Greyhounds as family pets.

Let's Take a Look

My Gordon Setter Ruby came home one day after a run, tossing her head sideways, back and forth. She'd gotten a foxtail deep in her ear, but like a dummy I didn't realize it until several days later. We got the problem fixed, and from then on I've always checked her ears. At the time, though, having one of these professional-quality earscopes would've helped. It comes with a veterinary 4mm viewing tip and detailed instruction booklet about usage and what to do about common ear ailments. Same features as human models.

Vet Earscope, $24.95 + $2.50 S&H
(CA res. add 7.25% sales tax)

Notoco
P.O. Box 300
Ferndale, CA 95536
(707) 786-4400

Cracker Still Lives Here

The agony of losing a dog can persist for months, even years. Encouraging and supporting the expression of emotion about the loss is one of the best ways to get through it. This book empathically takes readers through feelings of grief over the loss, the anxiety of caring for ill and aging pets, how to discuss a loss or impending loss with children, dealing with sudden, unexpected loss, and a frank discussion of euthanasia. Includes a lengthy journal section entitled "Memories of My Loved One" for readers to express their own feelings. Help when you need it most.

By Susan Cummings, 1995, 94 pp., $7.95 + $1 S&H (FL res. add sales tax)

Rivers Edge Publishing
P.O. Box 7343
Fort Myers, FL 33911
(941) 332-2941

Cracker Still Lives Here

A Story of Living, Loving, and Healing
by
Connie Cummings

The Treatment of Animals

The use of animals for experimental medical work is highly controversial. The Nature of Wellness is an organization that questions the necessity of animal experimentation related to human health. Their work is solely supported through tax-deductible public contributions. They offer a 78-minute VHS documentary called *Hidden Crimes* and a newsletter, *The Vanguard*. Both offer a no-holds-barred look at animal experimentation that's factual but very heavy. Free information available as well.

The Nature of Wellness
P.O. Box 10400
Glendale, CA 91209
(800) 545-5848
http://home.earthlink.net/~supress

Hot Product for a Cold Winter ®

Next winter, consider putting Safe Paw on your sidewalk instead of rock salt. Salt and chemicals can get between your dog's toes, causing irritation. Your dog will lick his paws to relieve the irritation, ingesting those chemicals. Safe Paw is a patented mixture of pet-safe glycols and crystalline amides. It melts ice down to 0° F, and according to the manufacturer, its nontoxic formula won't hurt your dog even if he swallows it accidentally. That's why they make it.

Safe Paw, $15.99 + UPS (PA res. add sales tax)

International Performance Industries
P.O. Box 812
Richboro, PA 18954
(800) 783-7841

Easy Hose-Off ®

Washing your dog outside with a hose just got a lot easier. Fill up the clear reservoir on the Shampette with shampoo, give a quick massage with the bristles, squeeze the handle for water and shampoo, then rinse with clear water. A completely one-handed operation. For indoor use, an adapter is available.

Shampette, $36 + UPS (TX res. add sales tax)

Aquaculture Technologies
440 Benmar
Suite 1200
Houston, TX 77060
(713) 447-0205
E-mail: redseafish@aol.com

"Not Carnegie, Vanderbilt, and Astor together could have raised money enough to buy a quarter share in my little dog."
—Ernest Thompson Seton

TRUE DOG TALE

FLEA FACTS IV: FLEA CONTROL

There is no reason to resort to heavy poisonous chemicals to control fleas. That old way of doing things—dousing everything, you, the dog, the kids, with a mess of poisonous chemicals—is bad for everybody.

The Flea-Control Rule: Get Rid of the Fleas on Your Dog and Where You Live *All at Once.*

Start with your dog and other household pets. Treat all your pets at the same time, and stay with it. If you don't, some fleas will survive by jumping from one pet to another.

At the same time, treat your pet's sleeping areas, your carpets, home, and yard. View eradication of fleas as a daily commitment, a war with a pest that causes nothing but problems and will resist your efforts. Think it out in advance. Buy everything you need to eliminate fleas at one time, with one purchase.

Many excellent natural products exist for ridding dogs of fleas.

- **Natural herbal products.** Shampoos with conditioning and cleansing agents plus flea-killing and -repelling properties are very effective. Natural ingredients such as orange oil can kill both larvae and adult fleas. Essential oils of citronella, cedar, eucalyptus, and bay have been shown to be effective repellents against most insects. Dried, pulverized leaves of certain plants make excellent herbal flea powders. The safest and most effective herbal powders contain botanical pyrethrum, a product made from the dried and crushed flowers of the chrysanthemum. Many pyrethrin products contain the synergist piperonyl butonoxide (PBO) or synthetic pyrethroids, which may have enhanced toxicity and should be used cautiously or avoided. Other herbs effective in deferring or repelling insects are wormwood, rosemary, lemongrass, and rue.
- **Herbal collars.** These contain safe, natural oils that can be effective in keeping fleas off your dog. They offer an alternative to the more toxic chemical collars commonly available, and they help avoid the possibility of allergic or toxic reactions.
- **Brewer's yeast and garlic.** Many pet owners report positive results in controlling fleas when their pets are fed products containing brewer's yeast and garlic. This hasn't been scientifically proven, but then again, if it works, it works. Both can be found in specialized dog foods, dog treats, and supplements.

Healthy Dog, Happy Dog ®

The dog with a bandaged paw on the front cover sets the tone for this guide to dog diseases and their treatments. With the help of 40 full-color photos and 50 quality drawings, veterinarian Uwe Streitferdt explains most common dog illnesses and their corresponding conventional and homeopathic treatments. Includes suggested contents of a home medical kit, first-aid tips in case of poisoning, how to take care of a sick dog, and a wonderful chapter on nutrition, including how to cook homemade dog food to meet your best friend's protein, carbohydrate, fat, and mineral needs. Keep it around just in case, or while traveling.

By Dr. Uwe Streitferdt, 1994, 128 pp., $9.95 + UPS (NY res. add sales tax)

Barron's Educational Series
250 Wireless Blvd.
Hauppauge, NY 11788
(800) 645-3476

Training Your Dog: A Day-by-Day Program ®

Training your dog works one day at a time. Whether you want her to heel alongside you on a city street without a leash, or stop barking incessantly, or lay off chewing up the furniture—whatever it is will require training and a commitment of time. The payoff is a reliable dog. Many, many training tips in this 6-week program, as well as suggestions on picking a puppy, modifying behavior through nutrition, and working to turn your dog into your best friend, loyal companion, and obedient pet. The effort is always worth it.

By Kathleen Berman and Bill Landesman, 1994, 160 pp., $12.95 + UPS (NY res. add sales tax)

Sterling Publishing Co.
387 Park Ave. South
New York, NY 10016
(800) 367-9692

Sound Control

There's a strong connection between dog training and sound. You can control dog behavior (chewing, jumping on people, digging, house soiling, hyperactivity, most bad behaviors) with the careful, timely use of sound. The Dog Stopper consists of a 30-minute VHS video and two red plastic shakers from Paul Moran, frequently seen on national TV discussing the best way to train the perfect dog. At what age do you start? Around 8 weeks.

Dog Stopper, $19.95
+ $4.95 S&H
(CA res. add 8.25% sales tax)

Black Shamrock Productions
P.O. Box 4292
West Covina, CA 91791
(818) 339-9559
http://www.ultrapet.com

14,000 Animal Items

The Omaha Vaccine Company isn't just about vaccines. They have an enormous collection of health products, toys, beds, and almost everything conceivable for dogs—and other animals. This is the catalog that farm and country folks keep for their dogs, cats, horses, sheep, and cattle. If it walks and breathes and has any dealings with humanity, it's in here. Good folks, interesting free catalog for browsing.

Omaha Vaccine Co.
3030 L St.
Omaha, NE 68107
(800) 367-4444

Toothy Story ®

While your dog's noshing this tasty rubber bone, the toy is actually removing plaque and food debris from his teeth and exercising his gums. Cleverly concealed in the packaging is a 2.5-oz. tube of tasty enzymatic toothpaste. Make that chewing even more rewarding: Spread some toothpaste on the toy, then hand it back. Dogs like the taste.

Petrodex Dental Chew Bone, $15.69 + UPS
(WA res. add sales tax)

Information:
St. Jon Laboratories
1656 W. 240th St.
Harbor City, WA 90710
(310) 326-2720

Wet Deterrent ®

It's 3 A.M. The dogs (or raccoons) are in the garbage, again, and the racket is keeping you up. It's time for a brief, harmless lesson. Scarecrow is a battery-powered, motion-sensing lawn sprinkler. When animals come within its range, it briefly (for 3 seconds) squirts water from a pulsating sprinkler head up to 30′ over a 90° arc, covering nearly 1,000′ square. The combination of sudden noise and motion, plus a jet of cold water, startles unsuspecting animals, and they leave in a big hurry. Uses very little water (just hook it up to a garden hose). One-year warranty. Useful wherever you want to deter animals safely. Easy to move to another location.

Scarecrow,
$129 + $9.45 S&H
(BC res. add 7% sales tax)

Contech Electronics
P.O. Box 115
Saanichton, BC
Canada V8M 1Z5
(800) 767-8658

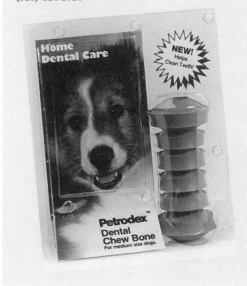

Disposable Poop Scoop Bag ®

Abandoned dog waste is more than unsightly—it's unhealthy. Roundworm eggs, which pass through the dog, remain in the ground, posing a risk to children who play in the area even when the waste has been washed away by rain. These small (6¼" l. × 4¼" w. × ⅛" thick) scooper bags include a cardboard scooping device. Manufactured in Europe from 100% recycled material and printed with water-based inks, they're 100% biodegradable. Scooper is entirely self-contained and can be securely closed after use. Slip one or two into your pocket for your next walk.

Eco-Scoop (10-pack), $3–3.50 + UPS
(CA res. add sales tax)

CGS Pet Products Ltd.
P.O. Box 491157
Los Angeles, CA 90049
(818) 981-2410

No See, No Touch Flea Collar

This is clever. The Sheath Pet Collar has a mesh pocket on its underside in which you insert the flea collar. No need to look at it, have the kids touch it, or risk losing it. Natural flea collars are healthy and effective. This sheath is a nice way to colorfully cover it up.

Sheath Pet Collar, $7.95 + UPS
(CA res. add 7% sales tax)

Roger's Visionary Pet Products
4538 Saratoga Ave.
San Diego, CA 92107
(800) 364-4537
http://www.rogerspet.com

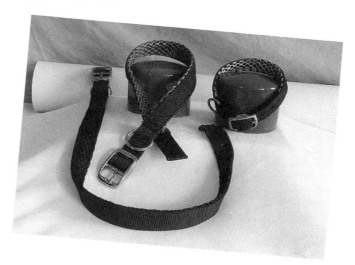

TRUE DOG TALE

Flea Facts V: Treating Your Home and Yard for Fleas

Treating your dog is the first step to flea eradication. But you must also simultaneously eliminate all stages of the flea life cycle in your home and yard. Thoroughly treat high-traffic areas and locations where your pet spends any time, especially shaded, protected areas where fleas like to incubate.

• **Inside.** Bedding should be washed and dried with high heat. Mop, vacuum and treat the basement, garage, and laundry room. Discard the vacuum bag outside, since hundreds of eggs may have been picked up during cleaning. Natural borate crystals are nontoxic and easy to apply to your carpet. They act as a desiccant to dehydrate and kill fleas.

Natural pyrethrum powders are very effective and can be used safely indoors. Apply them to floors, along baseboards, and under pet sleeping areas. Use pyrethrum indoors; it breaks down quickly and harmlessly outside when exposed to sunlight.
• **Outside.** Treat your yard with diatomaceous earth, especially spots where the dog likes to nap. This natural, nontoxic product is made from one-celled plants called diatoms. Mined from lake bottoms and dried, the inert, finely ground fossil material kills fleas by absorbing and removing the insects' outer covering.

What's the Diagnosis? Understanding Your Dog's Health Problems

You know these names. Race Foster and Marty Smith are practicing vets and the owners of the famous Drs. Foster and Smith catalog. Their very factual book is meant to educate pet owners about common disorders affecting their dog. Written in easy-to-understand language, it's *the* guide for dog owners who want to understand their choices when it comes to treatments for their dog, and who want to be a partner with their vet in choosing the most appropriate one. Fifteen chapters covering every inch of the dog.

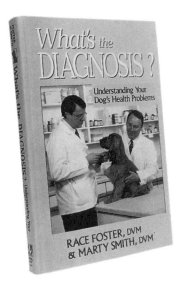

By Drs. Race Foster and Marty Smith, 1995, 278 pp., $17.99 + $5.99 S&H (WI res. add 5% sales tax)

Drs. Foster & Smith
P.O. Box 100
Rhinelander, WI 54501
(800) 826-7200

Scrambled Dog 🎲

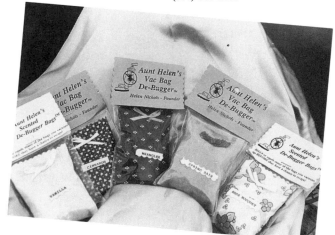

Dogs don't like weird or unusual noises. True story: One time I was walking around an oyster company near a remote bay in Northern California. A monster-sized irate dog came whipping around the corner and stopped, 5 feet from me in my summer shorts, growling, showing his teeth, and moving toward me very slowly. I talked calmly and avoided looking him in the eye; none of it seemed to work. Every step I took backward, he took another toward me. Finally, I grabbed my pager and turned it off, then back on. It emitted 5 loud beeps. I did it again and again and kept walking backward. The first beeps confused the dog and stopped him in his tracks, and there he stayed. Sound works! The Scraminal is a 3″ × 5″ rectangular dog-control device that senses motion and your dog's body, then gives a short loud blast. It resets itself and awaits the next incursion. Powered by a 9-volt battery, it's perfect for keeping your best friend off your favorite chair, away from dangerous machinery, or out of the garbage. It detects motion up to 15′ away, effectively covering an area of 3′ × 10′.

Scraminal, $69.95 + UPS
(CA res. add sales tax)

Amtek Pet Behavior Products
11025 Sorrento Valley Ct.
San Diego, CA 92121
(800) 762-7618
E-mail: USP@ix.netcom.com

It's in the Bag

If you vacuum fleas out of the carpet, they can survive the trip and wind up, alive, in the vacuum cleaner bag. They don't give up. They routinely bounce their way up through the hose, out the nozzle, and back into your house. The solution is to put one of these scented bags (mulberry, rose, cinnamon, vanilla, lavender, spring rain, or musk) into the vacuum bag. Contains an over-the-counter, EPA-approved bug killer that wipes out fleas in the vacuum bag so they can't reenter your house.

Aunt Helen's Scented Vac Bag De-Buggers, $1.75 each (1–12) + $2 S&H (VA res. add 4.25% sales tax)

Aunt Helen's Vac Bag De-Buggers
P.O. Box 386
Palmyra, VA 22963
(804) 589-1448

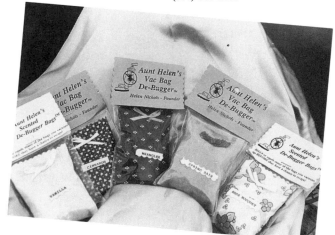

Dr. Ron™
The PET ADVISOR™

Dr. Ron on the Computer

The Pet Advisor is a powerful computer program that allows you to access information about your dog's health. Over 900 topics, including emergency information, personalized health records, a complete how-to section for at-home care, plus information on over 125 breeds. IBM-PC or compatibles, MS-DOS 3.1 or later, 1 MB RAM (minimum). Check your dog's health symptoms on your computer screen.

Dr. Ron The Pet Advisor, $29.99 (3″ disk), $44.99 (CD-ROM)
(includes S&H)
(CA res. add sales tax)

Pet Talk America
P.O. Box 9786
Bakersfield, CA 93389
(805) 834-3808

The Lost Pet Blues

It's no fun trying to find a lost dog. Driving around the neighborhood, sticking up posters, calling the nearest animal shelter, and worrying, worrying, worrying. Sign up with this service, and they send you an ID tag with a personalized number for your dog. Anybody who finds your dog can call their toll-free 800-number, 24 hours a day, and then they notify you. You can authorize the company to give out your credit card number for emergency medical or boarding costs. Special 911 service enables anyone who calls to find the nearest vet, even if their pet isn't registered with the company.

AT LAST,
911
FOR YOUR PET.

24-hour protection for your 24-hour friend.℠

1-800 HELP-4-PETS
(4 3 5 - 7 4 7 3)

1-800-HELP-4-PETS, $25
(one-year registration for 1 pet)

HELP-4-PETS
8721 Santa Monica Blvd.
Suite 710
Los Angeles, CA 90069
(800) HELP-4-PETS
http://www.1-800-help-4-pets.com

Vacuum the Dog

Thrills and chills await as you vacuum your skeptical dog for the first time! The teeth on this attachment are made of Kraton rubber, which helps to spread the fur, so the vacuum can suck up loose hair and dirt. Patented design keeps nozzle off the dog's skin. Also terrific at removing loose hair from clothing, car seats, upholstery. Fits onto any standard wand. (Adapters available for nonstandard vacuums.) Indicate your brand of vacuum when ordering.

Dogvac, $17.95 + $5 S&H

Dr. Smith's
329 Main St.
Frederickton, New Brunswick
Canada E3A 1E3
(506) 444-0004

Chapter Seven

The Gourmet Dog's Food and Drink

Thirsty Hiking Buddy

Headed for a long hike through the woods? Take along this watertight, folding water dish with a big 2-quart capacity. Made of heavy-duty nylon, it won't dry, crack, or puncture. When the trip's over, it's dishwasher safe. Colors include red, green, or blue; each with black trim and bottom.

Cool-lapsa-Bowl, $15 + UPS
(AZ res. add sales tax)

Dog Lover's Catalog:
(800) 990-9949

Cool Paw Productions
708 E. Solana Dr.
Tempe, AZ 85281
(800) 650-PAWS

Delightful Doggie Cookies ®

Yum, these look good enough for people to eat! Delicious, all-natural Carob Sandwich cookies with cream filling, and "peanutty" Peanut Butter cookies are a big snack hit with all dogs. They contain no preservatives, no by-products or fillers. Just unbleached whole wheat, pure vegetable shortening, and other selected quality ingredients. No chocolate (it's harmful to dogs), and they're lower in sugar and salt than regular cookies. Look for this company's dog cookies in the distinctive mini-Barking Bus package.

Exclusively Dog Cookies,
$2.69 (8 oz.)
Barking Bus, 99¢ (1.5 oz.)
+ UPS
(WI res. add sales tax)

Exclusively Pet
7711 N. 81st St.
Milwaukee, WI 53223
(414) 365-2933

Wacky Dog Mat and Bowl

Hey! Having some nutty fun with the pooch? Crazy art of doggy with butterfly is nutso but fun. Mat measures 12″ × 18″. The colorful bone-shaped bowl has nonskid feet and a 6″ dia. × 2½″ deep eating area. Dishwasher safe. Lighten up.

Dog and Butterfly Mat, $2.95
Bone-Shaped Dog Bowl, $4.95 + UPS
(WA res. add 8.2% sales tax)

Keller Design
P.O. Box 3854
Seattle, WA 98154
(206) 343-9515
E-mail: Petbuds@ix.netcom.com

Golden Goodies

Open the gold-foil wrapping of Lady Barkiva biscuits, and inside you'll find 100% natural carob and peanut butter biscuits made from the finest ingredients: whole wheat, rye flour, rolled oats, cornmeal, carob powder, peanut butter, vegetable shortening, nutritional yeast, and caramel coloring. Classy packaging with elegant gold-foil box and a gold bow makes this a natural for gift giving.

Lady Barkiva, $12.95 + UPS
(VT res. add sales tax)

Lucky Dog and Kitty, Too
Hunger Mountain Rd.
Gaysville, VT 05746
(800) 701-2297

Fidotastic Dishes and Treat Jars

Why slum around with cheapo dog dishes? Art Itself designer pet dishes were featured in the movie *Indecent Proposal* because the Hollywood prop people wanted the very best. High-quality handpainted stoneware with food-safe glazes make these Dog Dishes and Treat Jars jump into view. Small Dog Dish holds 2 cups; medium, 2½ cups; large, 3 cups; jumbo, 3½ cups. Treat Jar (approx. 9″ tall) matches bowl of your choice, both available in black, cobalt blue, red, green, or periwinkle on natural tan stoneware. Each is individually made to order. Many snappy designs.

Dog Dish, $35 (sm.), $38 (med.), $42 (lg.), $45 (jumbo)
Treat Jar, $42
(includes UPS in continental US)
(CO res. add 7.3% sales tax)

Art Itself
P.O. Box 12397
Denver, CO 80212
(303) 477-5423
E-mail: pcloyd@csn.net

A Cooling Drink

This is sooo cool! It's a little pet fountain that's the perfect height to provide your dog with a cool drink on a hot day. That cute small dog in the picture is drinking out of a bright yellow fountain (one of 7 available colors) made of solid "schedule 20″ steel pipe. Picture this in your back yard or—as a kind gesture—donated to a local park where dogs and people exercise. You can order the stand-alone fountain by itself, or attach the pet fountain to one of this company's people fountains. All acts of kindness are repaid.

The Pedestal Pet Fountain, $500
As an attachment to their existing fountain, $300 + UPS
(TN res. add sales tax)

Most Dependable Fountains
4697 Winchester
Memphis, TN 38118
(901) 794-4072
http://www.mostdependable.com

Humdinger Dog Bakery

At this very moment Dinger the Dachshund is cooking up a storm at the dog bakery in Naples, Florida. Bone-shaped carob Humdingers, Pinscher Pretzels coated with nonfat Parmesan cheese, onion, or garlic, and Beagle Bagels with nonfat cream cheese are a hit with any pup. All-natural, too. Beautiful color catalog with lots more tasty mail-order goodies and super gift baskets. Overnight shipping available.

Humdingers, $5.95 (½ doz.)
Pinscher Pretzels, $5.95 (½ doz.)
Beagle Bagels, $5.95 (½ doz.)
+ $5.75 S&H (orders
under $25), $7.75 S&H
(FL res. add sales tax)

Dingers Dog Bakery
2071 Pine Ridge Rd.
Naples, FL 33942
(800) 599-5829

The Dog's Dining Table

Why should your dog eat off the floor? You don't! Superb Pettables offer you a wide choice of eminently attractive canine dining furniture that's perfectly compatible with your home decor. Consider the following: Country Kitchen Pettable—decorated with a delightful dog resting on a mat—is finished in Old World crackle and warm woody earthtones in a kitchen setting. Classical Elegance is antiqued green (very unique) with warm earthy greens and honey tones. Either may be personalized with a portrait of your dog. Or choose the generic version shown. Matching bowls available with handpainting around rim. Many other design choices. Bone appètit!

Country Kitchen Pettable, $250 (M–L), $285 (XL)
Classical Elegance Pettable, $250 (M–L), $285 (XL)
Dishes (each), $6.95 (XS–S), $8.95 (M–L), $14.95 (XL)
Handpainting around dish rim, $10 (each)
+ UPS
(NJ res. add sales tax)

Millicent Cachepots
10 Leone Ct.
Glen Rock, NJ 07452
(201) 444-6098

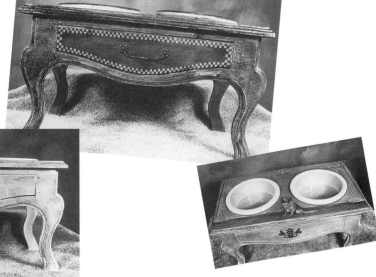

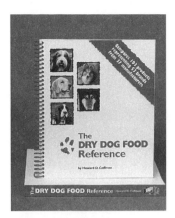

The Dry Dog Food Reference

It's amazing how people scrutinize food labels but don't have a clue about the ingredients in their dog's food. It is worth knowing. Exactly what is fish meal, egg product, meat by-products, poultry by-product meal? This exceedingly well-researched book (by a company with a very odd name) compares and analyzes 193 products representing 53 brands from 37 manufacturers. Think of it as the Consumer's Encyclopedia of dry dog food. Easy to use, with numerous cross-references examining everything from ingredients to nutrients, preservatives, food energy comparisons, feeding guidelines, price comparisons to calculate daily feeding costs, and more. Read your dog food bag lately? Do you know what that stuff is?

By Howard D. Coffman, 1995, 239 pp., $30 + $5 S&H (no sales tax in NH)

PigDog Press
427-3 Amherst St.
Suite 331
Nashua, NH 03063
(800) 775-0712, ext. 6111

Recycled Water and Fresh Food ®

You can do your part to help the environment by recycling a 2-liter soda bottle. Simply remove the label, fill it with water, and screw it into this self-dispensing water-dish-with-food bowl. Plus both bowls are removable for easy cleanup, and dishwasher safe. Unbreakable under normal use, and the price is right!

Food-n-Drink, $5.99

Stylette
P.O. Box 190
Oakdale, PA 15071
(800) 752-5650

Gourmet Sauces with a Cookie Dessert ®

All-natural Toppers are a lively addition to ordinary dry food. Pour on the roast turkey, chicken teriyaki, rack of lamb, or veggie marinara to perk up the interest of even the most jaded dog! Sauces contain no preservatives, artificial colors, or flavorings. A nice change, especially helpful if you're switching your dog to dry dog foods or changing brands. As a treat, follow up Pup's dinner with a Bear Bite cookie in chicken teriyaki or rack-of-lamb flavor. Dessert, too?

Toppers Gourmet Sauces for Dogs, $3.99 each
Toppers Bear Bites for Dogs, $1.99 + UPS (no sales tax in Ore.)

Toppers
14340 S.E. Industrial Way
Building B
Clackamas, OR 97015
(800) 973-6444
E-mail: info@toppers.com
http://www.awa.com/pets/

Those Montana Gourmutts

Melinda Maurisak and Jack, her "Gourmutt" chief taster, do their baking in Billings, Montana. They make some of the very best natural treats, all beautifully packaged. Odds are you don't have the time, recipes, ingredients, or inclination to do a whole lotta bakin' for the dog, so let her do it for you! Big Sky Buffalo Style Biscuits with Wooden Gift Box are buffalo-liver flavored, crunchy hexagonal biscuits that are irresistible to dogs. The Birthday Gift Box is practical and amusing: a huge cookie bone with Happy Birthday icing, 2 candles, 2 cookie cowboys, 2 hydrants, and some tasty crackers. Go first class with the 1-lb. Luv-a-Liva assortment packaged in a hand-thrown-porcelain Treat Jar with Lid you'll keep forever. All make great, unusual gifts, and the presentation—wooden boxes with handsome wrapping—adds to the occasion. She does it right.

Big Sky Buffalo/Wooden Gift Box (assorted treats), $14.99 + $3.95 S&H
Birthday Gift Box, $9.99 + $3.95 S&H
Blue Treat Jar with Lid (1 lb. Luv-a-Liva Crackers), $44.99 + $6.95 S&H (no sales tax in MT)

Gourmutt-Doggie Delights
510 Fourth St. West
Billings, MT 59101
(800) 4GOR-MUT (446-7688)

Animal Talk

Ever wondered what your dog/cat/giant tortoise, etc., is thinking? This book is devoted to what the author calls "tried and true telepathic communication techniques" to transform people's relationships with other species on all levels—physical, mental, emotional, and spiritual. Rather extraordinary stuff. Requires a big open mind. But is it really that strange? Most people talk to their pets, and perhaps nonverbal telepathic communication is possible between most living things. The only way to know is to try it yourself. The official road map to your pet's mind.

By Penelope Smith, 1995, 96 pp., $8.95 + $2.50 S&H (CA res. add 7.25% sales tax)

Pegasus Publications
P.O. Box 1060
Pt. Reyes Station, CA 94956
(800) 356-9315

TRUE DOG TALE

Natural vs. Unnatural Dog Foods

Read your dog food label lately? You've probably noticed the phrase "contains meat by-products." What the heck is that? If you really want to know: "tissue from dead, diseased, or disabled animals, including hair, hide, beaks, feathers and hooves." Is that something *you'd* eat? So why would you feed it to your dog? And nonnatural dog foods often include sodium nitrite, a preservative and coloring agent also found in hot dogs, bacon, and treated meats to give the product a reddish "meaty" tint. The color is added for you, for the sake of appearances, since most dogs appear to have only limited color perception.

Fortunately, you have a choice. All-natural dog foods contain no by-products, artificial preservatives, colors, or flavors; no sugar, and no nitrates; and they use vitamins C, D, and E to preserve the food, instead of the chemicals BHA, BHT, and benzoic acid. High-quality natural dry and moist dog foods are available at many retail stores and through mail-order sources. In this day and age it's completely unnecessary to feed chemically manufactured dog foods to your best friend.

One Bite at a Time 🎲

That's the way your dog will nibble these delicious peanut butter, garlic/chicken, or garlic/beef flavored cookies. Healthy ingredients include whole wheat flour, and no preservatives, by-products, added salt, or processed sugar. Only human-grade ingredients are used. Thirty cookies in each box. They won't last long!

Lov Bitez, $4.99 + UPS (TX res. add sales tax)

PetLink
13164 Memorial Dr.
Suite 134
Houston, TX 77079
(713) 973-8280

Heavy-Duty Dog Bowls

This solid handmade ceramic dog bowl is painted with your choice of a whimsical tennis ball or pawprint in the bottom. Matching painted rim and pawprint on the outside. Bowl is extra heavy for eaters who like to push it around, in your choice of navy blue, forest green, ruby red, or yellow and black tennis ball. Allow 2–3 weeks for shipping. Ask to have your dog's bowl personalized with his name.

Handmade Dog Feeder, $17 (sm.) + $6 S&H; $25 (med.) + $7 S&H; $35 (lg.) + $8 S&H; + $5 for personalization (GA res. add 6% sales tax)

Melia Enterprises
2103 N. Decatur Rd.
Suite 222
Decatur, GA 30033
(404) 315-6377

Living with More than One Dog

Sounds like a good idea to me. Especially in the country, lots of people own multiple dogs. But it can present a quandary to city folks with limited space. This modestly illustrated but helpful book, written by a dog-obedience instructor, tells what happens when dogs bunch up into groups, and it explains your role as the top dog. If you have more than five dogs, you can expect them to evolve into two separate dog packs that might or might not get along. There are right and wrong ways to add a companion to the life of your best friend, and it doesn't always work. Can you imagine returning a dog to the shelter or breeder because your dog and the new dog can't get along? Here's how to avoid that.

By Carol Cronan, 1995, 160 pp., $12.95 + $3.95 S&H
(WA res. add sales tax)

Canine Potentials Publishing
3979 E. Nixon Lane
Clinton, WA 98236
(360) 341-0581

Direct Book Service:
(800) 776-2665

Natural Liquid Aloe ®

Aloe vera has been called the "miracle plant." Used for centuries for healing, just a teaspoon a day in your dog's water adds vitamins, minerals, and amino acids. 100% natural aloe vera, comes in a tasty beef flavor. A natural pick-me-up for your dog; concentrated; 1-pint (30-day supply) size.

Aloe Vera Pet Drink (pint), $14.95 + $4.95 S&H
(CA res. add 8.25% sales tax)

Protect-a-Pet
P.O. Box 7547
Beverly Hills, CA 90212
(800) 835-9899

Clear Ears, Quiet Meal

What is this? A hot-water bottle for the dog's head? Some kind of inflatable life preserver? A backpack you stick around Rover's neck to carry kibble on long walks? Actually, it's a set of Ear Bibs. Slip 'em over your dog's ears, and it keeps them from getting wet and messy while he gobbles dinner! Indicate your dog's breed and head diameter at midear when ordering. Machine wash and dry. Long style shown. Presumably, wearing these, the dog also gets to eat in peace. Great for noisy households!

Ear Bibs, $8.95 + $2.95 S&H
(no sales tax in OR)

Pampered Pups Extraordinaire
647 S. 44th St.
Springfield, OR 97478
(541) 746-3801
E-mail: cavlady@pond.net

"A dog coming and staying in your house is an omen of wealth."
—Chinese proverb

Working Late?

Nobody wants their dog to go without a meal or water. If you're running late, that might happen. But there's no need to worry with this combo. Uses any recycled, cleaned, 1- or 2-liter soda bottle. Just fill the bottle with water and snap it next to the food bowl. Stable, wide, nontip base; convenient for trips and vacations, too!

Pet Bowl Food 'n Fountain, $5.95+ UPS
(IL res. add sales tax)

Molor Products Co.
1350-A Shore Rd.
Naperville, IL 60563
(800) 969-6656

TRUE DOG TALE

Dog Food Tales—Fat

I'm not sure you really want to know this, but you *should* know it. Much of the animal fat that's contained in both dry and wet dog foods is what's left over from the meat processing business—meaning fat and other meat products that are deemed unfit for human consumption. Because all meat products (including fat) spoil, they can be heavily treated with preservative chemicals such as ethoxyquin, BHA, and BHT. Your dog could be eating a chemical stew that's not only bad for him but very difficult to digest. Heavily preserved fat and meat products cause a range of problems in dogs: digestive upsets, vomiting, gas, bad breath, and diarrhea. Check out the natural choices.

Fresher Dry Food ®

Open that dry food bag every day, and eventually the food gets stale. One good solution is to pour a few pounds of food into this Lixit Dry Food Feeder. Just fill it up once a week, and your dog always has fresh food for nibbling.

Lixit Dry Food Feeder,
$9.95 + UPS
(CA res. add sales tax)

Lixit Animal Care Products
P.O. Box 2580
Napa, CA 94558
(800) 358-8254

Just Add Water

Warm up the oven, you're about to start baking. You'll have fun and probably save money, too, with this Gift Pack of Woofer's Dog Biscuit Mix. Contains no added salt or fat, no cornmeal, no sugar, just add water to make the dough. The biscuit cutter (for shaping the dough) and a cool stuffed dog toy, with bone-shaped tag, complete the package. Home-baked goodies for a friend.

Gift Pack: Woofers, Biscuit Cutter, and Toy with Tag, $20 + UPS
(OK res. add sales tax)

Just Bepaws
Laid Back Lifestyle Gifts
4020 Will Rogers Pkwy.
Suite 700
Oklahoma City, OK 73107
(800) 843-5242

Take Your Pet USA

The dog on the cover says it all. Traveling with your dog (or any pet) is getting easier, according to this travel guide. This enthusiastic book (in its 5th printing) contains detailed alphabetical listings by state and city of 4,000 hotels across the country that admit four-legged guests. Includes notations about on-site exercise areas, local vets, and outdoorsy attractions of interest to both man and beast. Did you know that Hawaii has a 120-day quarantine waiting period on all arriving pets? FYI: The Marriott Long Wharf hotel in Boston likes dogs but absolutely cannot stand snakes, so don't try to check in with one curled around your neck!

By Arthur Frank, 1995, 320 pp., $11.95 + UPS
(MA res. add sales tax)

Artco Publishing
12 Channel St.
Boston, MA 02210
(800) 255-8038

So Many Ways to Eat! ®

Recommended by vets and breeders, elevated bowls allow dogs to eat without gulping in extra air, which can cause bothersome gas. OurPet's Big Dog Feeder (left) includes 2 stainless steel bowls. Fill the legs with sand, if you like, to prevent tipping if you have a rowdy eater. Easy cleanup and disassembly for travel. OurPet's Cat and Dog Feeder is for smaller dogs and includes room for 2 stainless steel bowls. The reservoir below the bowls can be filled with cold water and ice cubes to keep food fresh (also automatically keeps water bowl filled). Easy cleanup, and with the plastic snap-on lids you can store or move it with the food and water intact. Earthtone recycled plastic for indoor/outdoor use. OurPet's Flexo Feeder works like an accordion, expanding in height from 10″ to 22″. Extended, it can be used as a food storage container to keep food fresh. Comes in an attractive plastic with a "gray stone finish" and a dark blue top, for indoor/outdoor use. Nice idea, especially for older dogs with arthritis.

OurPet's Big Dog Feeder, $42.95 (10″ h.), $45.95 (16″ h.)
OurPet's Cat and Dog Feeder, $19.95 (5¼″ h.)
OurPet's Flexo Feeder, $29.95 (10″–22″ h.)
+ UPS (OH res. add sales tax)

Virtu
1300 East St.
Fairport Harbor, OH 44077
(800) 565-BOWL

Who's Your Best Friend?

Show your love with this classy Loyal Friend glazed ceramic dog bowl. Wide lip with recessed, glazed design functions as a handle for easy care and keeps the dog's ears out. Two sizes: 6″ dia. with 1½-cup capacity, 10″ dia. with 8-cup capacity. Dishwasher safe; rich dark blue or hunter green colors. Superior quality.

Loyal Friend Dog Bowl,
$20 (sm.), $32 (lg.)
+ $5.25 S&H each
(IL res. add 8% sales tax)

Baxter and Charming, Ltd.
11 W. Main St.
Carpentersville, IL 60110
(800) 569-2761
E-mail: Baxterpets@aol.com

The Encyclopedia of the Dog

A dog owner's library should contain, at a bare minimum, two books—one health and emergency book, and this superbly photographed hardcover coffee-table book that illustrates, through photographs and charts, almost everything there is to know about dogs. Includes the history of the dog, from evolution to human companion more than 12,000 years ago; canine body language; and gorgeous pictures of hundreds of dog breeds, from primitive to domestic. Authoritative facts, figures, pictures, visual beauty, and design. It doesn't get much better than this.

By Bruce Fogle, D.V.M., 1995, 312 pp., $39.95 + UPS (NY res. add sales tax)

Dorling Kindersley Publishing
95 Madison Ave.
New York, NY 10016
(212) 213-4800

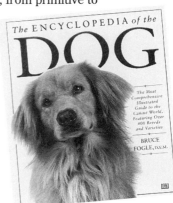

THE ENCYCLOPEDIA of the
DOG
The Most Comprehensive Illustrated Guide to the Canine World, Featuring Over 400 Breeds and Varieties

BRUCE FOGLE, D.V.M.

Rover's Own Treat Jar

Custom treat jar features artwork depicting the breed of your choice. Holds nearly 2 quarts of treat goodies. Detailed, intricate artwork on the front of each container. Made of heavy-duty glazed stoneware with an airtight seal, 6½″ dia. × 10″ h. in white. Be sure to specify the breed you want when ordering.

Breed Treat Jar, $32 + $5.95 S&H
(TX res. add 7.25% sales tax)

Accessory Pet
5836 Pathfinder Trail
Plano, TX 75093
(888) 558-7387

3-in-1 Feeder ®

This smart feeder combines a food scoop with a water bowl and a food bowl. Fill the scoop, place it on the post, and you instantly have an ant- and slug-proof feeding bowl. Large (¾-gal.) water capacity; 5-year replacement warranty; nontoxic and dishwasher safe; sun-resistant commercial-grade plastic. Available in black (shown) and ivory. High-tech look.

Three-Way Pet Feeder, $12.95 + UPS
(TX res. add sales tax)

Cinco Plastics
2409 Sabine St.
Houston, TX 77007
(713) 863-7632

> *"Dogs laugh, but they laugh with their tails."*
> —Max Eastman

Senior Years: Understanding Your Dog's Aging Process ®

We all get old—if we're lucky. It's nice to know what to expect as we, and our pets, age. Using a biomedical approach, this book explores aspects of aging and diseases common to aging dogs. It's a bit more complex and technical than some health books, but the author puts scientific terms into easy-to-understand language. There are many things we can do for our pets to help extend their lives. Think of this book as a look ahead for your middle-aged dog and a helpful resource for your older dog.

By Drs. John and Suzanne Hampton, 1993, 236 pp., $25 + UPS
(WA res. add sales tax)

Howell Book House
Kineto Press
P.O. Box 1080
Monroe, WA 98272
(360) 794-4019

Janet's Bakery ®

The pet industry is one giant but tiny business. Everybody knows what everybody else

is up to because their business and survival depends upon it. In this world, Janet Salimbene is considered a pioneer of organic, healthy biscuits for dogs, natural dietary supplements, and herbal flea control products. Her company, Wow-Bow, offers the highest-quality dog biscuits made from stone-ground whole wheat, fresh garlic, yeast, parsley, and eggs from free-range chickens. From her start in a garage more than eight years ago, she's kept the vision: organic, healthy food for pets without the chemicals,

pesticides, and additives found in many of the pet foods derived from factory farm animals. Dogs gobble these tasty, healthy goodies, and it's nice to know that pets, profits, and ethical philosophy can co-exist. Ask for them in better pet stores and health food stores.

Wow-Bow Health Biscuits, $4.95 (1 lb.), $19.50 (10 lbs.)
Gourmet cookies, $5.95

Wow-Bow Distributors
13 B Lucon Dr.
Deer Park, NY 11729
(800) 326-0230

Big Thirst Bowl ®

With a 14″ diameter and 2 recycled 2-liter soda bottles, this bowl should keep your dog in water for at least 4 days. It works on a vacuum principle: Water trickles down into the bowl as it's used. Cool idea: Put a couple of used soda bottles in the freezer ⅔ full of water. On a hot summer day, the cold water will drip down for a refreshing doggy drink. The bowl won't tip; with 2 full bottles it weighs nearly 10 lbs.! What a price!

Drip-Free Dog Fountain Self-Waterer, $6.49 + UPS (IL res. add sales tax)

Molor Products Co.
1350-A Shore Rd.
Naperville, IL 60563
(800) 969-6656

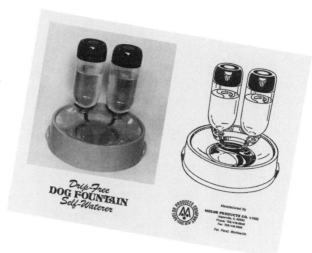

TRUE DOG TALE

Dog Food Tales—Artificial Color

That pleasing meaty-pink color of your dog's wet or dry food is just an illusion created for you, the buyer. No law says a manufacturer has to list artificial colors on the bag. So what you get is sodium nitrite, a coloring and preservative agent widely suspected to be a carcinogen. And then there's the coal tar dyes: blue #1 and 2, yellow #5 and 6, red# 3 and #40, and others synthetically manufactured from chemicals that are about as natural as gasoline. Some of these might be in your dog's food. While not all dog food manufacturers use these artificial colors—especially makers of "premium" dog foods—you won't be able to tell from the bag unless the manufacturer specifically says they don't use them. Many dog food companies have toll-free, 800-numbers you can call. Take a minute. Call and ask what's in the bag or can.

Bones Everywhere!

Having a light evening snack? Try serving these homemade bone treats on a bone-shaped placemat, followed by some kind words and petting. The Barker's Dozen collection contains 13 all-natural, large bone snacks. Or serve small, puppy-sized all-natural treats from the Bowser Bones bag. All bones are packaged in a reusable tin that opens and closes easily. If you want to bake your own bones, the Kanine Kitchen homemaker's recipe for all-natural bone treats includes a copper cutter in the shape of a bone. Packaged in a reusable clear plastic case with a tartan ribbon. Provide the perfect setting for your dog's treats with the Bone Mealmat in a beautiful dog tapestry fabric. Has an inner lining to soak up any accidents from the water bowl. Available in hunter or navy. Healthy food and an attractive setting. Candles, anyone?

Bowser Bones, $5.50
Barker's Dozen, $11
Kanine Kitchen, $11
Bone Mealmat, $16
+ $4.50 S&H ($1 for each addl. item)
(IL res. add sales tax)

Creature Comforts
Tyler and Russell, Ltd.
357 W. Erie St., 2nd Floor
Chicago, IL 60610
(312) 266-0907

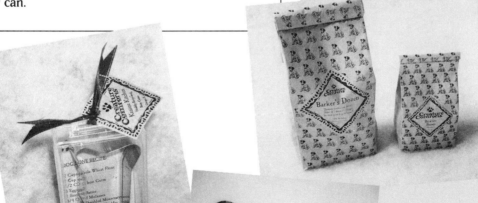

Café Dining ®

Cool Le Pet Café opens when your dog stands on the mat. Up goes the clear plastic lid, and it's mealtime. Down it goes when he's finished eating. Protects against flies, bugs, and birds, easily operated by dogs, two removable feeding bowls (dishwasher safe), smooth, effortless operation indoors or out.

Le Pet Café,
$34.95 + UPS
(CA res. add 7.75% sales tax)

Creative Pet Products
3140 Redhill Ave.
Suite 260
Costa Mesa, CA
92626
(800) 323-3251
http://www.buydrtv.com

What's for Dinner? ®

It's mealtime. Your dog looks up at you. He's thinking: "*I hope it's not the same old thing. You know—the dry food you've been serving me for YEARS that I have to eat because that's all there is.*" How would *you* like to eat the same bowl of cereal, twice a day, for ten years? Why not add some taste and lots of healthy vitamins with this gourmet gravy? Just pour it on dry food. It adds flavor, vitamins, minerals, and oils that most dog foods don't provide. Original lamb and poultry, or new hearty beef and liver flavors. Your dog will love the new menu!

Gravytime Gourmet Gravy, $4.89 + UPS
(VA res. add sales tax)

New England Serum Company
(800) 637-3786

Grateful Pet
P.O. Box 12064
Richmond, VA 23241
(800) 472-8984

Indestructible Happy Bowl

Contemporary stainless steel bowl with nonskid backing is for dogs of true pedigree. Features an embossed bones design on top, and offers all the benefits of stainless steel. Beautiful clean lines, 5¾″ dia. with 2½″-deep eating area. This just plain looks good. That's enough for me. Wrap it up!

Large Stainless Steel Bowl,
$14.95 + UPS
(WA res. add 8.2% sales tax)

Keller Design
P.O. Box 3854
Seattle, WA 98154
(206) 343-9515
E-mail: Petbuds@ix.netcom.com

Icey Bones ®

It's hot. You, the kids, and the dog need to cool off. Reach into the freezer for a nice frozen treat everyone can enjoy. Since you get two **Pup-i-Cool** trays in a package, the kids can have frozen pops and the dog gets fun, bone-shaped party ice for her water bowl.

Recipe booklet has twenty ideas for tasty frozen doggy delicacies.

Pup-i-Cool, $4.49 + $3 S&H
(CA res. add 8.25% sales tax)

Perfect Pet Products
24735 Ave. Rockefeller
Valencia, CA 91355
(805) 294-2266

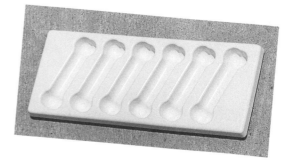

A Celebration of Rare Breeds, Vols. 1 & 2

There are more than 400 recognized dog breeds, many of which we rarely see in this country. These 2 remarkable volumes provide overviews, photographs, breed history, and behavioral analysis for 68 of the rarest breeds. It's a valuable reference work for anyone interested in learning more about or acquiring any of these unusual dogs. Ever heard of the Argentine Dogo, the Canaan Dog, the Castro Loboreiro, the Catahoula Leopard Dog, the Fila

Brasileiro, the Glen of Imaal Terrier, the Hovawart, or the Karelian Bear Dog? Neither had I. Now you can. These books will open your eyes to the incredible world of dogs.

Both by Cathy J. Flamholtz
Volume 1, 1986, 214 pp., $24.95 + $2.50 S&H
Volume 2, 1991, 208 pp., $24.95 + $2.50 S&H
(AL res. add sales tax)

OTR Publications
P.O. Box 481
Centreville, AL 35042
(800) 367-2174

Bonedango's Two-Minute Dog Crackers

Two minutes. That's how long it takes to bake 6 fresh dog crackers with this mix in your microwave oven. "Chewse" a texture—moist and chewy or crisp and crunchy—and enjoy the savory flavors of tomato, herbs, and garlic wafting through the air. All-natural ingredients include wheat flour, cornmeal, wheat bran, whey powder, tomato powder, garlic powder, natural flavor, salt, parsley, baking soda, and brewer's yeast. Easy to prepare, tasty dog goodies. Package makes 18 medium, bone-shaped crackers. Complete with nifty bone-shaped cookie cutter! Suddenly all the dogs in the neighborhood start arriving.

Mr. Bonedango's Dog Cracker Mix, $4.50 + UPS (CA res. add sales tax)

Love-n-Fun Foods
P.O. Box 7101
Fullerton, CA 92634
(714) 632-1595
E-mail:
foodtech@ix.netcom.com

A Bowl for Every Dog

These colorful, handpainted, heavy ceramic bowls from Color Pet Products are dishwasher and microwave safe. Completely nontoxic, with 100% lead-free glazes. Available in two sizes with 5 color

combinations, each features a raised "no sweat" bottom. The wide and low design helps prevent tipovers. Made in the USA since 1989.

Handpainted Dog Bowls, $17.80 (sm. 6″ × 2¼″), $22.50 (lg. 8″ × 3″) + UPS (NC res. add sales tax)

Color Pet Products
210 Old Dairy Rd.
Suite F
Wilmington, NC 28405
(800) 849-0276

The Consumer's Guide to Dog Food

"You are what you eat." It's an old refrain, and it makes sense. Question of the day: Is there some reason why food is the number-one business in this country—we all have to eat—and medicine is the second largest? Are the two related? It's good to see this book, because for too long people have blindly accepted food standards for their pets that often incorporate artificial ingredients, colorants, preservatives, and a stew of nasty by-products. An excellent start to finding out exactly what's in your pet's food. If you read labels, read this book. Straight information on what your dog is eating for dinner. It will surprise you.

By Liz Palika, 1996, 120 pp., $9.95 + UPS
(IN res. add sales tax)

Howell Book House
201 W. 103rd St.
Indianapolis, IN 46290
(800) 428-5331

Smoked Chewing Goodies ®

Smokehouse, a company serving cooked and smoked meats to the food trade, now makes smoked dog treats—all kinds and sizes of smoked bones, chew sticks, and other smoked products. All are slowly roasted for up to 40 hours (cooking out most of the fat), smoked with real hickory wood (leav- ing no bitter aftertaste or oils), and packaged so you can surprise your dog with a great big tasty chew stick.

Smokehouse Dog Treats
17 W. Magnolia Blvd.
Burbank, CA 91502
(818) 845-4807

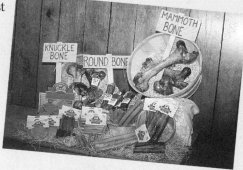

The Australian Shepherd: Champion of Versatility ®

Any owner of one will agree—pound for pound, the Australian Shepherd is one of the most intelligent and train- able dogs on earth. Lovingly written by pet author and columnist Liz Palika, the book is packed with tons of cute black and white and color pictures. It begins with the selec- tion of an Australian Shepherd puppy and moves on to train- ing, care, and health, with a special emphasis on breeding considerations. Historically, a gentleman cowboy named Jay Sisler introduced Aussies into America, taking his "blue dogs" around to rodeos in the 1950s and 1960s, where they amazed crowds with tricks like standing on their heads, bal- ancing on boards, jumping ropes, and climbing ladders. These superbright, fabulous companions radiate optimism and joy. Simply the best book for anyone considering an Aussie. Includes a sample puppy sales contract.

By Liz Palika, 1995, 222 pp.,
$29.95 + UPS
(IN res. add sales tax)

Howell Book House
201 W. 103rd St.
Indianapolis, IN 46290
(800) 428-5331

No-Water Worries ®

Now you'll never drive away wondering, "Does the dog have water?" I've used one of these for the past year. Just fill up this sim- ple, automatic, gravity-feed drinking system with fresh water, and the dog's covered. Hot weather? Fill up a bottle, and pop in the fridge/freezer at night for a cool drink during hot summer days. Durable indoor/outdoor use, antitip, antispill base; slate blue, mauve, or almond colors. Five-year warranty.

Water Fount, $5.96 (16 oz.), $7.80 (32 oz.) + UPS
(CA res. add sales tax)

Lixit Animal Care Products
P.O. Box 2580
Napa, CA 94558
(800) 358-8254

Suzanne Loves California

Need a consumable dog memento of California? Suzanne Simmons bakes dog cookies shaped like California with the letters CA stamped into them. They come attached to a greeting card! Or for a bigger treat, try her 6-oz. pkg. of California-shaped dog biscuits packaged with festive shredded plastic. Far-out fun stuff; cool to send to out-of-state guests who left their heart in San Francisco. A very different Christmas gift!

Three-Piece California Dog Biscuit Gift Card, $2.50
California Dog Biscuits (6-oz. pkg.), $4.50
+ UPS
(CA res. add 8.25% sales tax)

Purr-fect Growlings
P.O. Box 90275
Los Angeles, CA 90009
(213) 751-3613
E-mail: prfctgrwl@aol.com

Off the Floor, into the Bowl

That's the new mealtime trend—raising the dog bowl supposedly helps prevent digestive problems and, for older dogs, makes it easier for them to bend down at chow time. Here are two interesting choices. The rustic wooden Doggie Picnic Diner keeps food and water bowls in place while providing posture-perfect dining for your pet. Includes two dishwasher-safe crock-style bowls. Heights from 4″ to 15″ off the floor. The fancier Doggie Bone Diner has wooden legs, a white

trimmed surface, and 2 tough crock-style bowls for easy cleanup. Heights from 4″ to 15″ off the floor. Both come in a variety of surface sizes and bowl sizes.

Doggie Picnic Diner
(4″–15″ h., 14″ × 16″ top, with 19-oz. bowls), $68.95
Doggie Bone Diner
(4″–15″ h., 28″ × 15″ top, with 53-oz. bowls), $62.95
+ UPS (CA res. add sales tax)

Xadra Pet Accessories
P.O. Box 808
Carpinteria, CA 93014
(805) 566-9023

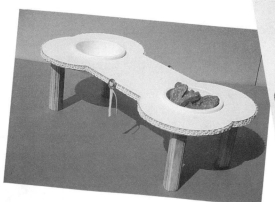

Where the Biscuits Live

I love this classy biscuit box from artist Janet Parker. The Dog Box is 7″ l., 5″ h. × 4″ d. in blue, orange, and green, with a brown dog with gold spots. He's got a bone in his mouth! Made from belalu wood, which is similar to balsa. A functional, beautiful work of art.

Dog Box, $23 + $7 S&H
  (ID res. add 5% sales tax)

Flying Circus
P.O. Box 503
Victor, ID 83455
(208) 787-9898

Go Anywhere Meal

Accessory Pet has everything for your dog's next meal—on the trail or in the kitchen! The Pet Travel Canteen is a durable container that will hold a quart of liquid without leaking or spilling. Ideal for traveling or hiking. Removable nylon strap, assorted colors. The handpainted personalized Stoneware Bowl will last a lifetime. A very solid, heavy white bowl with blue hand lettering for all those meals to come. Personalize it! The large bowl will hold up to 15 characters including spaces; the small bowl has room for 12 characters including spaces. Classy solid-pine Dog Dining Table maintains your dog's proper skeletal and muscular alignment while she noshes. Includes two 8-cup stainless steel bowls. Waterproof nontoxic topcoat; table size is 21″ l. × 11½″ w. Your choice of 8″ height for medium dogs or 12″ height for large dogs.

Pet Travel Canteen, $20 + $4.95 S&H
Personalized Stoneware Bowl, $17 (5″ dia.),
$20 (7″ dia.) + $4.95 S&H
Dog Dining Table, $60 + $6.95 S&H
(TX res. add 7.25% sales tax)

Accessory Pet
5836 Pathfinder Trail
Plano, TX 75093
(800) 558-7387

TRUE DOG TALE

The Oldest Breed?

One of the oldest breeds on earth, the Pug originated at least 5,000 years ago in China. Over the past 2,500 years it's shrunk from the size of a huge Mastiff to the toy version we see today. In the 1500s the dog made its way to Holland, thence to England in the 19th century, and to America in the last 70 years. Long-lived (up to 15 years), small (15–20 lbs., 10″ tall), whimsical, loyal, quiet—but always ready to play—pugs have become wildly popular in the U.S. They've always been a companion dog—first to royalty for thousands of years and now to kids and older folks who want a steady friend who is willing to do absolutely everything with them. Pugs take some getting used to—it might be that compressed face and those big eyes—but loyal owners extol their virtues on every occasion. I have friends who are fanatics about these dogs—they seem to acquire packs of them!

The Natural Dog: A Complete Guide for Caring Owners ®

Slowly, as this book will attest, people are trying organic, natural health and healing methods with their dogs. Now you can explore most of the natural choices available to you and your dog, from pesticide-free flea control, acupuncture and chiropractic treatments, homeopathy, aromatherapy, healing foods, preventive diets, and Bach flower and herbal remedies—it's staggering and gratifying that we have so many good choices. Make no mistake: Nothing beats the emergency room medical care your dog can receive. But for maintaining health and modifying behavior problems, more and more dog owners are taking a serious look at alternative, natural approaches that work.

By Mary L. Brennan, D.V.M., 1994, 350 pp., $15.95 + UPS
(NY res. add sales tax)

Penguin Books USA
375 Hudson St.
New York, NY 10014
(212) 366-2000

Stop Feeding the Ants

Feed your dog outside, and you've got ants in the bowl. They crawl in, you throw away the food—wasting money—move the bowl, and start over. Not with this patented Bowzer Bowl. It traps ants in water at the base of the bowl, away from the food and your dog. Dishwasher safe, nontoxic materials, antiskid feet for stability, neon green color, good price.

Bowzer Bowl (5″ h. × 10½″ w.), $12.95 + $3.50 S&H
(FL res. add sales tax)

Bowzer Products
3395 Fisher Rd.
Palm Harbor, FL 34683
(813) 781-0073

Keep It Fresh

The most economical way to buy dry dog food is in those big 40-lb. bags. Naturally, by the time you get to the bottom, it's invariably stale. Think about what happens to crackers and other baked goods after a few days, much less a month or more. Soft Store keeps food fresh with a heavy-duty, easy-opening lid to keep dog food airtight, pest free, and safe from moisture. Green, blue, and maroon colors; durable inner liner. Holds up to 50 lbs. of dry food.

Soft Store, $22.95 + UPS
(CA res. add 7% sales tax)

Roger's Visionary Pet Products
4538 Saratoga Ave.
San Diego, CA 92107
(800) 364-4537
http://www.rogerspet.com

The Dog Who Loved Too Much: Tales, Treatments and the Psychology of Dogs ®

At last an admission that dogs—like most people—have hang-ups. Most people have an irrational fear of something—heights, thunderstorms, water, something. The list is endless, just as it is for some very nice, otherwise normal dogs. The author is a veterinarian at the esteemed Tufts University School of Medicine. He understands why mild-mannered Fluffy might be put over the edge by an approaching thunderstorm. Dogs from northern breeds (such as Huskies and Samoyeds) and some of the larger breeds (Labs, Retrievers, and

German Shepherds) do show a consistent fear of thunderstorms, he says. They pace the floor, demanding attention from their owners. On rare occasions some dogs even throw themselves out of windows in a vain attempt to escape an approaching storm. Add in blanket-sucking Dachshunds, rage syndrome in Retrievers, anxiety in Afghans, and obsessive-compulsive disorders in Golden Retrievers, and you get the picture. It's all here in a fascinating, compassionate overview that provides loving insight on what might be bothering your dog—and ways to treat it.

By Dr. Nicholas Dodman, 1996, 258 pp.,
$22.95 + UPS
(NY res. add sales tax)

Bantam Books
1540 Broadway
New York, NY 10036
(212) 354-6500

Rustic Automatic Feeder

Like that "woody" look in a feeder? The Pet Nanny is an automatic, electronically controlled feeder in your choice of provincial or washed-oak finishes. Recommended for use with dry or canned food, it automatically opens and feeds your dog one meal while you're gone. You set the time. Good idea if you need to make a one-day getaway. Personalized with your dog's name and portrait, too!

Pet Nanny, $149.95 + UPS
(NJ res. add 6% sales tax)

Weiland Feeders
84 Bissell Rd.
Lebanon, NJ 08833
(888) PET-EASE

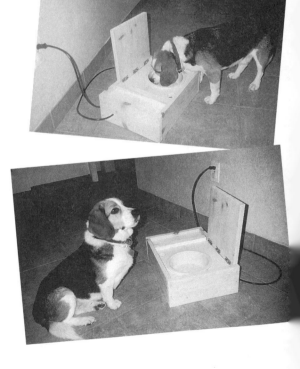

Big Dog Food

The Big Dog Glass Dog Treat Canister proudly displays up to ½ lb. of dog goodies, making it easy for the dog to keep an eye on his cookie inventory. Shiny cover has embossed bones and "Big Dog Treats" printed on the handle. Big Dog Stainless Steel Dog Bowl is decorated with pewter castings of the classic Big Dog with his favorite bones, 32-oz. capacity, dishwasher safe. Big Dog is always good.

Big Dog Glass Dog Treat Canister, $29.99
Big Dog Stainless Steel Dog Bowl, $29.99
+ $6.95 S&H each
(CA res. add 8.25% sales tax)

Big Dog Sportswear
3112 Seaborg Ave.
Ventura, CA 93003
(800) 642-DOGS (3647)
http://www.bigdogs.com

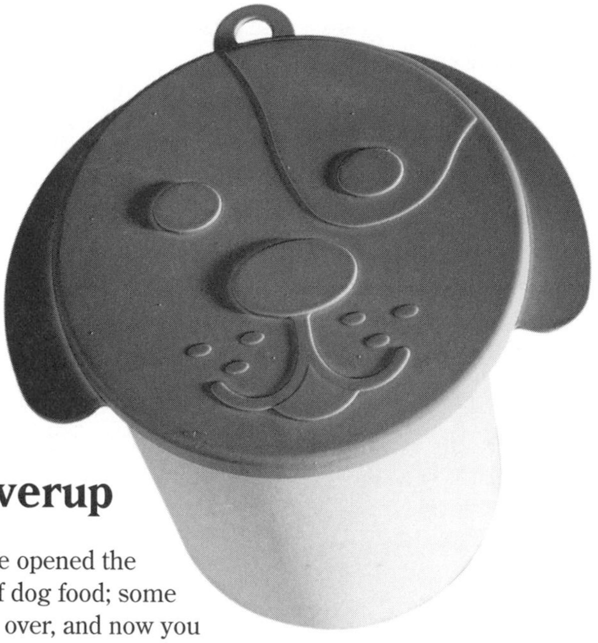

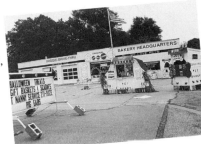

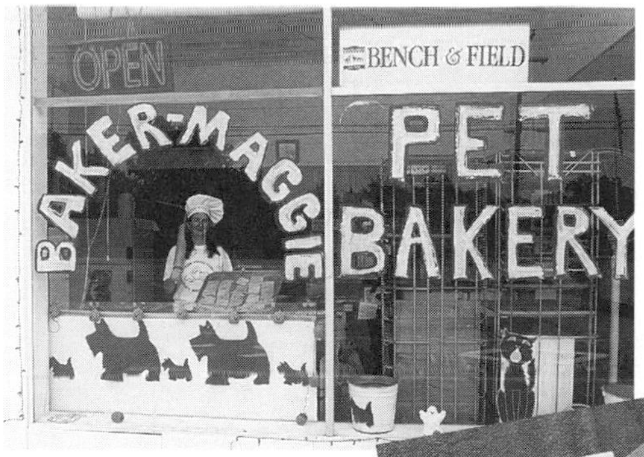

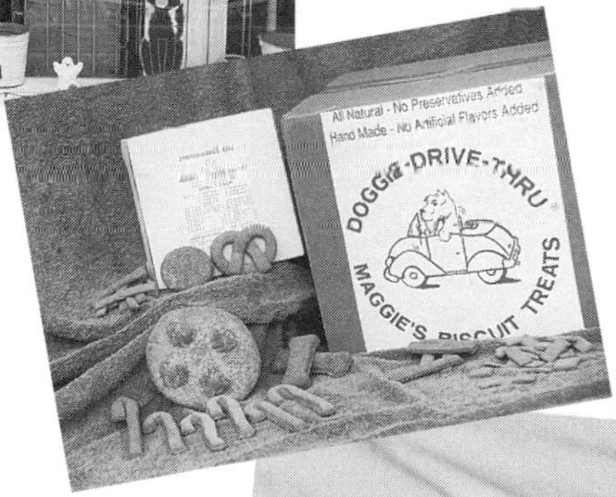

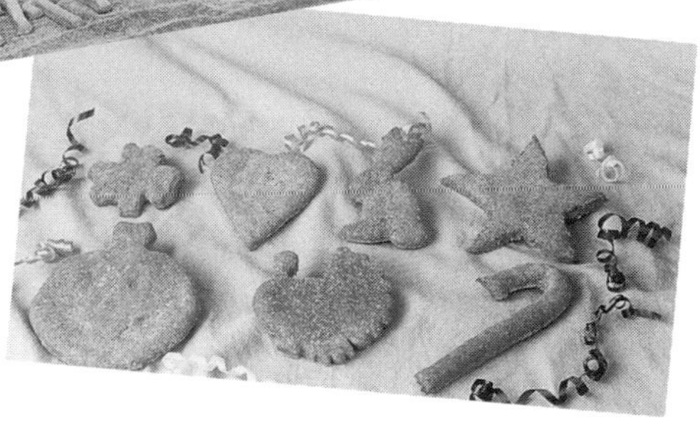

Coverup

You've opened the can of dog food; some is left over, and now you start searching for a lid or a piece of aluminum foil or plastic wrap or *something*. Not anymore. Get a couple of these cool dog-face lids, snap 'em on, that's it. Fits short and tall cans.

Dog Face Food Can Cover,
$2.95 + UPS
(WA res. add 8.2% sales tax)

Keller Design
P.O. Box 3854
Seattle, WA 98154
(206) 343-9515
E-mail:
Petbuds@ix.netcom.com

TRUE DOG TALE

The Thirsty Dog Test

Planning on camping with your best friend? Bring plenty of water, and make sure there are "safe" streams from which the dog can drink, meaning: no *Giardia lamblia*—an intestinal parasite—or pollution. Check to make sure he's getting enough water by using this simple test. Lift the fur above the dog's shoulder blades, then release. The fur should drop immediately back onto the shoulder blades. But if a dog is 5% or more dehydrated, the fur will sink back slowly. Check the dog's gums. They should be healthy and pink, not sticky or dark. If you see any of these signs, give your dog plenty of water and immediate rest.

All About Maggie

Maggie Patterson is the owner and wonderfully eccentric genius behind the Original Doggie-Drive-Thru in South Bend, Indiana. Baking away each day, she makes top-quality, all-natural dog treats—biscuits, cookies, and other edible goodies—for customers who cruise through her parking lot. She also sells her natural (no artificial flavors or preservatives) handmade goodies by mail in shapes like pizzas, pretzels, burgers, and fries in whole wheat and cheese flavors, so your dog—wherever you live—can enjoy these great fresh-baked goodies the next day. Ask for her free catalog of healthy, fun treats. (Enclose #10 SASE.)

Holiday Pack
(12 cheese holiday shapes), $5.99
Gift Baskets, $9.99 (sm.), $14.99 (lg.)
Cheese Cake! (9″), $10 + $5 S&H
(IN res. add sales tax)

Maggie Patterson
Doggie-Drive-Thru
50570 U.S. 31 North
South Bend, IN 46637
(219) 271-0022
(800) 273-3591
http://www.doggie-drive-thru.com

> *"Where are the dogs going? you people who pay so little attention ask. They are going about their business. And they are very punctilious, without wallets, notes . . . without briefcases."*
> —Charles Baudelaire

Winter Water

If you keep fresh water outside for your dog in wintertime, you need one of these. The **Thermobowl** holds 3 quarts, uses 30 watts household current, and at 0° Fahrenheit will keep the water a constant 44°. Includes neon indicator light to show you it's working. Fresh water in the snow.

Thermobowl, $29.95 + $3 S&H
(OH res. add sales tax)

Five Points Products
P.O. Box 387
Celina, OH 45822
(800) 633-0353

Dinner Art ®

Large Woof Dog Bowl sits comfortably on a recycled-rubber, 12″-dia. Round Bow Wow Petmat with a cute dog picture. Bowl is 7¾″ dia. by 3¼″ h. This company has a fun, modern, "arty" approach to dog stuff. Everything's special. It appears in better gift and housewares stores, and some hip pet stores. Worth asking for. If you can't find it, just call.

Large Woof Dog Bowl, $27.50
Round Bow Wow Petmat, $6
+ UPS (CA res. add sales tax)

O.R.E.
1330 Gladys Ave.
Long Beach, CA 90804
(310) 433-2683

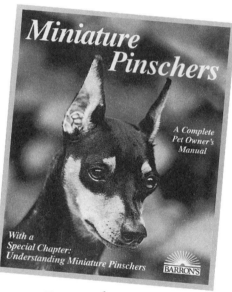

Miniature Pinschers

Is the Miniature Pinscher a shrunken version of the Doberman? Close, but no cigar. In fact, though they look alike, the Miniature is the older brother of these dogs' common ancestor, the German Pinscher. This book tells you all about that connection, plus the selection, raising, nutrition, and maintenance of Min Pins. Concludes with a convincing argument as to why you shouldn't breed this or any dog. When we have enough homes for all of the dogs out there now, we'll breed some more. . . .

By D. Caroline Coile, Ph.D., 1996,
88 pp., $6.95 + UPS
(NY res. add sales tax)

Barron's Educational Series
250 Wireless Blvd.
Hauppauge, NY 11788
(800) 645-3476

Bark for Joy!

A snack? For me? Store your doggie goodies in this fun treat jar. When you open the jar, out comes the sound of a dog barking! Guaranteed to get your dog's attention: She'll come running for a treat each time she hears the bark. Requires 2 AA batteries. Food fun!

Barking Dog Treat Jar, $24.95 + $5.38 S&H
(PA res. add 6% sales tax)

Fun-damental Too Ltd.
2381 Philmont Ave.
Suite 119
Huntingdon Valley, PA 19006
(800) 922-3110
http://www.shopperusa.com/
Fundamental

Chapter Eight

Glorious Gifts and Surprises

It Flies Through the Air!

Whimsical, spectacular Flying Dog is 12½″ in length, painted white with gold spots, wearing a blue, pink, and gold hat. Made from belalu wood, similar to balsa, by artist Janet Parker of Victor, Idaho. Where would it look great in your home?

Flying Dog, $20 + $7 S&H
(ID res. add 5% sales tax)

Flying Circus
P.O. Box 503
Victor, ID 83455
(208) 787-9898

Custom Saint Protection

Saint Francis of Assisi is the protector of pets. This cold-cast statue celebrates the blessing of a faithful friendship with the likeness of your dog displayed under his protective presence. Francis stands a proud 8″ tall in beige and gold robes, and your dog, custom-cold cast as a Charmstone figurine, sits loyally at his side. Just send your breed choice and your dog's name. Custom figures of mixed breeds also available. Just send along a good-quality color photo of your dog.

Saint Francis Pet Statue, $39.95
(includes S&H and sales tax)

Blue Ribbons
9390 Heartwellville Ave.
Englewood, FL 34224
(800) 552-BLUE

Spot Clock

See Spot Fetch lives on your wall in brilliant colors hand-painted on textured wood with an exciting recent find—an amusing bone—dangling just below. Measuring 12″ × 14″, it's a constant reminder from artist Andrea Paige that your dog has remarkable gifts—more of which you will doubtless discover in the next hour or so.

See Spot Fetch, $100 + $8 S&H
(TX res. add 8.25% sales tax)

What Will the Neighbors Think?
P.O. Box 80677
Austin, TX 78708
(512) 832-9989

Canine Cruising

Interested in putting the dog to work, even if only for fun with the kids? Because of the unique design and engineering of this 60-lb. carbon-steel cart, the dog in this picture is actually pulling just a few pounds on level ground. Coated with a baked-on epoxy finish, the cart is equipped with a sophisticated finesse brake system to assist rider and dog in various terrain situations. Heavy-duty Cordura fabric keeps arms and legs away from spokes, also protecting the rider from debris and standing water. Includes zippered cargo bag and a sturdy wood floor. Three years of development ensure an intelligent cart that provides optimum balance with a passenger weighing 50 to 250 lbs. Double shaft incorporates "floating shaft" principle. Model option available for a 3-minute setup or breakdown to allow transportation in your automobile trunk. A cab enclosure kit is coming to allow usage during inclement weather. Superb engineering throughout. Allow 8 weeks for delivery. The kids will have fun with this!

Short Cart, Single Dog, $850
Optional Cargo Trailer (single trace), $410
+ UPS (no sales tax in OR)

Canine Carriages
4636 S.E. 30th St.
Portland, OR 97202
(503) 232-3745
E-mail: Grahammo@ohsu.edu

Wave the Flag

Love flags waving in the wind? How about a large dog flag of your favorite breed? Each high-quality, 28″ × 40″ nylon appliquéd flag is hand-crafted with realistic details that portray features of each distinctive breed—more than 20 of the most popular available—including the breed name in bold type. A percent of each sale is donated to the ASPCA. Great big colorful flags to run up the pole or tack to your wall. Run one up a friend's flagpole, then bring her outside for a look! Snappy.

Best of Breed Flags,
$29.95 + $4.95 S&H
(NJ res. add 6% sales tax)

Chad Management
777 Passaic Ave.
Clifton, NJ 07012
(800) 929-7330
http://aspca.org

Golden Retriever

Dog (and Cat!) Greetings

These extremely hip hand-made cards by Northwest artist Paul Bennett are *fabulous*. Each includes a humorous canine color photo printed on fine-quality recycled paper, no message (that's for you to write) inside. Dog in a Ditch watercolor captures the lunacy and wonder of dogs; Crazy Eyes watercolor features a smiling cat and a zany dog with ears flying.

Mix and match. Order a dozen of one or six of each. Great whimsical, colorful, handmade cards.

Dog in a Ditch or **Crazy Eyes Greeting Cards** (box of 12), $33 + $3 S&H (no sales tax in OR)

Crazy Eyes
P.O. Box 1301
Sisters, OR 97759
(541) 549-9756

2,000 + Years in the Middle East

The Canaan Dog is a very old breed that has survived among desert tribes for thousands of years. In the 1930s the Israelis began developing this intelligent breed as a watchdog for Jewish settlements. A versatile, companionable animal of medium build (35–50 lbs., 20″–24″ at the shoulder), it now serves primarily as a herding, tracking, and search-and-rescue dog. Rare in this country, you see it occasionally at dog shows since its modest introduction into the U.S. in the late 1960s.

Wooden Dogs for a Song

E. C. Calvin makes attractive wooden dogs for what seems like peanuts. What a value—a handpainted dog individually crafted of pine in your choice of 15 of the most popular breeds: Collie, 5″ ($12), Dachshund, 3″ ($9), Dalmatian, 5″ ($12), Heinz/Mixed Hound, 3″ ($10), Husky, 5″ ($10), Labrador, 5″ ($10), Maltese, 3″ ($8), Poodle (sm.), 3″ ($8), Poodle (lg.), 7″ ($12), Sheepdog, 6″ ($12), Shepherd, 6″ ($10), Cocker Spaniel, 4″ ($9), Saint Bernard, 5″ ($15), Wire Terrier, 4″ ($10), Yorkshire Terrier, 4″ ($10). You can also order a natural-wood breed of your choice, paint it to resemble your dog, and take $2 off the price. Great affordable gift idea!

Wooden Dog, $12–$15 + $4 S&H
(HI, AK, and Canada add 50% to S&H)
(PA res. add 6% sales tax)

Free brochure (include SASE):
E. C. Calvin
4175 Marion Hill Rd.
New Brighton, PA 15066

Virtually Pettable Pets

Cyber-Pet is a big commercial site for pet owners on the World Wide Web. You can surf the Breeder's Showcase and Referral to check out a new puppy, browse through Pet Products and Services, read monthly articles, learn the latest health and nutrition information, or see what's up with rescue organizations and breed clubs. Also provides links to other web pet-sites.

Cyber-Pet
P.O. Box 11209
Costa Mesa, CA 11209
(800) 523-PETS
http://www.cyberpet.com

http://www.cyberpet.com
The Leader in Internet Pet Information

TRUE DOG TALE

Bred to Bite, Bred to Bark

Many dog breeds have worked for centuries, bred to physical standards that enable them to perform specific jobs. Consider dogs in the land of Down Under. The Australian Cattle Dog is a very tough, medium-size, reddish dog that runs all day on the huge ranches of Australia, herding cattle who would pay it no heed except for its awesome, powerful jaws. It's been bred to herd and nip reluctant 8oo-lb. cattle on the legs while avoiding their kicks. Another Australian herder, the Kelpie, herds sheep and has been bred to *never* bite. Each dog's behavior is a refinement of natural traits put to work.

Hollywood Squeaks

Visualize your dog munching on this fun, soft, leopard-print bone, looking like a million dollars, reclining on the couch, nibbling on the ends, chewing the squeaker in the middle. Ritzy gift.

Hollywood Squeaker Bone, $14 + $3.50 S&H
(includes MN sales tax)

L. Coffey Ltd.
4244 Linden Hills Blvd.
Minneapolis, MN 55410
(800) 448-4PET

Clifford's Sports Day ®

Little Emily Elizabeth has a giant red dog named Clifford. Today, he's visiting school on Sports Day, joining in the hurdle race, tug-of-war, baseball, tumbling, sack race. Playing with the children, listening to the coach. The gentle, friendly hero of Sports Day for children under 5.

By Norman Bridwell, 1996, 30 pp., $2.99 + UPS
(NY res. add sales tax)

Scholastic
555 Broadway
New York, NY 10012
(800) 392-2179

Sweeter to Me ®

Giving cologne for the holidays? It's as easy to give as to receive with this pleasant cologne in a 3-oz. container. Crisp spray-on fragrance lasts up to 24 hours. Amusing yet practical, it *is* for the dog—but I suppose you could foist it off, as a joke, on some guy and see if he bites . . . or sprays.

Four Paws Cologne,
$9.99 + UPS
(NY res. add sales tax)

Four Paws Products Ltd.
50 Wireless Blvd.
Hauppauge, NY 11788
(516) 434-1100

Labrador Retrievers: A Complete Pet Owner's Manual ®

Labs are the most popular dog in America. Before you buy your pup, consult this book for tips on basic rules of Lab care, feeding, grooming, health, understanding your Lab, training, and breeding requirements. Because this dog is so intelligent and versatile, give some thought to whether you want a companion dog, show dog, field trial dog, or hunting dog. Labs wear lots of hats. Superb and thorough introduction to this fabulous companion.

By Kerry V. Kern, 1995, 94 pp.,
$6.95 + UPS
(NY res. add sales tax)

Barron's Educational Series
250 Wireless Blvd.
Hauppauge, NY 11788
(800) 645-3476

The Gift of Sight

Guide Dogs for the Blind is a nonprofit charitable organization dedicated to training and providing skilled guide dogs to qualified applicants throughout the U.S. and Canada. All services—including training, equipment, the dog, transportation to and from the school, room and board, yearly follow-up visits, veterinary stipend, etc.—are provided *free of charge* to the recipient. There are two training facilities, one in San Rafael, California, and the other in Boring, Oregon. Tours are available. Monthly graduation ceremonies are open to the public.

More than 1,000 puppy raisers in eight Western states socialize the puppies in their homes for a year to prepare them for formal training. Purebred German Shepherds, Labs, Golden Retrievers, and LabXGoldens are then returned to the school for five months of formal training in guidework with licensed instructors. Then they are introduced to visually impaired students for a final month of training.

This remarkable organization helps hundreds of people each year. They receive nothing in state or federal funding and depend totally upon the tax-deductible support and generosity of people like you. To contribute, raise a puppy, volunteer, apply for a guide dog, or receive more information or a copy of their newsletter, *Guide Dog News,* contact:

Guide Dogs for the Blind, Inc.
P.O. Box 151200
San Rafael, CA 94915
(800) 295-4050

Doggie Essentials!

The folks at Small Town Ideas have plenty of cool gifts for dogs. Fake Fur Toys (clockwise from left) include Squirrel, Black Cat, large, hairy Disk, and crazy, furry Baseball (lower right). Assorted fake fur colors. They'll choose one for you. Bathtime over? High-quality Bath Towel, trimmed with dog-theme cotton print, is definitely the dog's towel. You'll probably never use it by mistake. Big—measures 46″ × 25″. Washable *cotton* Bone-Shaped Placemat with batting (24″ × 9″) includes sporting dog themes, just right for cleanups after the next canine feeding frenzy. Cotton Fish Placemat (9″ × 13″), with a clear fishing theme, is very popular with aquatically inclined pups. Dog Photo Frame (8½″ × 13″) holds a 4″ × 6″ photo of your dog in a handpainted wooden frame with a ribbon hanger. Can be personalized with your dog's name and/or your favorite quote, or the expression: "Bless my pet, Oh Lord I pray, Keep it safe both night and day!" Your choice of rust, green, or blue trim.

Fake Fur Toys, $5.95 (with squeaker), $5.50 (without) + $3 S&H; 3 toys for $15 + $3 S&H
Bath Towel, $8.95 + $2 S&H
Bone-Shaped Placemat, $12.95 + $2 S&H
Cotton Fish Placemat, $9.95 + $2 S&H
Dog Photo Frame, $19.95 + $3 S&H
(CA res. add 7.25% sales tax)

Small Town Ideas
P.O. Box 1905
Lower Lake, CA 95457
(800) 994-0552

It's Goodies Time! ®

Cherry-red cast-iron Treet Machine is a scream, dispensing a little handful of your dog's favorite snack each time he pushes down on the bone handle. Vends most dry dog foods; 13″ high; instructions included for training your dog. Very cool. Includes an application for diploma and entrance into the Yuppy Puppy Hall of Fame.

Yuppy Puppy Treet Machine (reg. size), $29.95 + UPS (IL res. add sales tax)

Lucky Yuppy Puppy Company
571 W. Golf Rd.
Arlington Heights, IL 60005
(800) 762-7836

Take Me Along!

Now you can carry your toy dog along on your next walk, bike ride, or even Rollerblading. (Just don't fall backward!) Snug pouch is available in black, navy, maroon, or blue, made of 1,000-denier Cordura Plus, strong nylon, with a removable interior pad for easy cleaning. Small (3–8 lb.) and large (10–18 lb.) sizes. Contoured shape for pup comfort, 4 adjustable straps for a good fit. Padded neck collar provides comfort while watching the world go by. C'mon. Perfect gift to surprise your fitness-friend who has a small dog!

Kuddle Shuttle, $45 + $4.50 S&H (NY res. add sales tax)

Kuddle Shuttle
402 E. 78th St., #15
New York, NY 10021
(212) 794-3010

189

La Cantina Wine Chest

Who can forget their first glimpse of this humorous but practical and exquisitely designed wine chest with sculptured dog heads? *La Cantina del Vida de Vino* by artist Suzanne Simpson has painted embellishments, accented in burgundy, plum, and chardonnay colors. The dog head knobs and drawer pulls are in natural clay with black glaze. There's a diorama of Wil E. Coyote trying to seduce Chi Chi Zamora, crafted of different woods and clays. Stands 78″ h. × 24″ w. × 12″ l.

La Cantina del Vida de Vino,
$2,300 + UPS
(CA res. add 7.25% sales tax)

Whimsical Art
54 Issaquah Dock
Sausalito, CA 94965
(415) 331-7414

Photographs: George Post

More Than 300 Million Bytes!

That's bytes, as in the computer CD-ROM *Multimedia Dogs* 2.0. Here's the multimedia, interactive world of dog information ad infinitum. Use the many interactive features to search for your perfect dog, or just browse the many breeds, enjoying the full-motion video, CD-quality audio, and stunning photography. Great for your computer friends who never sleep.

Multimedia Dogs (interactive CD-ROM for Mac/Win),
$29.95 + $5.95 S&H
(CO res. add 7.5% sales tax)

Inroads Interactive
1050 Walnut St.
Suite 301
Boulder, CO 80302
(888) IN-ROADS
E-mail: inroads@inroadsint.com

Dog Deals

What's going on here? Playing cards with the dog? Gambling on his dinner? Unh-unh. Bomby the Black Lab is busy watching the interpretation of 32 full-color tarot cards, made for owners who seek greater understanding of their pet's future and "inner being." Designed for easy interpretation, even if you were out of the room when the metaphysical and psychic skills were handed out. Fun New Age gift from, where else, California.

Pet Owner's Tarot Deck, $15.95 + $3 S&H
(CA res. add 8.5% sales tax)

Pet Owner's Tarot Deck Co.
P.O. Box 5661
Santa Monica, CA 90409
(800) 482-4733

Dressed for Success!

Nicholas Tines is a genius at creating elaborately dressed dogs with wonderful props. Wolf Lawyer is superbly dressed in suit and tie with small wooden attaché case. A wolf—dressed as a lawyer. He's perfect. He sits about 12″ h., with legs hanging approx. 8″ below the seat. The innocuous Beagle Golfer sports a tartan sweater and just the right golfing getup, including a driver. Also available are hunters, fishers, judges, surgeons, dentists, chefs, and skiers. I've seen these up close, and they are terrific, with fabulous detailing. Handmade, large limited editions, with collector potential. A highly unusual and amusing gift for your dog-owning friends, whatever they do for a living! Humorous free catalog of bizarrely dressed animals! The perfect present for your attorney's office after a big settlement.

Wolf Lawyer, $99.50
Beagle Golfer, $99.50
+ $10 S&H each

Condor Handcrafted Gifts
1605–1552 Esquimalt Ave.
W. Vancouver, BC
Canada V7V 1R3
(604) 926-7324

Mug Face

Pour steaming high-octane java into an affordable mug featuring the breed of your choice. Add the matching coaster set (4 per package, not shown), and after the coffee takes effect, you're ready for anything. Dishwasher and microwave safe. Over 60 mug and coaster breeds. Makes a terrific housewarming or new puppy gift.

Dalmatian Dog Breed Mug, $6.95
Dog Coasters (set of 4), $6.95
+ $4 S&H each
(MA res. add 5% sales tax)

Liliane's Creations
P.O. Box 1004
Oak Bluffs, MA 02557
(508) 693-2515

Dog Law: ®
A Legal Guide for Dog Owners and Their Neighbors

Dog law? Who needs it? As you wander through this fascinating 336-page tome by attorney Mary Randolph, you'll be amazed at the legal situations that arise that involve dogs. What are your rights if a dog nips a mail carrier? Who do you call to mediate a dog dispute with your neighbor? What are your rights when you buy a sick puppy? Here's the big one: Can you leave money or property in a will to your dog? Unh-unh. The law considers dogs to be property. However, you can leave money in your will to a trusted friend to care for your dog, and there are even provisions to prepay any future vet bills. A great book covering all your doggone legal rights, including what you should expect when Fido travels on an airline. Who said life was simple?

By Mary Randolph, 1994, 336 pp., $12.95 + UPS
(CA res. add sales tax)

Nolo Press
950 Parker St.
Berkeley, CA 94710
(800) 992-6656

Wildly Practical Dog Luggage

Who's the genius who thought this up? The Bone Voyage Travel Case carries every thing you'll need while traveling. Plus, the bottom of the case is a actually a padded, fur-lined bed with a removable bottom cushion, for a dog to sleep in. It's a portable bed!!! Top of case holds 2 Rubbermaid resealable containers for food or water, a refillable lotion or shampoo bottle, a refillable spray bottle for flea spray, and a flea comb. Extra space available for a prescription bottle. There are also two deep mesh pockets on the top of the case, which can be unzipped from the bottom/bed. Machine washable, available in classy Dalmatian or cheetah fur. Note the faux leopard sleeping pad that rolls up for easy travel. Rather incredible! This luggage also makes a clever get-away bag for the dog: Just prepack it with food and goodies, zip it up, and store it in the event you need to leave in a hurry (hurricane, earthquake, relatives). Great product.

Bone Voyage Travel Case, $78 (sm.) + $5 S&H; $96 (med.) + $7 S&H; $110 (lg.) + $10 S&H (CA res. add 7.75% sales tax)

M&M Productions
2781 W. MacArthur Blvd.
Suite B-307
Santa Ana, CA 92704
(888) 645-1613
E-mail: MnMPrd@aol.com

> "A good dog deserves a good bone."
> —Ben Jonson

Dog Screen

Put your dog's face on your computer at work! How? Just mail these people the pictures you want on the screen—dog photographs from that camping trip, your latest dog art sculpture, your love letter to your dog as text—and you get back a disk with the images as a screen saver. Demo disk available. System requirements: VGA/SVGA monitor (256 colors). On IBM compatibles: Windows 3.1 or Windows 95. On Mac: System 7. Perfect for those long Friday afternoons.

Persona Screen Saver, $19.95 (for the program) + $5 (each photo) + $3.95 S&H (CO res. add 3% sales tax)

Personal Software
1205 W. Elizabeth St.
Suite E-200
Fort Collins, CO 80521
(970) 484-5972

Wild Dogs: The Wolves, Coyotes, and Foxes of North America ®

In 130 color photographs, renowned nature photographers Erwin and Peggy Bauer capture the essence of your dog's ancestors: the 8 species of North American wolves, coyotes, and foxes at home, in the wild. From playful pups to savage hunting attacks, it's all here. Stunning photographs with minimal text.

By Erwin A. and Peggy Bauer, 1994, 120 pp., $16.95 + UPS (CA res. add sales tax)

Chronicle Books
275 Fifth Ave.
San Francisco, CA 94013
(800) 722-6657

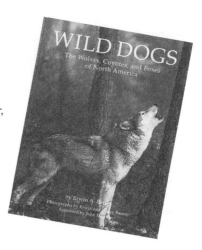

Photo Realism

Handcrafted pewter picture frames are the classy way to picture your pal. Each 4¼″ h. × 3¼″ w. frame depicts the breed of your choice below the branches of a flowering tree and includes a breed miniature—in a nice 3D effect—at the bottom of the frame. Specify your dog breed when calling. They have most.

Dog Pewter Frame, $22.99 + $6.99 S&H
(WI res. add 5% sales tax)

Drs. Foster & Smith
P.O. Box 100
Rhinelander, WI 54501
(800) 826-7206

It's Time to . . .

Handsome 9″-tall clock combines style and function, featuring quartz movement and an alarm that's as faithful as your best friend. Hand-carved of natural basswood; operates on 1 AA battery. Specify Yorkie, Boxer, or Schnauzer, though most AKC breeds are available by special order.

Hand-Carved Mantel Clock,
$125 + $12.95 S&H
(NY res. add sales tax)

In the Company of Dogs
P.O. Box 7071
Dover, DE 19903
(800) 924-5050

2,000 Dog Books

That's the number of dog books—give or take a few—that 4-M Enterprises sells, including in- and out-of-print and rare dog titles. Free 100+ page color catalog, free book locator service (by phone, fax, or e-mail). If they can't find it, nobody can. Calendars, too. Their motto: "If we don't have it, we'll do our doggonedest to get it for you." A rare dog book? Consider *Les Races des Cheins,* an 1897 2nd. ed. of 1,160 pp., including 1,392 engravings of 2,064 dogs of nearly every known breed. It will set you back a modest $1,950. These people live and breathe dog books.

Dog Book Catalog, free

4-M Enterprises
1280 Pacific St.
Union City, CA 94587
(800) 487-9867
E-mail: Books4M@aol.com

Mona's Pastels

Mona's a pro at pastel dog portraits. Pastel paintings consist of many layers and can outlast oils, which sometimes yellow with age. Send her your best close-up shot of your dog, and she'll take it from there. Your choice of a 8″ × 10″ portrait in an 11″ × 14″ frame, an 11″ × 14″ portrait in a 16″ × 20″ frame, or a 13″ × 18″ portrait in an 18″ × 24″ frame. Attractive. Affordable price includes frame and double matting. What a gift idea/surprise for a friend! Borrow a picture of their dog, and surprise them with a portrait.

Pastel Pet Portrait, $69 (8″ × 10″) + $5 S&H; $99 (11″ × 14″) + $6 S&H; $129 (13″ × 18″) + $7 S&H (includes sales tax)

Mona Truhlar
1911 W. Broadway, #13
Mesa, AZ 85202
(602) 985-6651

Never Leave Me!

I once found and adopted a dog who could not be left alone. She'd tear up the house when I was gone. It was a classic case of separation anxiety. I tried everything. One day, having driven a quarter-mile down a country road, I chanced to look in the rearview mirror, and there she was—running full speed, hundreds of yards behind, chasing my car down the road in the dust. She had jumped out an open window in the house. I eventually found a nice neighborhood family with three kids who adored her. They took care of her during the day. Then she started spending the night sleeping in the kids' beds, and eventually she adopted them. I was commuting long hours, and it made all of us happy that she was happy.

There are ways to treat separation anxiety, such as teaching the dog to stay or sit, then leaving briefly. (Put the dog in a room, close the door, then reopen it immediately.) Eventually stretch out the absences from a random minute or two to 5, 10, 15, 20 minutes, and so forth. Many training books can help. So does patience.

The Guilt-Free Dog Owner's Guide ®

Lest you be wracked by feelings of inadequacy, here's everything you need to know beforehand about obtaining, training, and keeping a dog, even with your busy schedule. It's not always easy. You might need a pet sitter to come in once a day, or perhaps you have a friendly neighbor with a dog who's home during the day. Maybe you can make it home for lunch and a walk; perhaps you'll need a dog walker if you work late. Plenty of busy people keep their dogs happy. Smart, creative arrangements that can work for both of you.

By Diana Delmar, 1994, 252 pp., $8.99 + UPS (NJ res. add sales tax)

Wings Books
Random House
Value Publishing
40 Engelhard Ave.
Avenel, NJ 07001
(800) 793-2665

Dogs on Parade

Thinking about buying a dog? Curious about individual breeds? This CD-ROM has tons of fun and interesting facts about the world's favorite dog breeds. Includes more than 35 minutes of high-quality videos. Photos include text and a voice-over narration (more than 1½ hours) in your choice of 3 languages (English, Spanish, or Japanese). System requirements: PC with Windows 3.1 or Windows 95, 386 or better, 256-color display, sound card, 4 megs. of RAM, double-speed CD-ROM (or faster), and a mouse. No files are copied to your hard drive. Mac version coming. A whole library on a disk.

101 Favorite Dog Breeds (CD-ROM), $19.95 + $4.95 S&H
(CA res. add 7.25% sales tax)

Centaur Multimedia
P.O. Box 1583
Ventura, CA 93002
(800) 730-4107
E-mail: gregb@europa.com

Carol's Cards

Send a nice color close-up of a favorite canine friend to Carol, and she'll print up beautiful color photo stationery, note sheets, address labels, hand-decorated flower cards, even business cards. Here's a sample card from a photo sent to her. Print that beautiful furry face and send it to friends!

Stationery (8½″ × 11″), 25¢ each
Address Labels (60), $9.95
Hand-Decorated Flower Cards, $1.25 each
Business Cards, 30¢ each
+ $2 S&H
(CA res. add 7.75% sales tax)

Free Brochure with SASE:
Carol Lynn Graphics
P.O. Box 2472
Temecula, CA 92593
(909) 676-2648

Big Red Surprise! ®

Very cool red fireplug is a great container for your dry dog food, with removable lid so you can dip into it, then cap it to keep food fresh. Big enough (24″ h. × 14″ dia.) to store dog toys and almost anything else, including kids' stuff. Best of all, it has no plastic smell: I know; I yanked the cap off and stuck my nose in it. Will easily accommodate 24 cans of soft drinks with ice, but really, leave it alone and give it to the dog. Amusing, practical gift that'll last forever. Big—it will pose a major difficulty for the gift-wrap challenged.

Fireplug Storage Container,
$24 + UPS
(OH res. add sales tax)

Huerter Toledo
P.O. Box 346
Bellevue, OH 44811
(800) 537-1601
E-mail: dogdooley@aol.com

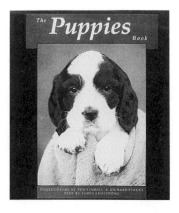

The Puppies Book ®

Only a meanie wouldn't like this sweet book. Tons of fluffy, sweet puppies in beautiful color photos with a just a little bit of text. Three very cute Golden Retrievers all in a row, snoozing next to one another; cute puppies in baskets and flowers; a cute Cocker sitting in a goldfish bowl. The only thing missing is the puppy breath and soft warm fur. Great sweet gift for kids and puppy fans!

Photos by Ron Kimball and Richard Stacks, text by James Armstrong, 1995, 80 pp., $14.95 + UPS
(CA res. add sales tax)

Cedco Publishing
2955 Kerner Blvd.
San Rafael, CA 94901
(800) 233-2624

Naturally Citrus ®

This stuff is amazing. One little squeeze releases a delightful, citrusy fragrance of oranges and lemons that masks any doggie odors. Each bottle contains the pure, all-natural oils of more than 1,000 lbs. of citrus fruit peels. We bought some to spray wet doggie smells and around the cat's litter box. But instead, everybody in my family just loves the smell, and the bottle keeps disappearing. It's one of the best all-natural air fragrances to be found anywhere. One can lasts forever.

Citrus Magic, $9.95 (minimum order 2 cans) + $3 S&H (GA res. add sales tax)

Beaumont Products
1560 Big Shanty Rd.
Kennesaw, GA 30144
(800) 451-7096
http://www.citrusmagic.com

TRUE DOG TALE

The Dogs of War

Playing with my sweet Golden Retriever, it's hard to imagine that dogs were used in warfare for thousands of years. That's how the expression "the dogs of war" originated. Roman, Persian, Egyptian, and British history is replete with stories of battles won or lost because of dogs. It is claimed that the Saint Bernard developed, as a breed, nearly 2,000 years ago from dogs that remained behind as Roman troops climbed through the Alps to attack Switzerland. And visualize this: A thousand or more huge Mastiffs, trained to fight men, weighing 100+ lbs., racing across the battlefield to fight enemy soldiers armed with spears and bows. The British used Mastiffs during the Middle Ages to pull heavily protected knights off their horses. It's a long, fascinating, and somewhat bizarre history, especially when you consider that many of these same breeds have evolved into the couch potatoes we know and love today!

Jack Russell Terriers Today ®

The Jack Russell Terrier is named after an English minister who began the breed in 1819 with a female named Trump, whom he spotted one day and bought on the spot from a milkman. This marvelous book is heavy on history and breeding standards but includes selection and adult care basics as well as old etchings and photos of the first "parson's terriers." In the early 20th century these same terriers were used in bizarre hunting rituals called badger digs. For an entire day, hundreds of civilized people, in suits, would take turns putting their terriers down a badger hole. On top of the hole people would begin digging down with picks and shovels—often going down 5' or more, then digging a trench to follow the barking of the terriers deep in the badger's warren. Ultimately, one or more of the terriers would drag out the badger, which would be caught and weighed! Exhausted and humiliated, the badger was then taken to an open spot and released.

By Sheila Atter, 1995, 192 pp., $29.95 + UPS
(IN res. add sales tax)

Howell Book House
201 W. 103rd St.
Indianapolis, IN 46290
(800) 428-5331

A Message from Your Dog

This lovely poem accompanies an attractive watercolor rendering made from the color photograph you provide of your dog or the pet of someone special. It comes unmatted and unframed in an 11″ × 14″ standard frame size. You select your own frame according to your personal taste and decor. Handwritten in beautiful calligraphy, personalized with your dog's name, it's the perfect gift for a dog-loving friend.

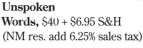

Unspoken Words, $40 + $6.95 S&H
(NM res. add 6.25% sales tax)

Kindred Spirits
1380 Rancho Blvd., #121
Rio Rancho, NM 87124
(800) 995-0796, ext. 1308

Puppy and Dog Gift Set ®

New puppy in the house? Just about everything you'll need to take care of her is included in this 17-piece kit, including a 25″ l. × 16″ h. × 14″ w. dog carrier, a grooming brush, an adjustable collar (⅝″ w. × 12″–16″ l.), a 48″ leash, 10 rawhide chew sticks, a twisted beef hide chew, a double dinner bowl, and last but not least, a squeak toy. Great instant gift for the new puppy owner.

Puppy & Dog Care Kit,
$34.99 + UPS
(PA res. add sales tax)

Stylette
P.O. Box 190
Oakdale, PA 15071
(800) 752-5650

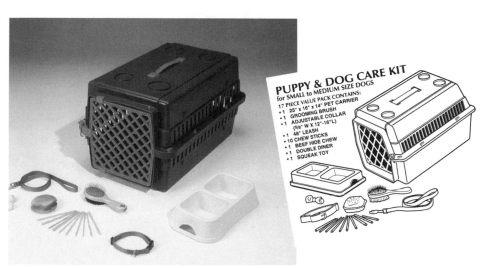

Champion Swimmer and Rescuer

The big black wonderful Newfoundland, weighing in at a hefty 100–145 lbs., is really a creampuff. A perennial favorite of families, especially those with young children. Even-tempered, with a mild, gentle disposition, this big bear of a dog can be trained to do just about anything—even pull carts! Originally their great strength was used on fishing boats to pull in the nets. Now these gentle giants are best known for saving people in the water. Superb swimmers, they have an endearing tendency to want to retrieve anyone (or anything!) afloat. They are still used today in Europe for water rescue work.

I'll Ride for a While, Thanks.

Riding your bike with the dog? Dogs need exercise, but young and old dogs often just don't have the endurance to keep up. Give them a nice break with this wildly cool bicycle trailer. It's lightweight (18 lbs.), with a colorful fringe canopy, a washable cushion, and a canteen-type water bottle. Snap in the red safety flag, and you're ready to hit the road. Or if you like, run the dog for a while, then have him rest while you do the pedaling. Take the dog along for the ride. One of a kind, rather incredible gift.

Pet-a-Lon Bicycle Trailer, $175 + UPS (MA res. add sales tax)

The Pet-a-Lon Co.
127 Orchard St.
Millis, MA 02054
(508) 376-4247

Dog Tales: Classic Stories About Smart Dogs 📚

The dogs in this book won't be making an appearance on David Letterman's "stupid pet tricks." These are stories about bright, even brilliant dogs, all from different eras, by nine authors. Includes colorful pictures of dogs in a variety of settings. If only they could talk. Move over, Lassie.

Introduction by Richard Wolters, Fly Productions, 1990, 86 pp., $9.99 + UPS (NJ res. add sales tax)

Wings Books
Random House Value
Publishing
40 Engelhard Ave.
Avenel, NJ 07001
(800) 793-2665

Doggie Blooms

Ready for a friendly dog to showcase your beautiful flowers? Cute, smiling dog planter in the breed of your choice comes in two sizes. Holds flowers, cherry tomatoes, anything you can grow in a pot. This is a happy dog, glad to be

helping, always ready with a smile. Small planter will hold up to 4″ pots, large up to 6″ pots. Request the breed of your choice when ordering.

Small Dog Planter (5″ w. × 8″ h. × 13″ l.), $26.95 + $4.85 S&H
Large Dog Planter (7″ w. × 12″ h. × 17″ l.), $31.95 + $5.85 S&H (WA res. add 7.8% sales tax)

Fantasy Farm Products Co.
P.O. Box 1262
Bellingham, WA
(360) 734-9770
E-mail: hermann@prodigy.com

Bichon Frise, Please

Everything Bichon Frise is what you get with this catalog. Bichon Christmas Cards portray a happy dog with Santa hat and cat with ribbon, pen and ink, set of 12. Welcome Slate is a friendly, stone hello always ready at your front door. It can even be customized with a photo of your Bichon! Standing Wooden Bichon is hand-carved of pine, then handpainted. It includes a colorful wooden base. Love Bichons? Just a small sampling from the catalog.

Bichon Christmas Cards, $14
Welcome Slate (customized), $60
Standing Wooden Bichon, $35
(all prices include S&H)
(MA res. add sales tax)

Rolande's/Talisman
68 Providence St.
Mendon, MA 01756
(508) 478-1889
E-mail:
cyberpet@ix.netcom.com
http://www.ads-online.com/
bichon.htm

Dinner *Was* Served

Does your furry friend stand around in the kitchen, maintaining eye contact, staring back and forth from her bowl to you? Does she do it with everybody who enters the kitchen? Professional moochers get very good at this! Now you no longer have to guess if the dog has eaten or whether she's just bluffing another meal. Just move the arrow to the sun when the pooch has had breakfast; move the arrow to the moon when she's been fed at night. Cute! Made of natural wood with a hanging hook.

Doggy Dial, $7.97 + $2 S&H
(CA res. add 8.5% sales tax)

The Smart Wood Company
1827 Haight St.
Suite 11
San Francisco, CA 94117
(415) 752-3282
E-mail: Bfattal@aol.com

Almost Everything You'll Ever Need to Know

I have, admittedly, a certain reluctance about chasing technology, and I only grudgingly learn new computer tricks. And I had some difficulty loading this baby, but I did it. Packed into more than 500 megabytes is a detailed database on 157 breeds with color photos, a 40-factor Breed Selector, 60 printable articles on topics from puppy temperament testing to service dogs (including almost one hour of professionally produced video and slide shows to enhance the articles), a massive catalog of over 2,000 dog books, and endless amounts of dog-related information. It's staggering how much info you can put on one CD. Both Mac and PC versions of this massive work encompassing the universe of dogs on one thin, shiny disk.

Telemark's Guide to Dogs (CD-ROM), $29.95 + UPS
(CA res. add 7.75% sales tax)

Telemark Productions
645 Cheshire Way
Sunnyvale, CA 94087
(408) 738-2386
E-mail: info@telemarkprod.com
http://telemarkprod.com

Calico Picks a Puppy ®

There. On the front cover. Among all those cute puppy faces, there's a smiling cat face. That's Calico, who's looking for the "purrfect" puppy. Whom to choose? Well, Poodles perform, Retrievers fetch things, Spaniels love to jump and splash, Sheepdogs and Shepherds love to work, the Hounds (Dachshunds, Beagles, and Bassets) have great sniffers, Collies can herd and count sheep or ducks or geese, Setters love to "point" when they get near a bird, and other breeds are good at something, too. How can a child pick the puppy of her dreams? The colorful artwork and short descriptions in this charming book can really help.

By Phyllis Limbacher Tildes, 1996, 32 pp. (large format), $6.95 + UPS (MA res. add sales tax)

Charlesbridge Publishing
85 Main St.
Watertown, MA 02172
(800) 225-3214

> *The one absolutely unselfish friend that man can have in this selfish world, the one that never deserts him, the one that never proves ungrateful or treacherous, is his dog."*
>
> —George G. Vest

The Greatest Gift You Will Ever Give ®

The nicest gift you will ever give your dog (or cat) is a tiny rice-size microchip that's painlessly injected by a vet between your pet's shoulders. The microchip has a unique identification code that can be read with a hand-held scanner, like the kind they use in grocery stores. More than 12,000 HomeAgain scanners have been placed with animal shelters and vets nationwide. When your lost dog is found and brought to a shelter or vet's office, the scanner reads the ID code imprinted in the chip, which is called into a national database center, open 24 hours a day, 365 days a year, through a toll-free 800-number. You, the owner, are contacted immediately, and every possible step is taken to reunite you with your homesick pet. Along with the microchip, you receive an identifying tag to be worn on your dog's collar. This is the future. Available from your veterinarian.

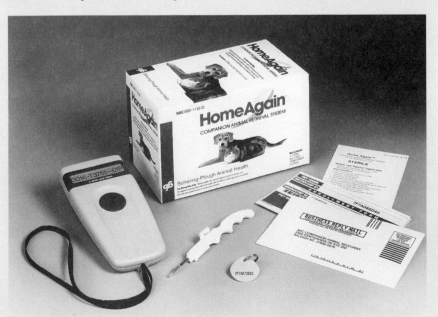

HomeAgain, $9 (one-time enrollment fee) + veterinarian fee

Free information kit:
HomeAgain
Companion Animal Retrieval System
Schering/Plough Animal Health
1095 Morris Ave.
Union, NJ 07083
(800) 2-FIND-PET

Jack Russells on the Go

Those clever Jack Russells. Scurrying about, using all that curious intelligence packed between those little ears. Check out the amusing caricatures of these bright, affectionate dogs on a 100% cotton canvas tote bag. Available in natural or red.

Jack Russell Ruffians Tote Bag, $14 + $3 S&H
($5 S&H for 2 items)
(PA res. add sales tax)

Up the Creek
1209 Rose Glen Rd.
Gladwyne, PA 19035
E-mail: jsmith4287@aol.com
http://home.navisoft.com/
utc/utc.htm

More Zamora Fun

Fun stuff from Pam Kaplan for your dog—and you! Dressing the dog for Turkey Day? The outrageous nylon Thanksgiving Turkey Collar features whimsical turkeys with feathers. If your dog wears hairbows, you can also get matching turkeys on a barrette. Looking for a great dog gift? The Bone Basket is filled with a dozen yogurt-dipped cookie bones, individually wrapped with colorful ribbon and presented in a reusable decorative basket. How about a frame for a picture of your best buddy? Picture that great fuzzy face in one of these frames. Bones, Bones, Bones has three layers of bones in a two-color combination (black and gold, red and gold, green and gold). Let's Walk is a black frame featuring a minileash with a rawhide accent; your choice of red or blue leash handle. Dog Charms is a frame with an eclectic collection of brass charms and multicolored

jewels. Each is a lively original! All three desk frames come complete with glass and easel backing.

Thanksgiving Turkey Collar,
$8 (8"–10"), $10 (12"–16"),
$12 (18"–24")
Bone Basket, $16
Picture Frame
(3" × 3", 4" × 6",
5" × 7", or 8" ×10"), $18–$36
+ $5 S&H
(TX res. add sales tax)

Zamora's
2527 Guerrero Dr.
Carrollton, TX 75006
(214) 245-1119

The New American Eskimo

The beautiful white American Eskimo dates all the way back to the Stone Age. Here are 7 fascinating chapters on famous owners and Eskie hero dogs, plus complete details on registering and showing your dog, more than 300 photographs, an extensive chapter on the standards for the breed, and what you'll need to know to select, care for, groom, breed, and train these dogs. Owners of Pomeranians, Keeshonds, Japanese Spitz, and Volpinos—all related to American Eskimo dogs—will also find this book valuable.

By Nancy J. Hofman and Cathy J. Flamholtz, 1995, 224 pp., $34.95 + $2.50 S&H
(AL res. add sales tax)

OTR Publications
P.O. Box 481
Centreville, AL 35042
(800) 367-2174

TRUE DOG TALE

Rasta Fur

You know those Jamaican dreadlocks, with the matted hair and bangs? The canine version comes naturally on Pulis and Komondors from Hungary. Komondors have incredibly matted fur that looks just like thick dreadlocks draped all the way to the ground. Their coat evolved to protect them against harsh weather and wolves as they guarded sheep. An extraordinary look you couldn't get with a month of grooming. Good old evolution always wins.

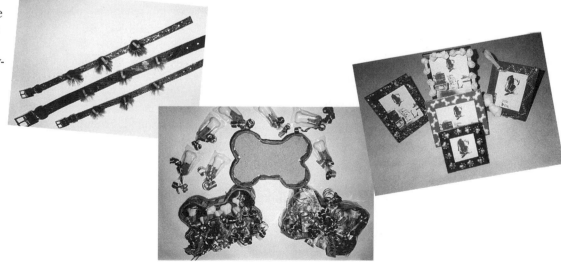

Smooth-Rolling Dog Pens ®

Colorful fine-point (0.5mm) dog pens are available in 24 of your favorite breeds, with permanent waterproof ink. These look especially nice and exude quality because a film image is directly affixed to the heavyweight plastic. Tungsten-carbide refills available in black and blue ink. Kids (and big kids) love 'em. Hand 'em out as gifts to your friends.

Our Best Friends Dog-Series Pens, $3.49 + UPS (CA res. add sales tax)

Writek U.S.A
6405 E. Alondra Blvd.
Paramount, CA 90723
(800) 230-2583

Four-Legged Romance

Ready for that hairy date? The high-fashion look of puppy love is just the beginning of this intriguing scent for dogs. Imaginative wording on the bottle talks about puppy love, first love, when we are young, romantic, and full of hope. Just dab it on your beloved dog.

puppy love (spray cologne for dogs, 2 oz.), $25 + UPS (AZ res. add 7.05% sales tax)

Philosophy
4602 E. Hammond Le.
Phoenix, AZ 85034
(888) 2NEW-AGE
Internet: http://philosophy.com

Tricks I Taught My Master

Who's in charge, you or the dog? Does someone need to be in charge? This massive book with black and white illustrations helps you answer that question, providing an enormous wealth of information on modifying owner thinking (that means you), why dogs develop bad behaviors, how dogs learn (a key chapter), eliminating destructiveness, correcting chewing problems, and more. Oddly, some dogs will chew up your house and everything in it simply because it smells like you. The solution? Offer one rawhide chewable toy, rub it around in your hands, and make that the primary object/scent your dog chews on. Remember their sense of smell: Touch anything, and it smells like you. Includes a million practical ideas and examples. Amusing sections in each chapter as the dog gives his canine perspective on the foibles, futility, and successes of training.

By Dr. Robert Andrysco, 1995, 400 pp., $12.99 + UPS (OH res. add sales tax)

Talking Pets
2662 Billingsley Rd.
Columbus, OH 43235
(614) 889-8972

http://www.smartpages.com/talkingpets

Wind Sounds ®

Wind chimes can be so soothing. These 4 full-bodied, dual-sided, raised designs are sand-cast in aluminum, hand sanded, and then polished with a pewterlike finish. They're big. Durable beauty with a great mellow tone. Each dog measures approx. 3.5″ × 5.5″. Your choice of more than 100 dog breeds to resonate in the wind.

Dog Wind Chimes,
$36.50 + UPS
(CA res. add 8.25% sales tax)

Dannyquest Designs
11782 Western Ave., #17
Stanton, CA 90680
(800) 215-9711

┌─────────────────────────┐
TRUE DOG TALE

Heading For China

Some dogs just have to dig. Every time you turn around, they're out in the yard tunneling to China. Irritated by all this rooting around? You can cover up errant excavations with boards, heavy canvas, a tarp, etc., so his favorite spot is no longer available, then maybe he'll forget about it. Admittedly, it can get obsessive when your yard starts looking like a construction site. If all else fails, give in and provide the dog with a spot to dig that's his own. Put a modest little fence around it, soften it up with a spade and some sand, and show it to him. Take one of his favorite rubber chew toys, wave it in front of his face, and, while he's looking, bury it in the new digging spot. He'll dig it out and keep digging whenever he gets the urge. Such a simple, harmless, amusing pleasure—if it's in the right place.
└─────────────────────────┘

The Dogs We Love, Every Day!

Is that a face you could love? Wellll . . . Petprints has dog calendars for everybody on your shopping list. Full color, almost every breed on earth, and they look great. It doesn't stop there. You can also order dog diaries, T-shirts, sweatshirts, posters, stickers, greeting cards, and other quality products, complete with pictures of our favorite friends. Start with a call for their catalog or browse their website.

Pug Calendar,
$10.95 + $4 S&H
(CA res. add 7.75% sales tax)

Petprints
P.O. Box 643
Corona del Mar, CA 92625
(714) 660-8895
http://www.petprints.com

The Complete Poodle ®

There, on the cover, is the quintessential white poodle—with shaved legs, pom-poms above her feet, brushed and coiffed with a fluffy little white ball of fur on the tip of her tail. A terrific resource book with a focus on grooming and breeding gorgeous poodles meant for show. Hundreds of black and white photos of champion poodles, grooming techniques galore. Just to prove this dog can be, and do, anything there's a great photo of John Suter of Alaska riding his sled pulled by a team of—get this—6 black poodles with ears flying in the annual Iditarod dog race! What a breed.

By Del Dahl, 1994, 270 pp., hardcover, $25.95 + UPS
(IN res. add sales tax)

Howell Book House
201 W. 103rd St.
Indianapolis, IN 46290
(800) 428-5331

See-Thru Dogs

Cool Doggy Lunch Box is a fun, practical gift for schoolkids. They look great and are made of a durable, clear plastic. Shows an amazing variety of dog breeds. Very cute. Pack up the peanut butter and juice!

Doggy Lunch Box
$12 + $4.99 S&H
(MN res. add 6.5% sales tax)

Tails
4708 Utah Ave. North
New Hope, MN 55428
(612) 535-3055
E-mail: tailsl@ix.netcom.com

Layers of Dogs

This cheerful guy is made from layers of fine woods glued together for a cool 3D effect. Small size (3" w. × 4½" h. × 3½" l.) is perfect for shelf or table decorations; the large (6" w. × 9" h. × 5½" l.) dog looks great on the porch or out in the yard. Bright red tail and ears, black eyes and nose, white legs and face. Sixteen happy breeds available.

Layered Dog, $11.95 (sm.) + $3.85 S&H; $21.95 (lg.) + $4.85 S&H (WA res. add 7.8% sales tax)

Fantasy Farm Products Co.
P.O. Box 1262
Bellingham, WA
(360) 734-9571
E-mail: hermann@prodigy.com

Major Personality Change

Take a good, close look at the Bulldog's face. His nose is pushed way up on his face, nearly to his eyes. In the 1600's dogs like these were trained to fight bulls by grabbing the animal's nose and holding it to the ground. The only way the dog could breathe—since he had his jaws locked onto the bull's nose—was to have a nose as far as possible from its mouth. This gruesome wager sport—with the Bulldog hanging on for dear life while being flailed around like a rag by the powerful bull—was finally outlawed in England in the early 19th century. Since then, careful breeding has totally changed the personality of this dog from a vicious, resolute fighter to a mellow family companion. But the change has come at a cost. Bulldogs have a somewhat abbreviated life span (9–11 years), and they can be prone to ailments like overheating and breathing problems. Don't let that stop you. They love their families and creature comforts, don't need a lot of room, aren't wild about exercise, and will generally prefer to take the car to the store.

Civilizing Your Puppy Ⓡ

Got a yard and a few acres? This is a book for folks who primarily keep their dogs outside and need the basics of puppy raising. Plenty of good hints and color pictures, especially on raising pups in a pen. Why build a pen? Outdoors it gives the dog a sense of home and a great place to trash (dig and destroy) at his or her leisure without touching the rest of your yard.

By Barbara J. Wrede, 1992, 96 pp., $5.95 + UPS (NY res. add sales tax)

Barron's Educational Series
250 Wireless Blvd.
Hauppauge, NY 11788
(800) 645-3476

Send a Letter, Keep a Letter Ⓡ

Fun Puppy Pads come in three sizes wrapped in a spring tartan ribbon with the classic saying: "Love Me, Love My Dog." Perfect for scribbling great thoughts and staying organized at home or in the office. Rustic Mail and Paper Metal Holder is available in a dog silhouette with hand-cut pawprints for design. You'll find them useful for storing and procrastinating on paying bills, keeping your love letters in one place, or holding stationery.

Puppy Pad, $14
Mail and Paper Metal Holder, $18
+ $4.50 S&H ($1 each addl. item) (IL res. add sales tax)

Creature Comforts
Tyler and Russell, Ltd.
357 W. Erie St., 2nd Floor
Chicago, IL 60610
(312) 266-0907

Let Me In!

What a cool idea. Your dog taps this Doggie Doorbell with his paw, and a chime sounds in your house! Time to let him in. Easy to install in three steps: Peel off the backing and attach it to the door (glass or wood) where your dog usually enters, snap the cover shut, and plug the remote receiver/ door chime into any electric wall outlet. That's it! Pretty easy to train most dogs to use it. Perfect gift for grand-parents getting up and down, letting the dog in and out. No more scratched doors, either!

Doggie Doorbell
$39.95 + $5 S&H
(MN res. add sales tax)

G-S Products
P.O. Box 1028
Lakefield, MN 56150
(507) 662-5078
E-mail:
happypaw@rconnect.com

Logan's Matisse

Imaginary art? This amusing greeting card, "The Poseur," places Steve, the dog of artist Logan Franklin, into a fantasy setting at Henri Matisse's studio. When folded, the blank notecards with brilliant Matisse-like colors measure 4½″ x 6⅜″. Made of sturdy, fine white stock with matching envelopes, these wry cards will carry your message nicely.

"The Poseur" Notecards (pkg. of 5, with envelopes)
$12 + $2 S&H
(CA res. add 7.25% sales tax)

Logan Franklin
4 Mt. Tenaya Ct.
San Rafael, CA 94903
(415) 499-0719
E-mail: LogPaints@aol.com

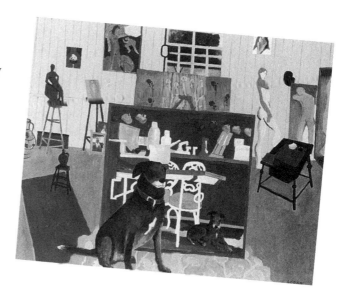

What Time Is It? ®

The dog's pacing around, to the door and back, giving you some nice eye contact. Must be time for a walk. Macho Mutt and Best Friend Leash Hooks are subtle reminders to get outside with the pup. The Walk Me Now Leash Hook positively screams for attention. Makes a great gift for anyone with a front door and a dog. No more hunting for the leash or car keys.

Best Friend or **Macho Mutt Leash Hook,** $8
Walk Me Now Leash Hook, $13
+ UPS
(OK res. add sales tax)

Just Bepaws
Laid Back Lifestyle Gifts
4020 Will Rogers Pkwy.
Suite 700
Oklahoma City, OK 73107
(800) 843-5242

It's a Puzzle

Ready for a long, quiet weekend? Turn off the phone, unplug the idiot box, shut down the computer, and dig into this cute 20″-dia. jigsaw puzzle of three Dalmatian pups with a red firehat. Includes more than 500 pieces for you—or a game-loving friend—to puzzle over.

Firehouse Frolic Jigsaw Puzzle, $9 + $4.95 S&H (TX res. add 7.25% sales tax)

Accessory Pet
5836 Pathfinder Trail
Plano, TX 75093
(800) 558-7387

Let's Explore

Is a puppy the right pet for your child? Maybe. Or maybe your child's not ready yet, and a low-maintenance guinea pig would be perfect. This 30-minute VHS for children ages 2–8 explores the magical world of more than 20 pets, somewhat like window shopping before you buy. Nice production values, narrated by a grandfatherly fellow who suggests some kind, practical advice to children so they understand the difference between an animal and a pet. Good idea before you buy that sweet puppy. 1995 Parent's Choice Honor Award. Watch it together so you can talk about it whenever the "I want a puppy" request arises.

Let's Explore (VHS video-tape) $14.95 + UPS (VA res. add sales tax)

Braun Film and Video
46444 Springwood Ct.
Sterling, VA 20165
(800) 815-6205

Functional Dogs ®

O.R.E.'s Crate o' Coasters Puppy Dog or Bone Coasters are extremely friendly, amusing little items made of recycled rubber. Four in a pack, large too: up to 3½″ × 5½″. How about 'em as a gift for a holiday party? Check out their fun recycled magnets for those fridge notes. Simple fun for kids. Great company, very "with it" products, no dull stuff.

Crate o' Coasters Puppy Dog or Bone Coasters (set of 4), $8.50
Puppy Dog or Bone Magnet, $1.99
+ UPS
(CA res. add sales tax)

O.R.E.
130 Gladys Ave.
Long Beach, CA 90804
(310) 433-2683

Where's the Dog Brush? ®

How often have you said that? It's easy to use a brush, put it down, and forget where you left it. Lucky dogs have lots of stuff—toys, brushes, grooming stuff, shampoos, clippers. Now you have a place to keep them. **Pet Pockets** is a heavy-duty, hanging nylon pet-supply organizer with 11 pockets. This is "home" to the dog stuff. Measures 35″ l. × 18″ w. × 3″ d., with sturdy hanger. Your choice of royal blue or forest green. A useful gift and organizer for your friends with lots of dogs and dog stuff.

Pet Pockets, $17.95 + $3 S&H (WA res. add 8.2% sales tax)

Together Enterprises
11905 124th Ave., N.E.
Kirkland, WA 98034
(800) 746-9604

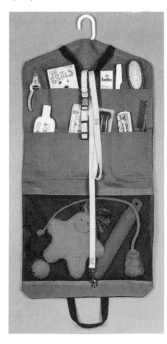

Silk Painting

Win Peterman's colorful silk paintings are unusual—they almost look like dog watercolors by a Grateful Dead artist who's gone straight. Wow, shimmering colors! The Silk Dog Pillow measures 18″ square with a custom-painted portrait of someone's special dog painted on the front, backed with satin polyester. A Velcro opening lets you remove the soft foam pillow insert (the material is called "Soft Touch" and feels like down) so the pillow can be washed by hand. Dog Scarf (above, center) is 15″ w. × 60″ l. in green china silk and can be painted either from your photo or in the breed of your choice. Running Dogs Scarf (above, right) is white crepe de chine. When the scarf is tied around the wearer's neck, the dogs on one end appear to be chasing the rabbit on the other end. Win uses French fabric dyes and each work is one of a kind. Ask about his silk Pet Portraits and Wall Hangings (not shown).

Silk Dog Pillow, $125
Dog Scarf, $55
Running Dogs Scarf, $75
+ UPS
(MD res. add sales tax)

Originals by Win
P.O. Box 1866
Prince Frederick, MD 20678
(410) 535-4976

Psychic Communication

Beverly Hale Watson communicates with animals telepathically. She frequently works with dog owners and the humane society in locating abused animals, lost pets, etc. Two stories of her paranormal experiences can be found in Brad Steiger's *Man and Dog,* reviewed on page 99. She has a psychic gift for finding and communicating with animals. Can she help you?

Beverly Hale Watson
215 Lake Trail Drive
Double Oak, TX 75067
(817) 430-3365

TRUE DOG TALE

The Eskimo Dog

For thousands of years, the Inuit people in northern Canada have raised this tough, aloof dog for hard work. Weighing 65–100 lbs., standing 21″–26″ at the shoulder, they've been bred by the Eskomos to be sled dogs and hunters who scavenge and feed themselves during summer. They will gladly excuse themselves from your warm living room—fireplace blazing—and curl up outside and sleep there, even during winter snowstorms.

Bag It

I love these totes. I've taken one to the beach and everywhere else for the last two years, and it still looks good. Pictured is the 12-oz. Chihuahua Canvas Tote Bag. Solid construction, tough, heavy canvas, made to last, and the price is right. Mine hasn't fallen apart yet. Available in over 60 breeds. Ask for a friend's favorite.

Chihuahua Canvas Tote Bag, $14.95 + $4 S&H
(MA res. add 5% sales tax)

Liliane's Creations
P.O. Box 1004
Oak Bluffs, MA 02557
(508) 693-2515

The Basic Guide to the American Cocker Spaniel

Cockers originated in Spain in the 12th century and arrived in America around 1900. They love family life and can live in a small house but require more attention (grooming and bathing) than many dogs. Forty of the top Spaniel breeders made contributions to this book, which covers the Cocker from puppy to training to show dog. Included are all the important details on health and diet, paperwork and registration, socialization and breed standards. Is the Cocker for you? Here's how to find out.

Edited by Michael R. Zervas, 1995, 118 pp., $9.95 + $3 S&H
(VA res. add 4.5% sales tax)

Dace Publishing
P.O. Box 91
Ruckersville, VA 22968
(888) 840-DACE

Wherever the Wind Blows

Spectacular black finish Dog Weathervane is 30″ tall with true-to-life handpainted colors of your favorite breed. The globes are painted gold, and the weathervane is available in all breeds. These lasting gifts look magnificent turning in the wind. The Dog Perma Sign is from the same company. It includes a metal dog sculpture of your favorite breed painted in realistic colors, and black-finish letters with up to 16 spaces per line painted in white. Your choice of standard-print or large-print lettering. Finding your house just got easier!

Dog Weathervane, $75 (without globes), $85 (with globes)
Dog Perma Sign, $69 (standard print), $82.50 (large print)
+ $5.95 S&H (Eastern/Central time zones)
or $6.95 S&H (Mountain/Pacific time zones)
(MI res. add 6% sales tax)

West Winds Trading Co.
3540 76th St.
Caledonia, MI 49316
(800) 635-5262

What's That You're Wearing? ®

Some people claim to prefer these colognes for dogs over nationally known people perfumes! Le Pooch (for males) is light and woodsy, with "a hint of leather and spice." La Pooch (for females) is "an elegant, yet light floral Lily of the Valley with a twist of apple." Pooch Puppy derives its full essence from the blossom of the Linden tree, "sweet yet very fresh." All are enriched with Panthenol and Lanexol, conditioners that leave your dog's coat shiny and smelling fresh. Packaged in beautiful crystal glass bottles with a nonaerosol pump. A Fifth Avenue gift. Also available in a Pooch Rawhide Gift Basket for rustic, woodsy types.

Le Pooch (for males),
$18 (50 ml.)
La Pooch (for females),
$20 (50 ml.)
Pooch Puppy, $28 (100 ml.)
+ UPS (NY res. add sales tax)

Les Pooches Boutique
P.O. Box 51
Tuxedo, NY 10987
(800) 745-4512

TRUE DOG TALE

Mixed Breeds

All dogs are ultimately related to wolves. Obviously, there have been some big, big changes since domestication 12,000 years ago—a Dachshund doesn't bear much resemblance to a wolf. Because both species possess 39 pairs of chromosomes, it is possible for dogs to mate with wolves. And, aside from the practical difficulties, it's possible for any dog breed to be mated to any other breed. That's how we ended up with more than 400 breeds worldwide!

Frisbee Dogs: Throwing Video
Frisbee Dogs: Training Video

What a life! Peter Bloeme actually gets paid to toss Frisbees to dogs, make videos, and write books. His 23-minute Throwing video teaches you and your dog how to enjoy the exciting and challenging sport of canine Frisbee. Covers all the basic concepts of throwing—grip, stance, arm, and body motion, as well as proper release. Bonus footage of 5 world champion teams included. The 30-minute Training video will both entertain and inform you. Whether your pet is a puppy or an adult, you'll learn how to enhance its natural instincts. You'll see leaping Labradors, pouncing Poodles, springing Spaniels, and a host of world champions with maneuvers that defy the laws of gravity. This guy plays for a living.

Frisbee Dogs: Throwing Video, $19.95
Frisbee Dogs: Training Video, $24.95
+ $5 S&H
(GA res. add 5% sales tax)

PRB and Associates
4060-D Peachtree Rd.
Suite 326F
Atlanta, GA 30319
(800) 786-9240

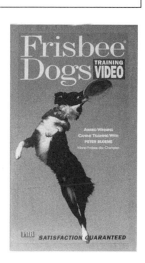

Dog Ownership Without the Dog

Dogz are little friends that live in your computer. They provide the joys of dog ownership, without the dog. On your computer desktop they scamper across applications, play games like "keep away," fetch, and chase, or nap in the corner of your screen while you're working. Dogz are unique looking and behaving and, YES, they can be taught by you to perform tricks! When you tire of "playing," retire them to their DogzHouse until next time. They also act as a screen saver or as GuardDogz, with password protection for your data. They start out as puppies that get bigger over time, growing into adults! Your choice of Terrier, Bulldog, Scottie, Setter, or Chihuahua. PC and Mac CD versions. Huge, imaginative hit with the computer crowd and kids of all ages.

Dogz, Your Computer Pet, $19.95 + UPS
(CA res. add sales tax)

PF.Magic
501 Second St.
Suite 400
San Francisco, CA 94107
(800) 48-ADOPT
http://www.pfmagic.com

Art on the Move

Show your love of dogs with C. Cookie Driscoll's dog decals on the windows of your car. Available in most of the major breeds. Just peel the decal, wet it, then place it on the inside of your window. No glue, easily removable so you can reapply it somewhere else when you feel like it. Fun gift for the windows in a child's room, too!

Cookie's Distinct Window Dog Art Decals, $4.50 each
(PA res. add sales tax)

Cookie's
530 Flohrs Church Rd.
Biglerville, PA 17307
(717) 334-4117

> *"To be followed home by a stray dog is a sign of impending wealth."*
> —Chinese proverb

Collectible Salts and Peppers ®

Clay Art in San Francisco makes whimsical, functional, decorative, and collectible dog salt and pepper shakers. Those two salty characters, handpainted in brilliant colors, are playing cards. Called Ruff's Bluff, they each measure 3½" high. Dog Racer is driving a bone with red wheels and black tires, and he's got a red crash helmet. Holes for dispensing salt or pepper. Amusing and attractive on any dining table.

Ruff's Bluff Salt and Pepper Shakers, $15.50
Dog Racer, $15.50
+ UPS
(CA res. add sales tax)

Clay Art
239 Utah Ave.
San Francisco, CA 94080
(415) 244-4970

Yorkshire Terriers: A Complete Pet Owner's Manual

Yorkshire Terriers were first recognized as a breed in England in 1886. Their history, detailed in this book, is interesting. For hundreds of years serfs were not allowed to own large dogs because they were prohibited from all forms of hunting. Small terriers were allowed, as long as they could fit through a 7″ dia. hoop held by the king's wardens, based upon the erroneous belief that a small dog couldn't catch anything of substance. More Yorkie history, care, feeding,

health, and personality attributes make this book a fascinating read. It's not a big book, but it's a solid overview of one of the prettiest companion dogs.

By Armin Kriechbaumer and Guger Grunn, 1990, 70 pp., $6.95 + UPS
(NY res. add sales tax)

Barron's Educational Series
250 Wireless Blvd.
Hauppauge, NY 11788
(800) 645-3476

A New Puppy!

Cute, pencil-illustrated Puppy Announcement Cards from Wild Earth include room on the inside for you to fill in the birth date and weight, like a birth announcement for a child. Nice cards (hand colored blue for boys, pink for girls) and quality paper. Artist Judy Vondriska also has whimsical 100% cotton Fruit of the Loom Agility T-shirts, featuring an original cartoon ("So Many Choices, So Little Time") in large or extra-large, your choice of yellow on turquoise or raspberry.

Puppy Announcement Cards (pkg. of 6), $6.50
Agility T-shirts, $15
+ $3.95 S&H (orders up to $20);
$5.50 S&H (orders $20.01–$40)
(WI res. add sales tax)

Wild Earth Design
924 County Rd. North
Hudson, WI 54016
(715) 749-9011

TRUE DOG TALE

Bag 'O Bird Tricks

Some dogs have extraordinary inherited traits that have been used by man over the centuries. The Kooiker, or Dutch Decoy Spaniel, has hunted ducks since the 1700s. Released from a duck blind, the dog runs around, waving its tail, racing back and forth, attracting curious ducks bemused by its odd behavior into traps where they are banded and released. It's not the only one with this gift. The Nova Scotia Duck-Tolling Retriever has his own bag of tricks. Released from the blind, this dog also races around, sometimes after a stick tossed from the blind up the shoreline. The dog retrieves it and fetches it, again and again. Ducks and geese find this interesting. As they approach, a hunter stands and fires, and the dog retrieves the birds from the water. Yet another, the Finnish Spitz—with a typical lush Spitz tail that curves over its back—listens for the flap of bird wings in the woods, runs to a tree where the bird has landed, waves its tail back and forth to hold the bird's attention, and yodels a bark until the hunter arrives.

Shed a Little Light

The lighted paper sculptures of artist Randy Marks utilize low-watt lighting and a variety of imported, brightly colored hand-dyed papers stretched over metal frames. *Arf,* in Dalmatian finish, stands 14″ tall. *Spike,* with provocative collar, is the same height. Wondrous, arty dogs aglow in the night.

Arf or **Spike,** $200 + UPS
(OK res. add sales tax)

Independent Vision
1717 Linwood Blvd.
Oklahoma City, OK 73106
(405) 236-1998

Some of This, Some of That . . .

The Boston Terrier, one of the most popular dogs in America, was created like a recipe. Add one part English Bulldog (which accounts for the pushed-in face), stir in some Bull Terrier (that's where all that energy comes from), and mix well with a Boxer (which defines the body shape). A wonderful, small (10–20 lbs., 15″ at the shoulder) dog that was bred down over the years from a size twice as large. It will go anywhere and do anything—as long as it's with you!

Just About Everything Dog

Mary Badenhop of Pipsqueak Productions is famous for the quality of her dog-inspired creations. Everything in this group makes a great gift, including her Greeting Cards (12 cards with envelopes, 4⅝″ × 6¾″), Photo Cards (same quantity and size), Stationery (10 printed cards, 10 blank), Magnets (three dimensional, 2½″ × 3¹⁄₁₆″), and Light Switch Cover (your choice of breed, finished for easy cleaning). Just a small sampling of her great dog products.

Greeting Cards, $9.95
Photo Cards, $9.95
Stationery, $6.95
Magnet, $5.95
Light Switch Cover, $9.95
+ $3.95 S&H
(orders up to $30);
$4.95 S&H ($30.01–$40)
(PA res. 6% sales tax)

Pipsqueak Productions
P.O. Box 1005
Honesdale, PA 18431
(717) 253-4330

> "All knowledge, the totality of all questions and answers, is contained in the dog."
> —Franz Kafka

Paws, Claws, Feathers, and Fins

With hot songs and lively graphics, this 30-minute video guides young viewers (ages 4–12) in choosing a pet, living with it, and dealing with loss. An award-winning video, it teaches kids responsibility and what's involved with owning a dog or any pet. Developed in consultation with the ASPCA, the American Humane Association, and American Veterinary Medical Association.

Kidvidz
618 Centre St.
Newton, MA 02158
(800) 637-6772

Paws, Claws, Feathers, and Fins, $14.95 + $5 S&H (MA res. add sales tax)

Dog Faces

Artist and designer Jon Stevenson of Petaluma, California, sells expressive, black-and-white-boxed dog cards of his buddy Scooter (a longhaired Jack Russell), Winnie (Bulldog with crown), and Noki with his party hat. Crisp quality, blank inside for your message. Humorous, friendly images. You provide the clever words.

Dog Cards (10 per box, with envelopes)
Scooter (longhaired Jack Russell)
Winnie (Bulldog with crown)
Noki (white dog with party hat)
$13 + $1.50 S&H
(includes CA sales tax)

Trumpette
108 Kentucky St.
Petaluma, CA 94952
(707) 769-1173

Salesman Eater ®

You might not have one of these guys with the big toothy smile, but hey, even if you have a Dachshund, the sign will still do the job! It will give anyone pause, including burglars and solicitors. Three-dimensional molded plaque with an "official" appearance, ½" thick, with complete hardware for hanging.

Bad Dog Plaque, $4.79 + UPS
(NY res. add sales tax)

Real Animal Friends Trading Corp.
101 Albany Ave.
Freeport, NY 11529
(800) 654-PETS

Make a Reservation for Two

Fresh from the kiln, hand-thrown and handpainted terracotta bowls feature a bone theme for dogs (and a fish theme for felines), available with matching placemats. Solid, dishwasher safe, heavy bowls that look and feel great. Makes every meal a special occasion. Placemats are low maintenance; just wipe off with a damp cloth. Part of the Northcreek line, which includes a comfy pillow bed, a sofa/car quilt, and more great canine products.

Northcreek Dog Bowl (bone pattern) $27
Matching Placemat, $10
+ $6.50 S&H (for both)
(includes MN sales tax)

L. Coffey
Ltd.
4244 Linden
Hills Blvd.
Minneapolis,
MN 55410
(800) 448-
4PET

Canine Companions for Independence

Since pioneering the concept of service dogs in 1975, Canine Companions for Independence has provided thousands of trained service, hearing, facility, and social dogs to people. The number of people involved in this national program is amazing: 520 active volunteer puppy raisers, 67 breeder caretakers, 3464 active volunteers nationwide, 97 full and part-time employees, four regional training centers (Santa Rosa, CA, Oceanside, CA, Delaware, OH, and Farmingdale, NY, with an additional service center in Orlando, FL), four satellite offices in Sacramento, Colorado Springs, Minneapolis, and Chicago . . . and 337 candidates

on the waiting list to receive a dog. I'd like to suggest you contact this wonderful nonprofit that has done so much for people over the years. Numerous tax-deductible giving programs are available, from memberships to bequests, estate planning and charitable trusts. They don't get a nickel from the government, depending totally upon charitable contributions for their good work. Look through their publication *The Courier.* Every single face of every new graduate, as they sit with their new dog companion, is smiling. Think of the good you can do.

Canine Companions for Independence
National Headquarters
P.O. Box 446
Santa Rosa, CA 95402
(800) 572-2275
(707) 577-1700 (V/TDD)
http://www.caninecompanions.org/

Stamp Fever!

What's stamp fever? The urge to run around the house stamping a dog on every scrap of paper you can find! Here's some great doggy stamps to help fulfill the urge. Mailbox Corgi is giving you the hint: Please send me a letter; Scotty holds a letter, sealed with a heart; Yorkie just looks beautiful. Stamp fan fun!

Mailbox Corgi, $8
Scotty with Letter, $8
Yorkie, $7
+ $3 S&H (orders under $15),
$4 S&H (orders $15.01–$30)
(NY res. add 8.5% sales tax)

Catch a Falling Star
344 N. Wyoming Ave.
N. Massapequa, NY 11758
(516) 249-8330

Everything's Coming up Dogs

Dog and cat books, that is. Charlene and Larry Woodward publish a massive user-friendly catalog (including e-mail ordering) of thousands of doggy and kitty books, smartly referenced in the front so everything's easy to find. Good overview on the best new titles, "Pick of the Litter" (best-of-breed books that come with their highest recommendation), dog videos, traveling with your pet, and absolutely everything else that's printed (including postcards and stickers) or that's on video or computer disks for dogs and cats. Fast, smart service.

Dog and Cat Book Catalog, free

Direct Book Service
P.O. Box 2778
Wenatchee, WA 98807
(800) 776-2665
E-mail: dgctbook@
cascade.net

Dog Time

Take a look at these cool dog clocks from artist Sheila Morrell! Send her a couple of good color photos, and she'll paint one to look like your dog. Each all-wood clock is individually hand made, then painted with acrylic, with a clear gloss coating. The price is extremely reasonable for a colorful, custom, functional work of art you'll keep for years. Great gift idea: Casually photograph a friend's dog, and surprise her with a beautiful, one-of-a-kind clock in the likeness of her dog.

Custom Dog Clock with Legs,
3″ square box with 8″ legs, $35
4½″ square box with 9″ legs, $55
6″ square box with 10″ legs, $75

6″ square box with ball feet, $55
+ $9 S&H in U.S.
(CA res. add 7.75% sales tax)

Sheila Morrell
2841 Verde Vista Dr.
Santa Barbara, CA 93105
E-mail: drgm@aol.com

Rolling Along

Need a wildly practical gift for a health nut with an active dog? From Norway comes the Springer, a device you attach to your bike so your dog can run alongside with you. Used by an amazing *12%* of the Scandinavian population, this exquisitely thought-out product can be mounted on either side of the bike, keeping the leash up high and away from your dog's paws and bike spokes. A spring absorbs and reduces as much as 90% of the shock of unexpected tugs if your dog lunges to the side, and a patented "safety release" frees the dog instantly in the event of emergency, such as the dog running on the wrong side of a lamppost. After initial installation you can attach or detach it in two seconds. Works with any size dog. Hot item.

Springer, $65.95
(includes S&H)
(IL res. add 7.75% sales tax)

Pet Supply Imports
P.O. Box 497
South Holland, IL 60473
(800) 346-1369

To Picture a Friend

Picture this at the office or on the mantel: a superior-quality, hand-finished wooden frame in rich green, red, brown, or black. Three popular sizes: $3\frac{1}{2}'' \times 5''$, $4'' \times 6''$, $5'' \times 7''$. Five solid-brass medallions set in pewter castings: 4 corner medallions and 1 centered oval medallion. Vertical or horizontal frames can be wall mounted or free standing. Gorgeous.

Picture Frame, $38 + $4.25 S&H
(IL res. add 8% sales tax)

Baxter and Charming, Ltd.
11 W. Main
Carpentersville, IL 60110
(800) 569-2761
E-mail: Baxterpets@aol.com

Putting the Cart After the Dog

Who makes the best dog carts on the planet? These people. They build them, compete with them, write books about them, and can show you how to get started with carting. Let's go from small to big. Can a little dog pull a cart? The PeeWee Chariot weighs $13\frac{1}{2}$ lbs. and has adjustable shafts, smooth precision bearings, 6″ black spoked wheels with a nonmarring tire (easy on floors), and counterbalanced shafts. Included is a fully adjustable nylon web harness in black or forest green, with lightweight hardware plus padding. Order the harness based upon your dog's weight. Handmade in Pennsylvania from oak plywood for strength. Believe it or not, it's suitable for most toy breeds! For larger dogs (a Newfoundland is shown here), the red Dog Works Competition Cart (with natural base/interior) weighs 50 lbs., has a capacity of 600 lbs., and can turn on a dime. Cart features removable shafts, wheels, and sides, solid maple and plywood construction, solid steel axle, and 20″ all-terrain pneumatic wheels. Measures: 33″ l. $\times$ 22″ w. $\times$ 9″ d. Fully adjustable—there's even an optional team kit that allows you to pair two dogs in a brace. Picture the kids being pulled around, by the dog, in their cart. Good buddies' fun. Want to learn more about canine carting? Order their professionally produced, 59-minute VHS video *An Introduction to Canine Carting,* which covers all the basics. Or get their book *Newfoundland Draft Work Book,* 91 pages of how carting works, on a practical level, for *all* dogs. Spiral bound, nothing fancy, just solid, reliable info.

PeeWee Chariot, $79 + UPS
PeeWee Harness, $29 + UPS
Dog Works Competition Cart, $289 + UPS
An Introduction to Canine Carting (VHS videotape) $35 + $4.50 S&H
Newfoundland Draft Work Book $18 + $4.50 Priority Mail
(PA res. add 6% sales tax)

Dog Works
14297 Curvin Dr.
Stewartstown, PA 17363
(800) 787-2788

Dachshund Dinner Guests

A pair of adorable Dachshunds handcrafted out of red cherry (a hardwood known for its rich color and durability) will be more than pleased to hold your dinner napkins. Approx. $4\frac{1}{2}''$ tall at the head, $6\frac{1}{2}''$ long nose to tail, with detailed features cut into the wood. Available in smooth-hair, long-hair, and wire-hair Dachshunds.

Dachshund Napkin Holder,
$25 + $3 S&H
(OH res. add 5.75% sales tax)

Dachshund Delights
P.O. Box 712
Burton, OH 44021
(216) 834-9557
E-mail:
74002.1656@copuserve.com
http://ourworld.compuserve.-com/homepages/stemnock

The New Dachshund ®

Who doesn't love these cute little wieners! My aunt and uncle always had two or three. As a kid, I played endless hours on the lawn with them, chasing them through the house, little legs flying. From its beginnings as a hunting hound, the book traces the long history and many breeders who have evolved the dog to its current standards. This is primarily a breeding history of Dachshunds, with hundreds of black and white photographs of past (and current) champions and their handlers, concluding with a very brief chapter on care and feeding. It's sure to appeal to Dachshund owners with an interest in the history of their favorite breed.

By Lois Meistrell, 1976, 288 pp.,
$25.95 + UPS
(IN res. add sales tax)

Howell Book House
201 W. 103rd St.
Indianapolis, IN 46290
(800) 428-5331

Refrigerator Art

Admit it. The only reason to have a fridge is to display dog magnets. Here's some new stuff for the collection. Magnetized photo frames come in eight whimsical designs for dogs and—uh, cats. Handpainted, they hold a cute 1½″ × 2″ photo of your furry friend(s). Each frame contains an easel back for a stand-up frame. There's a magnet on the back for your art gallery in the kitchen. Kids love to add handfuls of these to their collections.

Pet Photo Frame/Magnets, $4.95 + UPS
(VT res. add sales tax)

Lucky Dog and Kitty, Too
Hunger Mountain Rd.
Gaysville, VT 05746
(800) 701-2297

Plastic Bag Organizer ®

Since we are never going to get rid of plastic bags, you might as well find some way to store them. As odd as it seems, this product makes sense. The Grand Poo Bagh features dog images on a 16″ l. × 8″ w. cotton fabric tube, with elastic on each end. You hang it on the wall and stuff up to 35 used plastic bags inside. Next time you need a bag, you pull one out the bottom, one at a time. Attractive and durable, it can also be laid on its side in a drawer. Smart place to keep your litter-cleanup bags, by the front door, for your next walk.

The Grand Poo Bagh,
$10.95 + UPS
(CA res. add sales tax)

Accessory Pet, (800) 558-7387
KV Vet Supply, (800) 432-8211
Pet Warehouse, (800) 443-1160

Earthwhile Endeavors
P.O. Box 471060
San Francisco, CA 94147
(415) 771-1166
E-mail: earthbath@aol.com

TRUE DOG TALE

When Is a Squeaker Not a Squeaker?

There is actually a movement afoot to eliminate squeakers from dog toys. Some folks claim that the dog destroys the toy trying to get at the squeaker, which, in critics' minds, represents the plaintive cries of a helpless animal. As usual, it started in California, and now it's creeping east. Silent toys. How will you ever explain this to your dog?

Dog Watch

The ultimate go-anywhere, do-anything watch in your choice of bold Big Dog graphics. Durable, all-purpose watch with scratch-resistant crystal and quality Japanese quartz movement. Water resistant down to 5 atmospheres in case you decide to get really wet. Your choice of 4 fabulous designs: Big Kahuna, Big Dog Golf, Large in Charge, Big Dog Logo. Somebody you know would love one of these!

Big Dog Watch (sm. or lg.), $29.99 + UPS
(CA res. add 8.25% sales tax)

Big Dog Sportswear
3112 Seaborg Ave.
Ventura, CA 93003
(800) 642-DOGS
http://www.bigdogs.com

TRUE DOG TALE

Sleepless in Dogland

Some dogs are known for their snoring! The French Bulldog can really snort it up at night. Pugs, being more refined, snore gently while dreaming. Many dogs with scrunched-in faces and noses close to their eyes have breathing problems. Curled up, in the wrong position, they'll snore until they roll over!

Puppy Music

The sounds of heart-beats, whelping pups, and classical music on this 60-minute cassette tape are soothing to the ears of any young pup who misses Mom and can't seem to get to sleep. More than a novelty, this tape, played at low levels, soothes pups by replacing familiar sounds to keep them from becoming lonely. Helps when you have to leave them alone, too! No more lonely puppies!

Canine Lullabies (cassette tape), $6.99 + UPS
(CA res. add 7% sales tax)

Roger's Visionary Pet Products
4538 Saratoga Ave.
San Diego, CA 92107
(800) 364-4537
http://www.rogerspet.com

TRUE DOG TALE

Pit Bull Rules

In America anybody can own a Pit Bull. Bred to be fighting dogs, they make the newspapers now and then with stories of attacks on people and children. But some people feel that their loyalty and intelligence make them great pets. In England they have this interesting law—drafted by breeders in cooperation with the government—called the Dangerous Dogs Act. Want to own or import a Pit Bull into the U.K.? First, you'll need an exemption certificate, which states that—in part—you will comply with the following: The dog must be neutered and implanted with a transponder, and it must be on a leash and muzzled at all times in public, in the presence of a handler at least 16 years old. Oh yes, you'll need a special annual insurance policy in case the dog runs amok. They take this seriously. Violate the law, and the fines start. They can imprison you if the dog causes injury, and often the dog is destroyed. I'm not picking on Pit Bulls. The same laws apply to a few other dogs, including the mercurial, ferocious Tibetan Mastiff.

Dog Money

Make a statement the next time you write a check. Personalized checks from the Kansas Bank Note Company use a photograph or drawing of your dog. The cost is a one-time artwork charge, then the basic charge for checks. You get the photo back with your checks. Takes about 4 weeks unless you request first-class delivery. Their list of generic dog art for checks is lengthy—ask for it. Many sizes (3-to-a-page business checks, Canadian checks, duplicate styles), plus they have gift certificates. Incidentally, you might want to compare these costs with what your bank is charging. Generally these are *much* less expensive, and they work just fine. At last. Creative checks from a friendly bank! Wonders never cease. Surprise your spouse.

Custom Dog Checks,
$25 (one-time artwork charge)
+ $12 (200 personalized checks)
+ UPS
(KS res. add sales tax)

Kansas Bank Note Co.
P.O. Box 360
Fredonia, KS 66736
(316) 378-3026

The Long, Winding Road

Planning a getaway with a friend and the dog? Surprise your friend and leave the planning to Debra Dylan Yates of Pocomoke City. She'll head you down the right road. Her specialty is helping plan your trip so you and the pup don't get lots of blank stares and "no way's" when you try to check in for the night after a long day of driving. Tell her where you want to go, fill in her 2-page form, and she'll recommend great places to stay along your route that allow pets. Some do, some don't. A bargain at this price.

Pet Travel Resources,
$10 per travel plan

Pet Travel Resources
2327 Ward Rd.
Pocomoke City, MD 21851
(410) 632-3944

The Happy Dog

Racing for home, this running dog metal sculpture is one of the happiest dogs you'll ever see! And he'd love to live in your house. Superb handcrafted wall sculpture will keep your best friend's leashes and sweaters readily at hand. No two are alike. Approx. 9" × 20".

Running Dog Wall Rack, $65 + $8.95 S&H
(NY res. add sales tax)

In The Company of Dogs
P.O. Box 7071
Dover, DE 19903
(800) 924-5050

The Visual Leap Forward

What's the perfect dog gift that keeps on giving? How about a calendar for a friend with a picture of their pooch for each month? These folks publish a custom, full-color, 12-month Wall Calendar of any dog, with up to 30 special events of your choice printed on the calendar. They look good. Two sizes—9" × 11½" and 11½" × 18"—and they're laminated so you can hang them anywhere. In the mood for a message? Why not have them make you customized Greeting Cards—packs of 10 with matching envelopes, your text inside, and a nice photo of your dog's glorious face in full color on the outside. Personalized gifts are extra-special.

Imag-In Custom Screen Saver, $29.95
(includes 10 free scans)
Custom Color Wall Calendar, $34.95
(lg; addl. copies $24.95); $29.95
(sm.; addl. copies $19.95)
Custom Color Greeting Cards
(with matching envelopes), $14.95
(box of 10), $24.95 (20), $29.95 (30)
(includes S&H and TX sales tax)

Envision Publishing
P.O. Box 702925
Dallas, TX 75370
(888) IMAGIN-8
http://web2.airmail.net/jei/envision.html

Dogs on the Move!

Amazing Wind Machines are unique: a traditional folk art form re-interpreted with a contemporary design and materials. They're designed for outdoor use, but it's best to bring them inside when winds exceed 30 mph. Each includes a 16″ outdoor pole mount and an indoor display base. Outdoors, they operate like a weathervane, turning to show wind direction. The Dalmatian Wind Machine (15 l. × 16″ h. × 7″ w.) has ears that wiggle, a mouth that "barks," and a tail that wags. He makes a fabulous gift, with beautiful colors and detailed craftsmanship. The quality is so good, many wind machines are kept permanently indoors as dog art. Other breeds from which to choose. Ask for the catalog!

Dalmatian Wind Machine
$200 + UPS
(MA res. add sales tax)

Amazing Wind Machines
P.O. Box 619
Littleton, MA 01460
(508) 952-2478

Embossed Leather Dogs

Imagine giving either of these leather, heirloom-quality gifts to a friend. Raised relief (debossed) images of dogs are individually hand made of the finest leathers by Floriana Petersen of San Francisco—a Europe-trained leather maker. The image on the Photo Album and the box is a hunting dog/retriever in black leather. They are lined with handmade marbled paper. The Photo Album (which could also be a scrapbook) is 10″ × 12″ and contains 30 sheets of acid-free 80-lb. paper. The Box, 7½″ × 9″, is made from Spanish cedar, like the wood used in cigar boxes. It can be used for cigars, notepaper, or your treasures. Exquisite detail and quality. Eminently upscale.

Leather Bas-Relief Photo Album,
$64 + $3.50 S&H
Leather Bas-Relief Box,
$54 + $3 S&H
(CA res. add sales tax)

On Your Marque
459 Clementina
San Francisco, CA 94103
(415) 543-6700

Big Fun Wacko Talking Dog!

Just attach this crazy toy to your dog's collar. Hide the wireless, bone-shaped remote controller (works up to 50′ away) in your pocket. When a person walks up to pet your dog, you can make one of five lunatic phrases blare out of the collar. Sounds like the dog's talking! Yow! Two AAA batteries included. You supply a 9-volt battery.

Talking Dog Collar with Remote Control, $24.95 + $5.38 S&H
(PA res. add 6% sales tax)

Fun-damental Too Ltd
2381 Philmont Ave.
Suite 119
Huntingdon Valley, PA 19006
(800) 922-3110
http://www.shopperusa.com/Fundamental

TALKING DOG COLLAR WITH REMOTE CONTROL

TRUE DOG TALE

Truffle Dog?

Truffles are those fabulously expensive, outrageously delicious fungi that grow under the ground. In parts of Europe specially trained pigs find them by smell, often in proximity to oak trees. Word is there's a dog—the Italian Lagotto Romagnolo—that's a master at finding these precious gems with its keen nose. Specially trained, with superior sniffers, they root out truffles costing hundreds of dollars a pound.

Dog Mail!

Supercool dog mailbox is available in Hound Dog, Scottie Dog, and Dalmatian designs. Each is a colorful U.S.P.S.-approved mailbox that will mount with tamper-proof screws on any standard mailbox post. Made in the USA of weather-resistant painted metal, a wood face, and legs and tail painted with weatherproof enamel for long life. Ask about low-cost mailbox insurance (in case you run it over) and a color brochure of other wild and crazy mailboxes.

Dalmatian Mailbox,
$59 + $7.90 S&H
(CA res. add sales tax)

More-Than-a-Mailbox
617 B Second St.
Petaluma, CA 94952
(800) 331-3252

Glad Tidings

Send a nice letter on this attractive Dog Notes Stationery (blank inside for your message) and 5″x 8″ Memo Pads (100 pages with the screened image of your favorite dog, 50 breeds available), or stamp your own with a Dog Rubber Stamp from Tidings of San Francisco. Rubber stamps are great for kids and adult kids on letters and envelopes and to make greeting cards, party invitations, and favors. Dog fun!

Dog Notes Stationery (box), $9
Memo Pad, $6.50
Dog Rubber Stamp, $6 and up
+ UPS
(CA res. add sales tax)

Drs. Foster & Smith Catalog
(800) 826-7206

Amazing and Mysterious Dog Tale?

Have you read the story about the lost dog who traveled halfway across America to find its owners? How about the dog who could sense an earthquake coming? Or the trained dog who saved her unconscious owner by dialing 911 on her telephone? I would love to hear your own amazing, mysterious, and unusual dog stories.

Please write me, and thank you!

John Avalon Reed
P.O. Box 515
Mill Valley, CA 94942

"Heaven goes by favor. If it went by merit, you would stay out and your dog would go in."

—Mark Twain

Spot's Magical Christmas

Spot has joined the ranks of classic books for young children. Like most parents, I once read these to my infant son. In this story, Spot, with a little help from his animal friends, practically saves Christmas for all the puppies and kids around the world. Big job! Cute doggy family illustrations—and always a happy ending.

By Eric Hill, 1995, 28 pp.,
$11.95 + UPS
(NY res. add sales tax)
G.P. Putnam's Sons
200 Madison Ave.
New York, NY 10016
(800) 631-8571

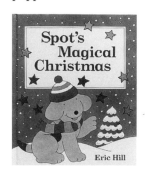

Your Dog's Toy Box

All those toys need a home! This wonderful wooden toy box, painted with a white background covered with blue paws, is just the place for the toys to rest. On the front is a red bone, personalized with your dog's name. Since there's no lid, the dog can mosey over and take whatever toy he wants! Very cute, nicely made. Self-serve toys. Mail orders only.

Doggy's Own Toy Box, $29.95 (8″ × 8″ × 6″ h.);
$34.95 (11″ × 11″ × 8″ h.); $4.50 S&H (NY res. add sales tax)

Doggy's Own Toy Box
1575 Military Rd., #13-111
Niagara Falls, NY 14304

What Goes Around Comes Around

Many non-profit organizations around the country need volunteers to raise puppies and to help with their many activities. The organizations listed below help provide service or guide dogs to those less fortunate than you. Your help—and tax-deductible contribution—are always needed and appreciated.

Assistance Dog Programs

Assistance Dog Institute
P.O. Box 2334
Rohnert Park, CA 94927
(707) 537-6391

Founded by Bonnie Bergin who started, worldwide, the concept of service and assistance dogs.

Canine Companions for Independence
P.O. Box 446
Santa Rosa, CA 95402
(707) 528-0830

Canine Partners for Life
Box 130, RD 2
Cochranville, PA 19330
(610) 869-4902

Freedom Service Dogs
P.O. Box 150217
Lakewood, CO 80215
(303) 234-9512

Handi-Dogs, Inc.
P.O. Box 12563
Tucson, AZ 85732
(602) 326-3412

Independence Dogs for the Mobility Handicapped
146 State Line Road
Chadds Ford, PA 19317
(215) 358-2723

Hearing Dog Programs

Dogs for the Deaf
10175 Wheeler Road
Central Point, OR 97502
(503) 826-9220

Intl. Hearing Dogs, Inc.
5901 E. 89th Avenue
Henderson, CO 80640
(303) 287-3277

Paws with a Cause
1235 100th Street, S.E.
Byron Center, MI 49315

Guide Dog Programs

Fidelco Guide Dogs
P.O. Box 142
Bloomfield, CT 06002
(203) 243-5200

Guide Dog Foundation for the Blind
371 E. Jericho Turnpike
Smithtown, NY 11787
(800) 548-4337

Guide Dogs for the Blind
P.O. Box 1512000
San Rafael, CA 94915
(415) 499-4000

Guide Dogs of America
13445 Glenoaks Blvd.
Sylmar, CA 91342

Guide Dogs of the Desert
P.O. Box 1692
Palm Springs, CA 92263

Guiding Eyes for the Blind
611 Granite Springs Road
Yorktown Heights, NY 10598
(914) 245-4024

Leader Dogs for the Blind
1039 S. Rochester Road
Rochester, MI 48307
(810) 651-9011

Pilot Dogs
625 W. Town Street
Columbus, OH 43215
(614) 221-6367

Seeing Eye Guide Dogs for the Blind
P.O. Box 375
Morristown, NJ 07963
(201) 539-4425

Southeastern Guide Dogs
4210 77th Street, East
Palmetto, FL 34221
(813) 729-5665

Animal-Assisted Therapy

Delta Society
Pet Partners Program
P.O. Box 1080
Renton, WA 98057
(206) 226-7357

Therapy Dogs Intl.
6 Hilltop Road
Mendham, NJ 07945
(908) 429-0670

Therapy Dogs Incorporated
P.O. Box 2786
Cheyenne, WY 82003
(307) 638-3223